A Caring Jurisprudence

Listening to Patients
at the Supreme Court

Susan M. Behuniak

ROWMAN & LITTLEFIELD PUBLISHERS, INC.
Lanham • Boulder • New York • Oxford

ROWMAN & LITTLEFIELD PUBLISHERS, INC.

Published in the United States of America
by Rowman & Littlefield Publishers, Inc.
4720 Boston Way, Lanham, Maryland 20706

12 Hid's Copse Road
Cumnor Hill, Oxford OX2 9JJ, England

British Library Cataloguing in Publication Information Available

Library of Congress Cataloging-in-Publication Data
Behuniak, Susan M., 1956–
    A caring jurisprudence : listening to patients at the Supreme
Court / Susan M. Behuniak.
      p.   cm.
    Includes index.
    ISBN 0-8476-9454-2 (alk. paper). — ISBN 0-8476-9455-0 (pbk. :
alk. paper)
      1. Patients—Legal status, laws, etc.—United States. 2. Medical
care—Law and legislation—United States. 3. United States—
Supreme Court—Decision making. I. Title.
KF3823.B44 1999
344.73'041—dc21   99-16198
                                                      CIP

Printed in the United States of America

©™ The paper used in this publication meets the minimum requirements of
American National Standard for Information Sciences—Permanence of Paper
for Printed Library Materials, ANSI Z39.48–1984.

To John

who practices and teaches the radical view
that understanding lies neither in the forest nor
the trees but in the roots

Contents

Acknowledgments   vii

Introduction   ix

1   Three Versions of a Story: The Medical, Legal, and Personal   1

2   The Abortion Cases: The Merging of Medical and Legal Knowledge   31

3   The Physician-Assisted Suicide Cases: The Triumph of Medical Knowledge over Patients' Knowledge   65

4   A Jurisprudence of Justice and Care: Enabling the Court to Hear the Knowledge of Patients   103

5   Listening to Patients: The Abortion and Physician-Assisted Suicide Cases Revisited   133

Notes   167

List of Cases   173

References   175

Index   185

About the Author   193

Acknowledgments

It's hard to say whether the impetus for this book lies in my experiences as a patient or in my academic study of law. As a patient who, at last count, has had five surgeries, I've seen some of the best in medical care as well as some glimpses of the worst. As a political scientist who watches with great interest the activities of the U.S. Supreme Court, I've applauded as well as decried its decisions. In both of these capacities, my concern over the ethic of justice and the ethic of care have been heightened by my observation of one particular shortcoming that is shared by too many professionals in medicine and law—the failure to listen to patients. I can think of few other things that can break a patient seeking treatment or a patient-litigant seeking help than being treated dismissively—as if one were ignorant, or invisible, or worthless. And it is not necessary; neither the standard of care in medicine nor the principle of justice in law requires it. In fact, there are doctors and nurses, lawyers and judges, who are passionately committed to discovering what patients know. It is these professionals who have led me to the premise of this book: that in the legal cases that involve them, patients' knowledge should be heard, weighed, and answered by the Justices of the Court. In fact, both the ethics of justice and care demand it.

The task, then, became one of making sense of these experiences, concerns, and concepts. It is here that I turned to feminism, a theory and practice that names oppression, gives voice to the voiceless, and is unstinting in its commitment to affect change. And so, I am grateful to the many feminist scholars and practitioners, those cited as sources as well as those unnamed, who have led the way.

My appreciation to the Le Moyne College Faculty Senate Committee on Research and Development for granting me a summer stipend and a one course load reduction as I worked on this book. Also to Inga-Lil Barnello, social science librarian, who patiently brought me up to speed on computerized research techniques, and to Dawn Curry, student aide to the Department of Political Science, who spent many an afternoon making photocopies and runs to the library for me. Students in my "Constitutional Law" and "U.S. Supreme Court" courses always give me much to think about, and I thank them for accompanying me on my journey to imagining how the ethics of justice and care should inform legal practice.

Every Tuesday afternoon during the school year, a group composed of some of the feminist women on campus gather to eat lunch and share stories. Through their commitments and their actions, they have taught me much about the ethics of care and justice and have provided me with friendship, support, and a safe haven amid the turmoil that is Le Moyne. My thanks to these colleagues: Lynne Arnault, Janet Bogdan, Maria DiTullio, Jennifer Glancy, Brenda Kirby, Kathleen Nash, and Beatrice Robinson.

I benefited greatly from the anonymous readers who reviewed early drafts of the manuscript. Their comments and suggestions helped me to fill in the holes, separate the wheat from the chafe, and sharpen the points. Just as importantly, their criticisms were expressed in a manner that energized rather than deflated me. While I tried to incorporate their suggestions and answer their concerns, the flaws that remain in the book are, of course, my responsibility alone.

Jennifer Knerr, my editor at Rowman & Littlefield, has been key in bringing this project to fruition. Her belief in the book and enthusiasm has been unshakable, and I appreciate having had the opportunity to work with her.

My sister, Carol Girard, has not only been my constant companion throughout my life but also in all the experiences that come from being DES daughters. We have been there for each other during some very scary times and from these experiences I have learned how medical crises profoundly touch not only the patient, but also their loved ones. I am grateful to her for her unwavering love and support and for all that she has taught me about relationships and care.

John F. Freie plays multiple roles in my life: husband, colleague, and intellectual muse. He is the person who insisted that I write this book, and then without complaint, lived with the consequences. Our life together is animated both by love and by work, and so I depend on his sense of knowing when it's time to put the work aside and take a spin in his Miata, or share a bottle of wine, or walk our faithful dog companions. For all that he does and all who he is, this book is dedicated to him.

Introduction

To be just, judicial decision making should be impartial, reasoned, and universally applied. This is the dominant understanding of justice that personifies the American legal system. It is the view symbolically depicted in statues of Lady Justice, whose blindfold, scales, and sword guard against subjectivity, emotion, and particularity. It is the process expected by those who enter the legal system, whether as litigant, lawyer, or judge. It is a commonly offered articulation of what fairness means and of what it requires. And it is an approach to judicial decision making that is adopted and largely followed by the U.S. Supreme Court.

It is also the perspective that I hope to challenge in this book.

Obviously, this is no easy task. The notion of justice as impartial, reasoned, and universal is embedded not only in American legal norms but also within the national psyche. And it has powerful appeal. Certainly we do not want legal cases to be decided by those who are personally involved with the litigants, those who rely on their feelings rather than on their intellects, and those who would refrain from applying the same rule to everyone who is similarly situated. After all, the opposite of justice is injustice, an outcome that should deliberately be avoided by any court. To call into question the wisdom of following an ethic of justice, therefore, is as great a heresy that one can imagine committing in the field of law.

My argument, however, is more nuanced than a call to overthrow the ethic of justice and is more complicated than a demand that the law be compassionate. What motivates my inquiry into the role that justice plays in judicial decision making is a feminist concern—that the exclusive reliance on the ethic of justice too narrowly confines that which is regarded as knowledge. In particular, the judicial system's demand for the impartial, the reasoned, and the universal results in the elevation of some types of knowledge and the undermining of other types of knowledge. While this empowerment of one form of knowledge over another takes place in most legal encounters (e.g., it is facts not hearsay, evidence not suppositions, and precedents not personal whims that are welcomed in courts), the result of this preference is particularly profound in cases involving biomedical issues because it is there that patients' voices are disregarded and physicians' voices are heard. When the legalities of medical treatments or practices are challenged in court, medical knowledge and not patients' knowledge readily fits the template of that which law regards as knowledge. Medicine's reliance on facts, reason, and universal rules makes it particularly well suited for seriously influencing judicial decision making. Within the medical community, physicians in particular are readily granted the status of expert. Their schooling in scientific method, with its hypothesis testing, objective observations, and definitive results, lends credibility to their opinions, observations, and conclusions.

Yet, every patient knows that there is another form of knowledge. This knowledge comes not from formal schooling and professional practice but from personal experience. As such, the formation of patients' knowledge frequently departs from scientific method: it is created and learned not by distancing oneself from the subject but from being the subject; it is concrete in nature rather than abstract; and it is informed as much by what is felt as by what is intellectualized. It is the type of knowledge more associated with an ethic of care than with an ethic of justice. Its source is personal relationships, emotions, and particulars, and it too can serve as the basis for decision making. In fact, in many of our personal encounters with family and friends we rely on the ethic of care to guide our behavior and to help us in making judgments. Within this personal context, we freely draw from the involved, emotional, and particular to form our knowledge.

But such a personal and experiential basis for knowledge strains at the parameters of that which is conventionally considered to be knowledge in the public realm. Perhaps no where is this more evident than in the U.S. Supreme Court where cases involving abortion and physician-assisted suicide (PAS) have been heard and decided. In both of these lines of cases, most of the Justices based their decisions on the knowledge presented to them by the mainstream medical associations while they dismissed the knowledge offered by the litigant-patients. This was as true in the abortion cases where the majority of the medical and patients' knowledge complemented each other as it was in the PAS cases where the majority of the medical and patients' knowledge contradicted each other. In the course of considering both of these issues, the Justices disregarded the subjective, interested, and particular knowledge of patients.

This preference for medical knowledge over patients' knowledge was not without consequences. First, it affected the Court's understanding of which constituency was at the center of the cases. In the abortion case of *Roe v. Wade* (1973), the Court seemed to favor women's reproductive freedom and grant them reproductive rights, but it seemed to focus more on the consequences for physicians than for the lives of the patients. In the PAS cases of *Washington v. Glucksberg* and *Vacco v. Quill* (1997), the requests of patients who asked the Court to legalize PAS were overshadowed by those of physicians who appealed to the Court to protect their profession. Second, the Court's preference for medical knowledge affected their understanding of the issues. While pregnant women and terminally ill adult patients asked the Court to consider the cultural contexts of their crises, the Court adopted the medical perspective that an unwanted pregnancy and a terminal condition are primarily *medical* events involving the doctor–patient relationship. Not only did this view reinforce the primacy of medical expertise, it also diverted the Court's attention from the economic, spiritual, familial, psychological, and political aspects of the issues—elements that might have affected the tone and reasoning of the opinions if not the decisions themselves. Third, the elevation of medical knowledge over patients' knowledge affected how well these decisions would meet the standard of justice. In directing its attention to physicians' needs rather than those of the litigant-patients, in considering physicians' knowledge to the exclusion of patients' knowledge, and in addressing the needs of physicians while leaving untouched the injuries claimed by patients, the Court did not seem to comport with its own ethic of justice.

Yet, given the legal norms that dictate that patients' knowledge be treated as suspect because it is involved, emotional, and particular, is the elevation of medical knowledge over patients' knowledge inevitable? I want to challenge the notion that it is. To do this, I question the dichotomy that forces zero-sum decisions to be made in choosing between different types of knowledge and different governing ethics. It is indeed possible to develop a jurisprudence that draws from not only the ethic of justice but also the ethic of care. The model I suggest, that of a "caring jurisprudence," maintains within judicial decision making the presence of the ethic of justice while also heightening the role played by the ethic of care. This approach is one way to ensure that patients' knowledge will be heard, evaluated, and answered in the Court.

Therefore, this book is an exploration of whether the legal norms of the U.S. Supreme Court can be modified to accommodate the personally involved, emotional, and particular knowledge of patients. Because I am very aware that I am posing a challenge to mainstream understandings of law in general, and to the Court's role in particular, I build my argument slowly as I progress from chapter to chapter. Therefore, a brief summary of the outline of my argument and how it unfolds in the chapters may be instructive.

I begin in chapter 1 by explaining how legal norms create a bias that favors medical knowledge and that weighs against patients' knowledge. To explore this, the construction of knowledge is studied from three different perspectives: the medical, the legal, and the patients'. Each of these perspectives adopts distinctive epistemologies and I study them not only to highlight their differences but their intersections as well. What I find is that the similar natures of legal and medical knowledge place patients and their knowledge at a distinct disadvantage before the Court. My point is not that patients' knowledge should control judicial decision making, but that its exclusion handicaps the Court's deliberations in that it limits the scope of the knowledge before it.

In the next two chapters the ramifications of this epistemological bias are explored by examining two distinctive lines of cases similarly situated as biomedical concerns—abortion, the subject of chapter 2, and PAS, the focus of chapter 3. I find that in both series of cases the Court framed the issues as predominantly *medical* issues and that this characterization all but excluded patients' knowledge. The consequences of amplifying medical knowledge are evident when *Roe's* progeny are studied: physicians' discretion is consistently protected while the harms suffered by patients are repeatedly ignored. In the PAS cases, the medical framework directed the Court's attention to the medical profession's plea that their integrity as healers be protected and away from the cries of patients who asked that their final wishes not be sacrificed on the altar of the slippery slope argument. Again, my point is not that patients' knowledge alone should have determined the outcome of these cases, but that in allowing medical and legal knowledge to automatically trump patients' knowledge the Court failed to consider fairly all the relevant information concerning the issues before it.

Therefore, chapter 4 begins by suggesting that the exclusion of patients' knowledge from judicial decision making is not only lacking in compassion, but lacking in justice as well. This chapter bears the burden of suggesting how law can in fact adopt a different approach from that of relying exclusively on the ethic of justice. Because feminist scholarship has addressed the tasks of challenging dichotomies, giving voice to the voiceless, questioning the meaning and the politics of "objectivity," and strengthening the "feminine" ethic of care, it is to this feminist literature that I turn for guidance. Using this scholarship as a springboard, a model for a "caring jurisprudence" is constructed and proposed. It is a model of judicial decision making that integrates the ethics of justice and of care as countervailing forces, like those of perpendicular threads on a weaving loom. Again, my goal is not to eradicate reason, impartiality, and universality from the law, but to temper them with knowledge founded in the emotional, involved, and particular experiences of patients. To this end, the model calls for judicial decision making to follow three steps: (1) a micro contextual analysis that is sensitive to the circumstances of the litigant-patients; (2) a macro contextual analysis that expands the sphere of reference beyond the constitutional issues of the case to the cultural forces that shape it; and (3) an integration of knowledge derived from both the ethics of justice and care.

Chapter 5 suggests how this theory could affect judicial practice. I revisit the abortion and PAS cases to demonstrate not only how a caring jurisprudence can be applied, but also how it can transform judicial decision making by broadening the sphere of knowledge considered. It is at this point that I introduce firsthand accounts by patients (and their loved ones) involved in the abortion and PAS issues to demonstrate what they can teach the Court about these issues, the meaning of justice, and how these lessons can affect judicial decision making. In applying the model, I attempt to show that a caring jurisprudence, while attentive to outcomes, is not a result-oriented approach (i.e., one that leads inevitably to one possible conclusion). While my evaluation of the medical, legal, and patients' knowledge leads me to favor pro-choice and pro-PAS resolutions of the cases, the Court need not adopt the same conclusions. Instead, I argue that regardless of whether the application of a caring jurisprudence would change the decisions in these cases, the incorporation of patients' voices would still alter judicial decision making in other significant ways. At minimum, the inclusion of patients' knowledge, from both the pro-choice and pro-life sides and from the pro-PAS and anti-PAS sides, would compel the Court to recognize that there is something seriously wrong with the way that we in American society treat pregnant women and respond to patients who are dying. But even more, the inclusion of this knowledge has the potential of affecting the nature and process of judicial reasoning and ultimately how the Court's opinions are themselves to be judged.

In the end, I suggest that we can move in the direction of a more balanced, more caring, and more just response to life and death issues if the Court listens to patients' knowledge when it considers cases involving them. One way of doing so is to adopt a caring jurisprudence. While I limit the study of its implications here to two issues within the field of biomedical law, I hope that the approach may sufficiently intrigue others that they will test its possibilities in other areas of law. A call for a more compassionate form of judicial decision making may strike a chord for those who struggle with issues stemming from the field of criminal justice (e.g., death penalty cases), within the arena of the First Amendment (e.g., the hate speech controversy), and within family law (e.g., child custody disputes). While hoping to provoke a larger debate over the role of care within the legal system, I stress again that the intent of a caring jurisprudence is not to supplant justice but to temper it. Rather than knocking Lady Justice from her pedestal, it is an approach that asks her to share it with the ethic of care.

· *1* ·

Three Versions of a Story:
The Medical, Legal, and Personal

The people that come to see us bring us their stories. They hope they tell them well enough so that we understand the truth of their lives. They hope we know how to interpret their stories correctly. We have to remember that what we hear is *their story*.

Dr. Alfred O. Ludwig to Robert Coles

A story unfolds. Something has happened to someone: she is pregnant but doesn't want to continue the pregnancy, or he or she is dying but death isn't coming fast enough. It is a personal story of a patient's life and a decision to be made. Chances are that in the midst of this crisis, the patient seeks the help of a physician. The story is now retold and reshaped by the process of recording it in the form of a medical record. Whether the physician can help the patient is another story, and it is one written as much by law as by medicine. If a conflict emerges over the legality of proceeding, the story will be told again, but this time as a legal case crafted in the legalese appropriate for a court. The one story now has three versions, each shaped by a different way of knowing—that of the personal, the medical, and the legal.

The question of who is telling or retelling the story is very important because the construction of knowledge is highly dependent on who it is that is claiming expertise. Where one stands on the issues of abortion or PAS is influenced (though not necessarily determined) by where one sits. Those who sit on the bench necessarily approach the cases with legal norms and processes in mind. Those who sit as medical care providers, poring over medical records, bring scientific knowledge and professional experiences to bear on the issues. Those who sit on examining tables know that they have entered in a profoundly personal way what was once for them an abstract issue. While there is in fact no clear dividing line between these perspectives, and while there are indeed individuals who rely on more than one or who cross into the realm of another, these approaches have distinctive qualities worth examining.

In this chapter, I study these three renderings of a story—the personal,[1] the medical,[2] and the legal. My ultimate goal is to explore how patients' knowledge and medical knowledge interact within the legal culture, and how this interaction

1

affects legal decision making. To get at these questions, I begin here by studying epistemological questions concerning each of the three perspectives: how is knowledge formed, articulated, and translated into practice by patients, physicians, and lawyers?

While I have focused on this troika of approaches to knowledge, I am well aware that there is not *a* personal, *a* medical, nor *a* legal perspective. Each of these approaches to knowledge is so broad that they include enough viewpoints to make difference, dissent, and conflict possible, and even probable, from within. Therefore, when I refer to *the* personal, *the* medical, or *the* legal perspective, the label is only intended to indicate the dominant, most common, or mainstream approach within the perspective and not that there is a uniform and unanimously accepted position in each.

I am also aware that there are other perspectives involved in these stories including the ethical, religious, economic, political, psychological, familial, and social. I focus on the medical, legal, and personal because they are tightly bound together both in knowledge and in practice: the law provides the criteria and the forum for decisions, medicine provides the information and the forum for practice, and the patient is the site for both the origination of the problem and its resolution. Since my goal is to study how these three forms of knowledge play out in court, I integrate the other perspectives only in terms of how they relate to the medical, legal, and personal.

The purpose, then, of this chapter is to uncover the distinctive characteristics of each of these three approaches to knowledge. How does the location of where one sits influence what one knows and where one stands on abortion and PAS? Within legal culture, knowledge forms a kind of continuum, ranging from the most certain to that most questionable. I therefore begin with an examination of medical knowledge since it has its origins in scientific method, a source of knowledge considered most reliable. Next, I study law and its attempts to model itself after the scientific construction of knowledge. Finally, I turn to patients' knowledge and examine how it departs from many of the norms of mainstream knowledge and is consequently not as readily heard as an expert voice. This chapter concludes by identifying the points at which the epistemologies of law, medicine, and patients intersect or clash. What emerges is a cult of expertise that shapes not only the abortion and PAS issues, but their resolution as well.

MEDICAL KNOWLEDGE

Something has happened to someone—either an unwanted pregnancy or a terminal condition. The patient seeks the aid of a physician who approaches the situation with a particular set of questions: What is the medical problem? What can

I, as a physician, do to help? This framing of the problem as a medical problem sets into motion a particular way to study the problem and highlights the relevancy of a particular type of information. How, then, does the medical profession construct and use knowledge in responding to these situations?

Science and Medical Knowledge

A common response to this question would be that medicine brings science to bear on these issues. At first blush, medicine certainly looks "scientific." Everything from the physician's white lab coat to the technical language of diagnosis and treatment speak of professionalism, rationality, and certainty. Examinations are performed, tests ordered, technologies used, results studied, and conclusions drawn. It all appears very precise, objective, and infallible. Almost weekly the mass media report on the new findings, even breakthroughs, that have been published by the top medical journals, further demonstrating the power of science to create new knowledge about the human body, its ailments, and appropriate treatments. Yet— and this is crucial to appreciate—medicine is not a science (Hunter 1991: 25).

That medicine is not a science probably flies in the face of what most people think or what they want to believe. Medicine does have a systematic connection to science and technology (Freidson 1970: xviii), but this is not enough to make it a science. The common mix-up has serious ramifications for medicine. If medicine is seen as a science, there is little room for uncertainty, failure, or mistakes. If physicians are regarded as scientists, they are afforded a deference regarding their knowledge that is in fact unwarranted, and are held to a standard of perfection that is impossible to meet.

To get at the question of what medical knowledge is, it's first important to recognize what it isn't. At the root of the "medicine as science" belief is a confusion about the relationship of medicine to science. Medicine is not a science itself but is an *applied* science. This is a matter not simply of semantics but of accuracy. Medicine itself does not construct scientific knowledge; instead, scientific method is used to form knowledge that is then applied to particular cases by physicians. While the general mission of medicine is to heal, the goal of science is to form reliable predictions that lead to understanding (Toulmin 1961; Lastrucci 1967). Put in simplest form, science produces knowledge and medicine uses knowledge.

While it is difficult to precisely define what constitutes a science, one attempt at a general definition suggests that science is "an objective, logical, and systematic method of analysis of phenomena, devised to permit the accumulation of reliable knowledge" (Lastrucci 1967: 6) It may also be instructive to note that the Latin root *scientia* is defined as knowledge, "often as opposed to intuition, belief, etc." (ibid.: 5). Science forms knowledge through a deliberate process by which to ensure accuracy and reliability—the scientific method.

Scientific method involves the "careful use of the empirical-inductive method of inquiry together with the imaginative use of the theoretical-deductive" (Conant 1964: 2). It is theoretical-deductive in that the scientist relies on observations, reasoning, and creativity to construct a hypothesis. A method is then devised for testing the validity of the hypothesis. The experiment is then conducted, data gathered and analyzed. The process is empirically inductive in that the data and analysis are used to either confirm or reject the hypothesis. If rejected, the scientist begins again with a new or adjusted hypothesis. If confirmed, it will be presented as a finding (new knowledge) that is always subject to new testing, revisions, and even rejection (see Lastrucci 1967: 55).

In contrast, medicine is not science but a use of science. As such, it is a craft that demands that the practitioner possess the skill of applying scientific knowledge to individuals for the purpose of healing (Brody 1982: 256). One physician writes of the profession in this way:

> Doctors are not scientists, at least not in their medical roles, because, though they certainly draw on science, what they do is neither objective enough nor oriented to the production of new knowledge—nor should it be. And they are certainly not artists, since aesthetic principles and independent creativity have little or no place in practice, despite everything that has been said about the "art" of medicine. But doctors are craftspeople of the higher order. (Konner 1987: xvii)

In its application, then, medicine does not possess the objectivity, precision, and certainty that science does. Instead, while medicine strives to achieve these attributes, it is in fact an imperfect craft where subjectivity emerges, best guesses are made, doubts are raised, patients healed—and mistakes made.

Science, however, does play an important role in medicine, since it forms the basis for medical practice and medical education. During the first two years of med school, students take science courses (like biochemistry, embryology, anatomy, histology, physiology, and rational psychology) that focus on "the science of the normal body" (Klass 1987: 27). During the second year, the study of the normal becomes the foundation for learning about pathologies and disease (ibid., 45). During these years, medical students are in fact learning by rote the knowledge currently accepted by a variety of sciences, and exams are used to test their learning. But then, after two years, a shift in emphasis takes place.

During the next two years, as well as during a doctor's internship and residency, the educational method changes from book learning and memorization to that of clinical experience—i.e., applied knowledge. Now it is that objective, scientific knowledge that is transformed into the subjective, practical reality of medical application (Freidson 1970: 344). When the learning moves from the textbook to the clinic, information is no longer enough. Skills are now required (see Coombs and St. John 1979: 128). "You can absolutely memorize your textbooks, you can earn a perfect score on every multiple-choice test, but none of that leaves you equipped to take care of patients" (Klass 1987: 55). One of the skills needed is that of inductive reasoning. When physicians treat patients, they reason from the particular case at hand backward to general principles in search of a rule or theory to apply. This inductive method requires an accurate gathering of patient information, an interpretation as to what the patient's condition is, and a careful course of reasoning that discounts possible theories while leading to a diagnosis. Only then is a recommendation made as to how to treat (and this recommendation itself being the product of scientific method).

Medical school education is as much process as it is content. It seems to teach by first breaking down students then building them back up again in the image of the profession. Students begin by "falling down the rabbit hole" (Coombs and St. John 1979: 44). Having graduated (usually with honors) from college, they are now at the very bottom of the medical hierarchy; they know nothing of medicine and they do nothing medical. Instead, they study, study, study volumes of material, even when it isn't clear why this information is important to know or how it will be used in the future. They experience things that separate them more and more from others: a new terminology, the trauma of dissecting a cadaver, and long hours of study, combined with financial pressures, stress, and the fear of failure. The beginning of the clinical years moves them to a new site and yet another fall—now the third-year student is at the bottom of the hospital hierarchy, the most inexperienced of practitioners, and probably as uncertain and frightened as the patients. In the clinical setting, they must learn to practice medicine, learn to deal with death, and learn a style for relating to patients as well as to other medical personnel. The stress, the lack of sleep, the financial pressures, and the isolation continue.

Yet, med school is teaching more than the application of scientific knowledge. Certain values and attitudes are also being communicated. First, students are learning the hospital hierarchy, their role within it, and how to adapt to it. They are being taught to respect authority and to stay within prescribed boundaries of acceptable conduct. Second, students are also being taught what knowledge to trust. The knowledge of outsiders, lay persons, and even patients are suspect since they lack the specialized knowledge and the emotional detachment necessary to qualify as reliable (Freidson 1970: 250). Third, students in clinic are introduced to economic and time constraints that require them to move patients through the hospital system efficiently. In its extreme form, this is referred to as the GROP (Get Rid of Patients) orientation (Mizrahi 1986).

Fourth, in the face of patient suffering and death, students also learn strategies for coping emotionally. Maintaining an emotional distance from patients and denying personal reactions are seen as necessary mechanisms that protect physicians emotionally so that they can continue practicing medicine. The desensitization includes humor, sometimes morbid, in circumstances that seem inappropriate.[3] Another distancing device is the reification of a condition and its substitution for the person who has the condition. The collapsed metonymy of patient and medical condition (as in, "take the broken leg to surgery" and "admit the bowel cancer") renders the patient invisible and "protects" the physician from dealing with the patient rather than the condition (see Hunter 1991: 135).

Medical school is also a sign of the professionalization of healing. It was not until the Middle Ages that university medical schools were introduced in Europe. Before such formalization, healing was traditionally a craft practiced by midwives, shamans, and witch doctors and taught through apprenticeship. These healers had earned a reputation within their community for their healing knowledge and skills. In the United States, the licensing of doctors and uniform training did not take root until the twentieth century (Freidson 1970: xviii). The professionalization of medicine in the United States not only moved the site of medical training but it bespoke a shift in medical practice and a transfer of medical knowledge from women to men. Medical schooling was only for men and licensing required medical schooling; hence, licensed practitioners of medicine were men and only men. Women who had served as healers for their families and their communities lost the authority to practice, the confidence of patients, and, eventually, the knowledge that they had preserved from mother to daughter.

Professionalization also caused a gender split within medicine as to who had knowledge and how it was to be used. Doctoring became male identified and nursing female identified. When Florence Nightingale established the profession of nursing, she was emphatic that it was the physician who was the medical expert and that the role of the nurse was to carry out doctor's orders. Nurses were to act only under doctor's orders and take no initiative on their own:

> Nightingale thus required that what the nurse did for the patient was a function of what the doctor felt was required for the care of the patient. Even such unskilled tasks as feeding a patient were thus defined as part of the medical regimen. All nursing work flowed from the doctor's orders, and thus nursing became a formal part of the doctor's work, a technical trade rather than a "natural" practice of femininity or a part of the exercise of charitable impulses. Nursing thus was defined as a subordinate part of the technical division of labor surrounding medicine. (Freidson 1970: 61)

While this gender division of knowledge and practice has been challenged today by female physicians and male nurses, by the rising number of physician assistants and nurse practitioners, and by a growing recognition of nursing as a profession with autonomous knowledge and responsibilities, a split between curing and caring still haunts medical practice (Anderson 1983: 173). Because of their caring role and frequent contact with patients, nurses have access to patients' knowledge in a way that most physicians do not. One study suggests that patients will discuss their concerns over prolonging or ending their lives with nurses much more often than with physicians (Brown 1971: 1415). Yet, the medical education of physicians continues to follow paradigms of knowledge inspired by the men who founded it.

What this brief history indicates is that trust in the knowledge and skills of formally trained physicians is a relatively recent phenomena. Four hundred years ago, physicians employed bleedings, leeches, incantations, quasi-religious rituals, and even snake broth to fend off illness (Ehrenreich and English 1979: 37–38). During the 1700s, water, air, and light were believed by physicians to be injurious to health (ibid., 43). During the early nineteenth century, bloodletting and purges induced by vomiting, laxatives, and enemas were common medical practices (ibid.: 46–47). It was only around 1912 "that a random patient with a random illness consulting a random physician had a better than 50–50 chance of being benefited by the encounter" (Cook 1975: xi).

Yet, faith in medical knowledge and technology grew, reinforced by state laws requiring that practitioners have formal training and stripping from "amateurs" any authorization to practice medicine. The result was that more and more physical occurrences were now viewed as reasons for medical interventions. During the twentieth century, giving birth at home and dying at home became anachronisms of another time as the hospital room filled with medical personnel and medical equipment replaced the front parlor filled with loved ones as the site for these events. The public's reliance on the medical profession also exhibited an unrealistic belief that a good physician can cure anything. During the 1990s, this faith has been shaken both by evidence to the contrary and by a growing concern that medical interventions can harm as well as heal. In an effort to again transfer medical knowledge from expert hands to those of patients, a concerned public is turning once again to alternative methods of healing—hence, the booming interest in herbal remedies, traditional cures, and self-healing techniques (see *Time*'s coverage of Dr. Andrew Weil and the popularity of alternative medicine, Kluger 1997). Yet, a serious tension exists between the desire for reliable medical treatment and the longing for less medical intervention. At the crux of the issue are questions concerning how medicine constructs and uses knowledge.

Medicine's Epistemology

The construction of knowledge is crucial to the practice of medicine as well as to the status of physicians and the medical profession. Patients obviously expect physicians to be schooled, knowledgeable, and skilled. The medical profession rejects information or techniques that are lacking in a scientific basis, and frowns upon attempts by the untrained to heal. While there are variations, medical knowledge possesses some distinctive characteristics:

Start with the Physical. The accurate collection of data, i.e., patient symptoms, is the basis for medical knowledge and practice. Medical practice is concerned with individual cases and so it is necessary for each case to be studied and assessed before any conclusions can be drawn or treatments prescribed. The beginning of knowledge, therefore, rests with the patient.

A Framework of Applied Science. Using scientific knowledge as the basis, the physician proceeds to frame the question as one of how to treat this patient. The problem, then, is one of making the proper diagnosis and then identifying the most appropriate medical responses.

Guiding Principles of Duties and Obligations. In studying the patient as a medical case, physicians are guided not only by scientific knowledge, but also by ethical obligations as to how to use that knowledge. The ancient Hippocratic oath continues to be administered to new physicians today and even in its updated forms it admonishes physicians to remember that their obligation is to heal and to avoid doing harm (see Edelstein 1943; Bonds 1990). Knowledge, then, is to be constrained in practice by principles, however, the interpretation of these principles, especially when they appear to conflict, opens the way to subjectivity and normative analysis—each seemingly as odds with objective science.

Methodology of Reason. In creating scientific knowledge from actual cases, physicians rely on inductive reasoning in that they reason backward from the particulars of the case in order to create general theories. This reasoning, then, is dependent on a complete and accurate medical record of the case, a command of scientific knowledge as to the normal body and its pathologies and diseases, and an ability to logically link the particular with the universal. In applying and testing this knowledge, medicine relies on deduction in reasoning from the general to the specific. Whether creating or applying knowledge, then, medical reasoning is an interpretive but systematic skill.

In sum, medical knowledge is based on the particulars presented by patients, is used to determine how to treat, is guided by avoidance of harm, and proceeds logically, inductively, and objectively in its use of data to properly diagnosis and treat the patient. Its scientific basis and its credo to heal give medical knowledge authority and status, while also inspiring trust.

The Limits of Medical Knowledge

As is true of any epistemology, not only is knowledge constructed, it is also constrained by the parameters set. Medical knowledge is subject to two specific boundaries as to its expertise: a blindness to patients' knowledge and an inability to answer ethical questions through science.

First, medicine emulates science's use of the particular to establish a knowledge of universals. Particulars, then, are viewed as "bearers of properties" rather than as "proper objects of knowledge" (Gorovitz and MacIntyre 1976: 60). Adopting this perspective in a medical context invites physicians to view patients in the same way, i.e., as "the bearers of properties" and not as "objects of knowledge." Patients, then, are culled for data rather than asked for the knowledge that they possess. The scientific method, therefore, leads physicians away from the view that the patient is a repository of knowledge and toward a limited notion of the patient as a collection of properties. It should also be acknowledged that this failing is a common problem but is not universal. Within medical practice, there are differences between how physicians approach the patient and their knowledge. Some physicians closely identify with their patients and listen to their knowledge (which suggests why Dr. Timothy Quill entered the PAS case on the side of his patients; see Quill 1996). Yet, the dominant perspective within medicine is to view patients as cases with symptoms.

Second, scientific method is a valuable way to assess what is wrong with a patient and how to treat a patient, yet, it offers no particular expertise for answering the question of whether a patient wants a service, or whether the treatment is ethical or not. These are questions for which "there is at present no reliable, systematic expertise" (Freidson 1970: 357). Science, then, cannot answer for the patient what is best for him or her, and neither can it answer what serves society best. Physicians, who play an important role in these issues, must address them through knowledge and reasoning apart from that of scientific method. Many turn to philosophy and the study of ethics to develop an approach to grapple with and resolve medicine's normative questions. Hospital ethics committees, governmental task forces, university and medical school ethics committees, and bioethics think tanks like the Hastings Center offer physicians the opportunity to combine the science of medical practice with the knowledge of the humanities and social sciences. It is therefore clear to even those who practice medicine that the certainty, the objectivity, and the systematic collection of scientific knowledge encompasses the question of what can be done, but does not extend to the question of what should be done. At that point, scientific knowledge has reached its limit.

Even with these limitations noted, the practice of medicine is more than the application of scientific knowledge—it is "a unique blend of epistemological and social factors (Gorovitz and MacIntyre 1976: 52). Knowledge of the profession is distinct from the circumstances and conditions under which it is applied (Freidson 1970: 344–46). Limitations on knowledge and its application, then, are also imposed by social factors. Two seem particularly relevant here—that of economics, and that of law and politics.

The practice of medicine is deeply affected by financial considerations. Economics exerts its power in many ways: medical students who graduate deeply in debt; patients who can't afford preventative or curative medical care; insurers who charge astronomical rates for malpractice insurance; managed care structures that limit medical tests, treatments, and options; and health insurance companies who contest doctor's orders or refuse to pay medical bills. Economics affects who becomes a doctor, who practices and what they practice, what research is conducted, what technologies and drugs are available, who is treated, how they are treated, and if and when they are treated. If a measure of objectivity is lost when science is applied by medicine, surely a measure of the healing power of medicine is lost when its practice is controlled by economics. The move from science to medicine to economics traces the shift in paradigms from objectivity to subjectivity to luck.

The practice of medicine is also constrained in several ways by the political and legal contexts. First is the political context that confines choices and influences how knowledge is used. A good example of this today is the tension between medicine's capacity to perform safe abortions and the political pressures aimed at stopping physicians from performing abortions. The pressures, ranging in form from polite discouragement to threatened and even enacted violence, are powerful political constraints on a legal medical practice.[4] However, law can also restrict medical practice. Malpractice law suits and statutes prohibiting a physician from performing certain procedures each constrain how medicine is practiced. The fear of legal actions may interfere with a physician's or a hospital's decision of how to treat or whether to treat a patient. This is particularly problematic when a proposed medical course of treatment conflicts with the wishes of the patient or of the family. Two physicians who have studied the problem suspect that "disagreements among physicians, and patients and families . . . [are] based not necessarily on the physician's real doubt about the wisdom of patient or family preferences but, in part, on the physicians' undisclosed fears of prosecution" (Duff and Campbell 1976: 490). When law actually forbids a medical procedure, as was true of abortion and is still true in most states regarding PAS today, the physician's choices are limited due to the threat of prosecution to those options allowed under law.

Medical knowledge, therefore, is circumscribed both by the science it uses and the social context within which it practices. When abortion and PAS leave the realm of medicine and enter the realm of the law, the structure of knowledge and its application shifts again. So does the story told.

LEGAL KNOWLEDGE

Something has happened to someone—either an unwanted pregnancy or a terminal condition. The patient in the former instance seeks a physician to perform an abortion; the patient in the latter instance seeks a physician who will give him or her the means to end his or her life. When the legality of such medical interventions are in question, it is to the courts that people turn for an answer. There, the personal medical crisis is transformed from a private problem to a public issue in the form of a law case. As legal controversies, the issues are necessarily reframed through the asking of certain questions, the consideration of particular concerns, and the following of a definite process of decision making. Now the question is whether the medical procedure sought can legally be obtained or performed. To answer this question, the legal system adheres to a distinctive epistemology and it is one that is quite deliberate in its design and explicit in its values and processes.

The Science of Law

To begin, it's probably most important to know that American law is guided by a very particular ethic—that of justice. While justice can be understood and practiced in various ways, two understandings are dominant within the American legal system. The first is that the administration of justice is a public and not a private matter, and the second is that the process used in judicial decision making must be fair.

The question of how to resolve personal disputes can be traced back at least as far as the ancient Greeks. As exemplified in Aeschylus' plays *The Oresteian Triology*, the Greeks attempted to explain how and why the administration of justice moved from the private realm of the family to the public order. Under the guidance of the goddess Athena, the characters ultimately accept an end to the cycle of personal revenge and place their trust in the judgment of a public tribunal. Although millenia apart, the American judicial system too is based on the assumption that the administration of justice is best assigned to the public order. When individuals ask the judicial system to intervene in a dispute, the responsibility of resolution shifts from private hands to the public courts.

In a democracy, such a transferal of the administration of justice from the private to the public is based on a sense of trust (rather than, for instance, on fear of force or pressure to adhere to religious mandates), and such trust is dependent on the belief that disputes will be handled fairly. At minimum, the ethic of justice seems to require three components. First, that those who pass judgment do so objectively—that neither discrimination nor favoritism bias the decision making. Second, that the decision be arrived at through reasoning—that logic and persuasion rule over personal whim or predilection. Third, that the rule established in resolving a dispute be universally applied—that all similar cases be treated similarly and different cases differently. The familiar image that captures these three norms is that of the Goddess of Justice—she who is blindfolded, who holds aloft balancing scales, and who bears the sword of public authority symbolizes how justice is to be done—with objectivity, reasoning, and universality.

The importance of these norms is heightened by constitutionalism. While the U.S. Constitution establishes a democratic form of government, it also sets limits as to what this government can do. When a clash emerges between democratic will and the constitutional language that imposes limits (especially in terms of minority rights), it is, as Chief Justice John Marshall once put it, "emphatically the province of the judicial department to say what the law is." Yet, in employing their power of judicial review, the Justices face what Alexander Bickel (1962) called the "countermajoritarian difficulty"—how should a Court that is appointed for life rather than elected employ the power to negate the actions of the elected branches? This concern has informed in several ways both the theory and practice of American law.

First, there is the commitment to principled decision making. The process by which the judiciary makes decisions is not the same as that followed by legislatures. Legislative representatives are tied by elections to constituents, party lines, and money, and thus their deliberations are overtly "political" as they choose from among policy options. In contrast, the countermajoritarian difficulty compels the Justices to appear as "apolitical" as possible, and this is accomplished by focusing on a fair and objective decision making process rather than on the selection of a particular result. In an influential article criticizing the decision making process (though not the decision) in *Brown v. Board of Education* (1954), Herbert Wechsler argued that a constitutional democracy requires that the Court use "neutral principles" in applying judicial review. He explained:

> A principled decision, in the sense I have in mind, is one that rests on reasons with respect to all the issues in the case, reasons that in their generality and their neutrality transcend any immediate result that is involved. When no sufficient reasons of this kind can be assigned for overturning value choices of the other branches of Government or of a state, those choices must, of course, survive. (1959: 1)

Igniting a heated debate over whether principles can really be neutral (see Miller and Howell 1960), as well as whether the result in *Brown* can be supported by principled reasoning (see Black 1960; Ely 1980), Wechsler's argument continues to exert influence as a way of legitimating judical review. As Stephen Wasby puts it, "the 'neutral principles' idea is . . . important because it proposes a goal—principled and reasoned opinions—to which judges should aspire even if they are not able to achieve it" (1993: 270).

A second response to the countermajoritarian difficulty is the development of American law as precedent-based, meaning that past cases serve as the source for determining a rule of law that will be applied to all new similar cases. This is not, however, the same as English common law where law was formed on the basis of judicial actions alone. The workings of American precedent-based law is distinguished by the establishment of and reference to textual records including constitutions, statutes, legislative histories including the intent of authors, as well as past cases. The judge is not only confined by past judicial decisions but by the applicable constitutional and statutory principles, language, and intent. Yet, looking backward is an essential part of shaping legal knowledge. In developing a consistency between past and present cases, the rule of law is to be neutrally applied to all by a judge who is guided by precedent rather than by personal whim.

The construction of knowledge, therefore, occurs in a very particular way. When a specific case presents itself, the facts are scrutinized and the main issue identified so that a search can begin for the rule to be applied. Edward Levi stated it simply: "The steps are these: similarity is seen between cases; next the rule of law inherent in the first case is announced; then the rule of law is made applicable to the second case" (1949: 2). Past cases become the terrain for the hunt, yet the judge must possess not only knowledge of the landscape but the skills to make reasoned decisions in choosing which paths to reject and which to follow. This is so because for most cases there is not a single path but many from which to choose. Decisions must be made as to similarity and difference, and therefore, a specific type of reasoning is employed in the creation of legal knowledge. As Cardozo described it, "its method is inductive, and it draws its generalizations from particulars" (1921: 23). Once legal principles are extracted from the specifics, deductive reasoning guides their application to new cases. This is a dynamic process in that the incorporation of new cases alters the case history as well as the law. As Levi states it, "the kind of reasoning involved in the legal process is one in which the classification changes as the classification is made" (1949: 3).

Yet, it is easy to oversimplify the process. Cardozo faulted jurists who viewed their own role as simply to search, compare, and apply:

> Their notion of duty is to match the colors of the case at hand against the colors of many sample cases spread out upon their desk. The sample nearest in shade supplies the applicable rule. . . . If that were all there was to our calling, there would be little of intellectual interest about it. The man who had the best card index of the cases would also be the wisest judge. It is when the colors do not match, when the references in the index fail, when there is no decisive precedent, that the serious business of the judge begins. He must then fashion law for the litigants before him. In fashioning it for them, he will be fashioning it for others. (1921: 20–21)

In so fashioning a direction for the law, judges draw on more than mere precedent since they are also guided by the logic of philosophy, the evolution of history, social customs and traditions, and a sense of morality (Cardozo 1921).

A third response to the countermajoritarian concern is the debate over how rigorously judicial review should be employed. Should the Justices approach their task with judicial restraint or judicial activism? Proponents of judical restraint, like Justice Antonin Scalia and Judge Robert Bork emphasize the democratic elements of the Constitution and argue that the Court should limit overruling of federal and state laws only when the text of the Constitution is clearly violated. To do otherwise, they maintain, is to usurp legislative power. Yet, advocates of judicial activism like Justice William Brennan and law professor Laurence Tribe, have urged the Court to accept the constitutional responsibility of protecting the rights of (numerical) minorities from oppressive majorities, by reading generously the individual rights both stated and implied by the text of the Constitution. To do otherwise, they maintain, is to shirk their responsibility to upholding the people's compact.

What should be evident from this discussion is that there are political reasons as to why the legal system strives to be (or critics would say strives to appear to be) above politics as well as immune to personal influence. Given their unelected status, their power to void the actions of the other branches, and their placement within a constitutional republic, the Court has adopted both norms and practices to legitimate its role. Within this context, there is a close fit between the counter-majoritarian difficulty and the ethic of justice. With its emphasis on objectivity, reason, and universal application, the ethic of justice conforms to the political constraints imposed on the judiciary by the constitutional system even as it guides judicial decision making.

While the focus so far has been on judges, it is lawyers who will represent patients and their interests in court. To do so effectively, lawyers must understand how judges go about judging and how in turn they as lawyers must argue their cases. In other words, they must learn legal reasoning. This is an expertise not left to chance.

Law schools train students to think like lawyers. In that it is necessary to teach them to think in a particular way is one indication that there are other ways to think and that many, if not most of us, do not "naturally" think like lawyers. Law school "valorizes sorting, rewards people who think fast but not always those who think deeply, and relies upon uniform rules and standards" (Guinier et al. 1997: 2). Students learn to quickly identify the legal issue in a case, aggressively argue one side, and conduct an attack on the other side—while remaining emotionally detached from the foray. Advocacy, then, is neutral since one must be able to persuasively defend either position, and it is bipolar since there are only two sides to the issue, and only won can win. Argumentation is based on the issue spotted, the logical application of relevant precedents and rules, the destruction of the other side, and the persuasiveness of delivery. Students who successfully learn to think like lawyers are rewarded with high class rankings within a system that is decidedly hierarchical and competitive. The objective of legal training is to produce students with the capacity to make sound decisions and to take action (Conant 1964: 60).

Like med school, law school reshapes a student by dropping them into an unfamiliar environment, disabusing them of the belief that they are already knowledgeable, submerging them in an ocean of information, and reshaping them according to the standards of the profession. Fear, stress, fatigue, and competition combine to isolate the student from those not in law school while pushing the student to identity with other law students and the profession at large. The process of learning to become a lawyer, then, entails a separation, a breaking, a rebuilding, and a new bonding. The teaching of law is designed to accomplish all of these.

Law's construction of knowledge is heavily influenced by the case study method of instruction that was first introduced at Harvard University in 1870 by Professor Christopher Columbus Langdell. Until that time, students learned law through reading textbooks and listening to lectures that identified for them the general legal principles. Langdell's case study method in essence threw out the book and started over. Instead of textbooks, students would now read cases, the primary sources of law, and would be guided by the instructor's questioning to discover for themselves the rule of law. There were several objectives and assumptions behind the introduction of this new legal pedagogy. Edwin Patterson identifies them as: (1) a deliberate move to teach law based on scientific method; (2) a belief that students learn better as active problem-solvers; (3) a pragmatism that legal education should resemble legal practice; and (4) a belief that the historical development of precedent could more easily be taught by the tracing of cases (1951: 2–10). The case study method, then, revolutionized not only what was taught as legal knowledge, but how it was taught.

That law was now being taught using a "scientific" method is important for how that shaped law's concept of knowledge. What made it scientific was that the law student employed the same inductive method as the student of the physical sciences in approaching "law as a science consisting of a body of principles to be found in the adjudged cases" (Keener as quoted in Patterson 1951: 3). Instead of chemistry experiments, the law student studied legal experiments (i.e., cases), and learned how to derive general principles from them (Patterson 1951: 5). Legal knowledge, therefore, was not a matter of memorized legal norms, but was the result of a carefully followed process, drawn from scientific method, that employed thinking through inductive reasoning to discover generalizations that could then be applied through deductive reasoning in the future.

The most popular method of teaching students this method of thinking is the "ritualized combat" known as the Socratic Method, still pervasive in "almost *all* first year instruction" (Guinier et al. 1997: 13, 28). Through a question-and-answer process where the teacher asks and usually one particular student answers (frequently not having volunteered to do so), the Socratic Method challenges students to think for themselves and to employ legal reasoning. After a case is summarized by the student, the instructor will then challenge the offered interpretation or ask a student to extend the rule of law to a new hypothetical case. In the course of the questioning and answering, students are working out conclusions and are gaining experience in spotting the issue and in problem solving. This is an active pedagogy that demands student participation. At its best, the Socratic Method teaches students how to think quickly and logically; at its worst, it uses intimidation and humiliation to form (critics would say to destroy) students' thought processes. Noting that this is not an equal or fair forum for discourse, critics point out that the questioner, who never abdicates the role, controls the discussion and uses this power to corner or to "pin" the student who is answering. Some students find the method frustrating and game-like in that no matter how they answer, the instructor shifts the discourse to their disadvantage. At times, the method seems more intent on "hiding the ball" from the student than in illuminating the law (Jaff 1986: 67).

Increasingly, the form and substance of law school education and the traditional processes and assumptions that form legal reasoning are being criticized, challenged, and even reformed by those within the legal community. In particular, the Critical Legal Studies (CLS), Feminist Jurisprudence, and the Critical Race Studies (CRS) movements have challenged whether this "scientific" method of legal reasoning is truly as unbiased and objectively discoverable as it claims. Noting the political nature of law, advocates of CLS maintain that law's support of the status quo is not coincidental and neither are its claims to disinterested neutrality (see Unger 1975; Kennedy and Klare 1984; Minow 1986; Tushnet 1991; Minda 1995). Fem Crits (feminists drawing on parts of the CLS tradition) question the masculine bias for constructing and resolving legal disputes in adversarial terms when more feminine-based resolutions such as negotiation, compromise, and counseling may better serve clients and the community (see Scales 1981; Menkel-Meadow 1985; MacKinnon 1987, 1989; Matsuda 1988; West 1988; Baer 1990; Bartlett and Kennedy 1991). Scholars who adopt the CRS perspective have been vocal in criticizing the capacity of traditional law to silence people who construct knowledge in other ways (Crenshaw 1988; Matsuda 1988; Delgado 1989; Delgado and Stefancic 1993; Williams 1991). For instance, legal knowledge about discrimination is limited and actually uninformed if it does not include and seriously consider the concrete and personal knowledge of those who are treated and viewed as outsiders (Matsuda 1988: 8–9). Within law, then, there are voices who question the model of law as objective science.

Law's Distinctive Epistemology

Yet, the traditional approaches to the law remain dominant. Within the mainstream approach, legal knowledge is formed within the following parameters:

Begin with the Facts. The facts form the starting line of the contest that is about to begin. They are explicitly stated, neutrally formed, and accepted as accurate by both sides to the case. Out of them is drawn a question or issue that becomes the point of contention. Lawyers are taught to rely on factual information that cannot be disputed, that which can be proved or corroborated, and that which cannot be seriously challenged.

A Framework of Rights. The facts of the case are studied with the purpose of identifying the controlling legal issue. Issues are framed as yes/no questions following the typical pattern of "Does this law that requires (whatever) constitute a violation of the plaintiff's constitutional right to (whatever)?" Controversies, therefore, are formed as a clash of interests or of rights (see Glendon 1991) whose resolution is a zero-sum game with only one side able to win and the other destined to lose. *Guiding Principles of Objectivity and Distance.* In that judicial interpretation is based on written texts and past decisions, judges are expected to be objective and impartial in their decision making, and disinterested as to the outcome of the case. It is to the process that judges owe allegiance, and not to a particular set of values. Law, then, is not results oriented but process oriented in its uniform application of general principles.

Methodology of Logical Reason. In order to create knowledge, law employs inductive reasoning that begins with spotting the issue at hand and moving backward to survey past similar cases in order to discover a general rule. In applying knowledge, deductive reasoning moves from the generalized rule in order to apply it to the case at hand. While this method may not always be open to a jurist (e.g., because of the introduction of a unique case or a case that challenges the correctness of past decisions), the decision must still be grounded in the legal form of textual interpretation or intent, the evaluation of competing legal claims, the interpretation of language, and the self-consciousness of the Court that it is in fact constructing legal knowledge.

The Limits of Legal Knowledge

In all, the legal perspective is concerned with constitutional and statutory interpretation, the application of precedents, and the assessment of individual and states rights. Knowledge is therefore constructed through interpretation and reasoning within the constraints of neutrality and objectivity. In adhering to this construction of knowledge, law is limited in several ways. First, law's adversarial nature demands that issues be articulated and defined in binary terms. Such a framing precludes the consideration of more than two sides to an issue, the possibility of reconciliation or compromise, or a discussion of the multitude of factors that have led to this point of conflict. Instead, law's focus is on the dispute and which side will prevail.

Second, legal education devalues personal knowledge (see Van Praagh 1992; Pickard 1987–88). Students are taught to leave their personal feelings behind and to utilize instead their skills in reasoning. The very structure and terminology of legal reasoning and argumentation leave no room and no language for the expression of the personal. As Lucinda Finley points out:

> There are some things that just cannot be said by using the legal voice. Its terms depoliticize, decharge and dampen. Rage, pain, elation, the aching, thirsting, hungering for freedom on one's own terms, love and its joys and terrors, fear, utter frustration at being contained and constrained by legal language—all are diffused by legal language. (1989: 904)

In dividing knowledge into the categories of subjective (i.e., emotionally based and therefore unreliable and not really knowledge) and objective (i.e., rationally based and therefore reliable knowledge), law narrows what it can see, hear, and feel. It therefore narrows what it can know.

These limitations are obvious in the abortion and PAS cases. Law highlights rights, power, and rules. The question of what is "best" for society, for physicians, or for patients is never overtly asked or considered; neither is an analysis of what brought all the parties to this point and what can be done to negotiate a resolution. Instead, when abortion and PAS are addressed from the legal perspective, the questions that arise concern text, previous rulings, founders' intent, and the facts and issues at hand. The Court has neither the luxury to ponder all the factors that a legislature could consider nor the obligation to resolve all the aspects of an issue. Like medicine, it has no expertise in asking the question of should a course of treatment be performed, since its reach extends only as far as the legality of the course of treatment. The subjective, the emotive, the normative are not part of law's domain. Instead, law is concrete, inductive, reasoned, universal, and at least in theory, impartial.

So, while an unwanted pregnancy, a medical option of having an abortion, and a state law outlawing the procedure constituted a personal dilemma for Jane Roe, it had to be reinterpreted as a legal matter for it to become a law case. She could not argue that because she wanted or needed an abortion that she has a legal right to procure the procedure. The physicians could not argue that medical knowledge made them alone qualified to judge what to do. Instead, the personal, medical, and moral dimensions had to be submerged and the legal aspects formulated to create a justiciable case and controversy: Roe charged that the Texas statute abridged her right of personal privacy, protected by the First, Fourth, Fifth, Ninth, and Fourteenth Amendments. In so arguing, Roe quite literally made a "federal case" out of her problem. As presented, the legal issue demanded a yes or no answer. Either the Texas statute abridged her constitutional rights, or it did not. (The Court's answer to this question is analyzed in chapter 2.)

A similar reformulation occurred in the *Quill* and *Glucksberg* cases. Rather than phrase the issue in terms of the moral, religious, economic, personal, or medical aspects of PAS, the attorneys framed their clients' concerns as legal questions: Do the New York state and Washington state laws that pronounce it manslaughter (New York) or a felony (Washington) to knowingly aid another person to attempt suicide violate a patient's right to liberty and equal protection of the law as guaranteed under the Fourteenth Amendment to the Constitution? Again, either the statutes are a violation or they are not. (The Court's answer to these questions is the subject of chapter 3.)

While the Court, then, addresses abortion and PAS by invoking the principles of legal reasoning, the knowledge of the personal is but a footnote in the record.

Why a woman would want an abortion, why someone who is dying would want to commit suicide, are not proper legal questions. Instead, they are questions that construct another type of knowledge. Another story to be told.

PATIENTS' KNOWLEDGE

Something has happened to someone—either an unwanted pregnancy or a terminal condition. The patient in the former instance seeks a physician to perform an abortion; the patient in the latter instance seeks a physician who will give him or her the means to end his or her life. But, the legality of such medical interventions is in question so the issue goes to court. As medicine and law wrestle over the greater issues of abortion and PAS, the patient asks a far more personal question: What about me? What is happening to me? What are my choices? The patient wants to add his or her story to the medical and legal records and urges the doctors and lawyers to "Listen to what I know." But it's hard for patients to be heard. Discredited for lacking objectivity, disregarded as having little reliable knowledge, and dismissed for lack of a disciplined method of study, patients struggle for recognition of their knowledge. So, rather than begin my inquiry here by asking how patients construct knowledge, my first task is to question how we can even speak of the personal knowledge of patients.

The Limits of Patients' Knowledge

In many ways, it is easier to talk of legal or medical knowledge than personal knowledge regarding abortion or PAS. While there are clear disagreements over these issues within both law and medicine, there are also commonly agreed upon standards of how to construct and use information. Law and medicine are recognized disciplines of study that have developed a way to construct paradigms of knowledge and approaches to practice. The experiences of patients are not organized into an academic discipline. As contrasted with law or medicine, no one aspires to become a patient. It is not a vocation; there are no schools to instruct patients how to obtain knowledge or make sense of their experiences. How, then, can we speak of patients' knowledge?

Another limitation is that patients are an exceptionally diverse group of people. Some need only a specific treatment while others require continual medical care until their deaths. Some are elderly; others tragically young. Some have great resources upon which to draw—financial, relational, religious and spiritual, while others are limited in any of these or all of them. Some are blamed by others or even by themselves for their medical condition; others are afforded the blessing of innocence. Some suffer from the stigmas associated with gender, class, race/ethnicity,

sexual orientation, age, or disability even as others are not so defined. Some patients accept their condition, some seek a cure, some deny the problem, some fight
it, some adopt all these attitudes at some point. Some patients seek certainty of information and of outcome; others do not. Some trust their physicians, family
members, friends, or a court to decide what is best for them; others insist on self-
determination. Clearly, there is no one patient perspective as there is no universal
patient. How, then, can we speak of the patients' knowledge?

It is also difficult to find the patient's story. While some accounts do exist (see
Rollin 1976; Selzer 1993; Bauby 1997; Reardon 1987; Kushner 1997), the voice
of patients regarding abortion and PAS are particularly difficult to uncover. The
terminally ill are usually unable to write of their experience, and many women
who have had abortions are silenced by their fear of exposure or their desire for
privacy. Frequently, patients' stories are told by others: physicians (Hilfiker 1985;
Brody 1987; Quill 1996); attorneys (Alderman and Kennedy 1997; Weddington
1992); family members (Humphry 1978; Rollin 1998; Allende 1994); activists
(Humphry 1991); and journalists (McCorvey with Meisler 1994; Stabiner 1997;
Albom 1997). In court, the presence of the patient's voice is often only an illusion.
Medical experts claim to represent it in speaking about the best interests of their
patients. The voice of lawyers are merged with that of their clients so that lin-
guistically the lawyer actually becomes the patient (and this fiction is duly reported
in the transcripts that say "Roe argued that . . ."; "Cruzan refuted that . . ."). Under
these circumstances, it is difficult to know if the voice heard is that of the patient.
How, then, can we speak of the patients' knowledge?

Yet we can. We can because the realm of the patients' perspective does exist—
and it is called personal experience. We can because we must—some information
crucial to our knowledge about abortion and PAS can only be found in the patients' realm.

Patients and Experiential Knowledge

Enter that realm, and amid the diversity, experience creates a common connection. A woman considering an abortion or a terminally ill patient considering suicide are experiencing crisis situations. They are at a crossroads in their lives. The
questions that confront them are of the most urgent, intimate, and poignant
kind—they demand that a decision be made between life and death. No matter
the answer to the question, the patient's life will be altered in a dramatic way. For
most, the experience itself will be transformative. Even if a patient has thought before about the "what ifs," the actual confrontation with a harsh reality is quite different. Abstract hypotheticals are only useful to a certain degree when real life
clicks in. To hear a medical diagnosis and know that it refers to you, to hear the
hope, consolation, plan of action or condolences offered by a medical provider, to

feel the psychological, emotional, and physical effects of a medical condition or procedure are gateways into the realm of the patients' perspective. Become a patient, and you are changed. In writing for the *New York Times Book Review* about Karen Stabiner's book on breast cancer, *To Dance with the Devil*, Susan Bolotin gives us insight into how profound that change can be:

> A diagnosis of breast cancer fills up a woman's calendar. So much to do, so little time: always someone to call, somewhere to drive, some magazine to flip through in yet another waiting room. Initial visits, second opinions, a whole new Rolodex of people to refer, and defer, to: the oncologist, radiologist, surgeon, the shrink, nutritionist, healer. There are the treatments: radiation, chemotherapy. The procedures: biopsy, lumpectomy, mastectomy, reconstruction, transplant. The shopping: prosthesis, wig, bra. The vomit. The rage.
>
> But when the surgery is over and the treatment is complete, how is a woman to fill the pages of her date book? What can she do but wait, never knowing, until she's dying of some other disease, if the cancer will come back? (Bolotin 1997: 8)

Yes, experience begets knowledge. Even physicians, who are certainly more accustomed than most people to the medical environment, emerge with new insights when they become the patient. Rafael Campo's *The Poetry of Healing* offers a testimonial of how dramatic are the insights gleaned from the realm of the patients' perspective. When faced with his own diagnosis of a cancerous cyst on his arm, he writes, "Ironically, anything I may have learned in medical school that might have helped me combat this disease seemed ineffectual and irrelevant. It was to poetry that I instinctively and immediately turned" (Campo 1997: 243). The documentary "Cancer: A Personal Voyage" (1997) traces the final years of the life of Dr. Peter Morgan who drew on his knowledge of medicine and his experiences as a cancer patient to teach other doctors the necessity of developing empathy toward the patients' perspective. He discovered that while doctors can master diseases and order tests, they don't really know about the tests: whether it hurts, what it means, how much trouble it puts a patient through. His lesson, though seemingly simple, profoundly changed his colleagues: "Thoughtful compassion, empathy and the laying on of hands is the art of medicine." So different, then, is the patients' perspective, that even physicians can be changed.

Enter the patients' realm, and commonalities become clear. Patients do not wish to suffer, lose their dignity, or be treated as an object, thing, or disease. They want access to competent medical treatment and alternatives, kind and compassionate medical care, and a trusting relationship with their care provider. In all, they ask that care be given to them and harm be avoided.

It is therefore drawing on this realm of experience that I speak of patients' knowledge. Yet, the difficulties inherent in this discussion are only beginning since traditionally and even currently, reason, not experience, is the road to knowledge

(Cassell 1991: 217). Reason is a trusted source of knowledge because of its claims to objectivity, its emotional distance, its reliance on facts, and its systematic procession from informational bits to solid conclusion. In contrast, experience is seen as an unreliable source of expertise since it is distorted by passions and emotions (ibid.), fooled by sensations, limited in scope to an individual occurrence, and missing any systematic process by which to build theory or suggest conclusions.

This conflict between reason and experience is illustrated nicely by two very different sources. Brian Clark's play, "Whose Life Is It Anyway?" contains a scene where two physicians disagree about whether a paraplegic patient can refuse to take prescribed medication. One insists that qualified opinions can only reside in those trained to use the objective knowledge of science, while the other attempts to refute this by arguing that since patients alone can directly feel their bodies, their knowledge trumps medical opinion. This fictionalized depiction of the tension that exists between types of knowledge and of the tendency for medical knowledge to supersede the knowledge of patients, is echoed in How We Die (1993) by Sherwin B. Nuland. Noting how the art of dying is usually subverted in favor of the art of saving life, Dr. Nuland considers the extent of medical knowledge:

> When I have a major illness requiring highly specialized treatment, I will seek out a doctor skilled in its provision. But I will not expect of him that he understand my values, my expectations for myself and those I love, my spiritual nature, or my philosophy of life. That is not what he is trained for and that is not what he will be good at. It is not what drives those engines of his excellence.
>
> For those reasons, I will not allow a specialist to decide when to let go. I will choose my own way. (266)

Both Clark and Nuland identify a cultural reluctance to recognize the limits of medical knowledge and to validate patients' knowledge. Indeed, the message of both playwright and doctor is that such an appreciation would require innovation in health care as well as modification in cultural attitudes. Thus, to attribute any expertise to the patient is to challenge some of the accepted norms for the construction of knowledge. It is to question knowledge itself.

Yet, this is precisely my intent. As I've suggested in the two previous sections of this chapter, the fields of medicine and law are becoming increasingly sensitive to the fact that important and useful knowledge is held by marginalized people (like patients, people of color, women, children). (Concerning medicine see Cassell 1991; Freidson 1970; May 1991; concerning law see Matsuda 1988; Crenshaw 1988; MacKinnon 1989; Delgado 1989; Minow 1990; Williams 1991.) Richard Delgado uses the term "outgroup" to refer to "any group whose consciousness is other than that of the dominant one" (1989: 2412). They are people "whose voice and perspective—whose consciousness—has been suppressed, devalued, and abnormalized" (ibid.). But make no mistake about it, the addition of marginalized voices is not so much about inclusion as it is about changing what we know. These voices challenge the mainstream and insist on being integrated through a dialectical discourse, not assimilated to conform to current knowledge.

Feminism serves as a particularly powerful example of using voice to challenge such marginalization and to promote change. The feminist critique of dualisms such as those of expert/nonexpert, public/private, and scientific/emotional, was built on the *experiences* of women (see Jaggar 1983). One method of building new knowledge based on experience is the feminist technique of consciousness raising that attributes value to what the individual knows through experience, and grounds theory on actual practice (see Sarachild 1995). The point of feminist theorists is not that the nonexpert person, the private realm or the emotional mode is better than the expert, public, and scientific, but that the latter cannot and should not be privileged over the former, and that the distinctions collapse under the scrutiny supplied by experience. Knowledge, then, is best formed with attention to the reciprocal and complementary nature of both reason and experience.

Therefore, I am purposefully including patients' knowledge for its potential to change both medicine and law. Inclusion of the patient's voice adds to our information at two levels. First, it offers particularized knowledge that may challenge more generalized knowledge. Patients' accounts of disease inform physicians of how varied symptoms can be. Their descriptions of the hardships imposed by certain treatments remind physicians that some attempts to heal are as (and sometimes more) frightening and painful as the medical condition being treated. Physicians who perform abortions should know that the motion of the suctioning instrument used during an abortion procedure resembles the thrusting of sexual intercourse. Physicians who treat terminal cancer patients should know that the collapse of a vein can be the final straw for a patient who endured surgery and several rounds of chemotherapy. Second, collectively these personal accounts may be instructive in placing an issue within a larger social context. The perspective offered by patients may present the possibility of seeing the issues of abortion and PAS, as well as their resolutions, in new ways. Indeed, the questions of why women want to terminate pregnancies or why terminal patients want to hasten their deaths can only be understood as part of larger social problems such as women's status in society or social attitudes toward dying. Patients, then, not only possess knowledge, it is necessary knowledge, and any accounting of these issues without it remains incomplete.

As was evident in the first section of this chapter on the medical perspective, this approach of valuing the experiential is not in fact contrary to that of medical knowledge, since it is almost impossible for physicians to form knowledge without the building block of patients' experience and their reporting of it. Indeed, as Sir William Osler, author of an early authoritative medical text wrote, "it is a safe rule to have no teaching without a patient for a text, and the best teaching is that taught by the patient himself" (1903: 50). This is to recognize that a physician cannot treat the body without an appreciation for the person (Cassell 1991). Put differently, medical knowledge cannot work without patients' knowledge. Yet, the same might be said of legal knowledge. There too, patients' knowledge can serve as the building blocks for the legal record. However, it may be more difficult for law to hear patients' knowledge because inclusion of their voices seems to threaten to undermine the mandates of the ethic of justice—that knowledge be impartial, reasoned, and universal.

It is with these understandings that patients do construct and use knowledge, though in ways different than that of law or medicine, that I maintain that we can and we must speak of patients' knowledge.

Patients' Distinctive Epistemology

Patients, then, construct knowledge in a very intimate way. Their experiences are paths to information that most others do not have. In stressing experience over reason (but not to its exclusion) the patients' way of knowing possesses several distinctive characteristics:

Begin with the Concrete, the Particular, the Self. Am I pregnant? or Is there something wrong with me? These are the questions with which the status of patient begins. They are questions phrased in terms of the self: I, me. The condition is not an abstraction, a hypothetical, or a case among many. It is real for the patient in that it is happening to him or her and it is involving his or her body—and this is a powerful site for information. Contrary to Cartesian theory, we don't just inhabit our bodies, we *are* our bodies (see Bordo 1987). Our bodies are the way we move and shape the world, the way we sense the world, and the way we disclose ourselves to the world (May 1991: 9).

In stressing the experiential it should also be noted that many patients add to this form of knowledge by gathering and integrating scientific information about their condition, their treatment, and their prognosis. The mass popularity of medical books like *Gray's Anatomy* and *The Physicians' Desk Reference* and instructional self-help books like *Our Bodies, Ourselves* demonstrate how individuals link the experiential with the scientific. Others reach out to those who are or have been similarly situated in order to exchange stories, draw strength, and build knowledge. Formalized patient support groups or patient advocacy organizations illustrate well that patients' knowledge is not unidimensional. Still, the distinctive and dominant feature of patients' knowledge remains the singular, concrete, and particular experience.

Within a Framework of Autonomy, Choice, and Self-Determination. What are my choices for treatment? This question is foremost in the minds of patients, but it only makes sense when there are (1) options, and (2) the patient's decision is determinative. As the professionalization of medicine grew, patients gained treatment based on science, but they lost some of their power over determining the course of treatment. Science trumps the personal. Law trumps the personal. While both law and medicine require that a patient give informed consent before treatment, the range of choices has already been narrowed by that which is legally and medically acceptable.

Personal knowledge does not always conform to these restrictions. When abortion or PAS have been denied to patients who want them, some patients reclaim their power to decide by taking matters into their own hands and proceeding with underground or illegal activities. Within the abortion rights movement the coat hanger is the symbol of such legal defiance, while in the PAS movement the plastic bag stands as the emblem of those who challenge law's authority. Both illustrate the isolation and danger that some patients are willing to endure in order to preserve their autonomy in determining their own fate. Patients' knowledge, therefore, is framed not in legal or medical terms, but as a personal decision that he or she is ultimately entitled to make.

Guiding Principles of Relationships and Caring. While the physical issue is experienced by the patient alone, those who have a relationship with the patient are also affected by the medical condition and treatment. Patients tend to worry not only about what is best for them, but what is best for those they love. An unwanted pregnancy, or a terminal illness is set within the context of how a patient's life is connected to the lives of others. While an abortion or impending death can invoke fear in a patient, sometimes the more compelling fear is that of the anticipated impact that not making these choices will have on loved ones. Because of this relational context, there can at times be tension between caring for the self and caring for others. What constitutes a tolerable condition or course of action for one patient can be intolerable for another. Patients' construction of knowledge may therefore take into consideration the suffering of others: emotionally, economically, physically, and spiritually. These others can even include the medical and legal professionals who are trying to help them (even as they are casting doubt on the patient's knowledge).

Drawing on the Emotional, Partial, Intuitive. These issues are not just physical, and neither are they just legal. There is some degree of distress or suffering going on, and it is relevant and informative. As Cassell urges us to remember, "bodies do not suffer, persons suffer" (1991: vii). Patients know that suffering is not the same as physical pain. Suffering can take the form of anguish, doubt, sorrow, disappointment, shame, guilt, or anger. It can also mean physical pain, emotional pain, psychological pain, or spiritual pain. Feelings, intuition, gut reactions may not be open to validation, replication, and study, but they can contain knowledge. Hence, the exasperated patient who tells the physician, "I don't care what the test results say. I know what I feel." Feelings, then are not the opposite of knowledge; they can be its source.

In sum, the patients' way of knowing is derived from the concrete and the particular, caring for oneself as well as for others, and the affective mode. There is no claim of science here; no rule-orientation; no unifying theory or system of discovery. Instead, knowledge is subjectively, personally, and individually discovered.

INTERSECTIONS AND DIVISIONS

At various points and in a variety of ways, the medical, legal, and personal approaches to knowledge converge, conflict, and interact. Before assessing the specific dimension of how these perspectives compare, I turn first to the environment shared by all three—that of American culture. In assessing how we form and use knowledge concerning the issues of abortion and PAS, the distinctiveness of the three epistemologies is important, but so is the cultural context that constrains and shapes these ways of knowing. Within this context, gender is important and death is feared, and these societal factors affect what we think we know.

The Cultural Context of Knowledge

Culture as Gendered. While not all women will face the abortion decision, all those who do face this crisis will be women. Yet access to abortion is mostly controlled by men (who still constitute the majority of Congress, state legislatures, the Supreme Court, federal and state judgeships, and physicians) while it is women who bear the burden of the procedure or of bringing to term an unwanted pregnancy. At first glance, it would seem that PAS is not so gendered. After all, as Justice Sandra Day O'Connor put it during oral argument of the *Quill* case, dying is "an issue every one of us faces, young and old, male and female, whatever it may be" (Greenhouse 1997). Yet gender appears to play a role in PAS culture, too. When dying occurred at home, women cared for the dying. If the image of death could be said to take the masculine form of the Grim Reaper, then comfort and care could be said to adopt the feminine form of mother, sister, daughter, midwife, or nurse. Women cared for and comforted the young and the old alike, and once death claimed their patient, it was often they who prepared the body for whatever mourning ritual followed (Bender 1992). With the medicalization of death, power shifted to men. Lawmakers, judges, physicians, pharmacists, ministers, and undertakers control the circumstances of death. We need to question, then, how this gendered nature of our culture also shapes our knowledge about abortion and PAS.

Culture as Death Defying. Each culture has established beliefs and rituals concerning what Kutner has termed the "pornography of death" (1976: 39). Death has been shielded and ritualized by repressive imageries and taboos. In the United States, despite the diverse ancestral mix of the citizenry, there is a definite cultural response to death—it is one of fear. Death is regarded as an enemy to be avoided or defeated (Hoffman 1975: 78). In the 1960s, Dr. Elizabeth Kubler-Ross broke the taboo against public discussion of death and began to sensitize the public to the harm perpetuated by society's fear of death. She traced five stages in attitudes toward death and dying and argued that the initial denial and anger can lead to a peaceful acceptance (1969). She developed this study into a theory that maintains that death is, in fact, the "final stage of growth" because the knowledge that we are not immortal encourages us to use what time we have to accomplish all that we can (1975).

It is hard to say whether this fear of death is at the root of medicine's obsession with defeating it, or that medical triumphs over death encourage us to fear our mortality. But what is certain is that today the fear of dying and the medicalization of death feed each other. The result is that a "good death," usually perceived as taking place at home surrounded by loved ones, has become the exception rather than the rule, thereby giving us even more reason to fear our demise. There are, of course, other ways to respond to and to characterize death. Death can be the cause for a spiritual awakening; an ultimate sacrifice; an opportunity for rebirth; a predetermined event; the lesser of other evils, an escape from suffering; and so on.

We are also conflicted about purposely causing death. While American culture loudly proclaims its commitment to life, it perpetuates death in subtle and not so subtle ways: war, murder, the availability of guns, capital punishment, suicide, the self-defense exception, poverty, inadequate protection of the physically abused, environmental pollution, lack of universal medical coverage, the marketing of and government subsidization of tobacco, glorified violence in our entertainment. And legalized abortion. And legalized PAS. How, then, do we apply our knowledge to death issues, when we fear it so and are so conflicted over when death is "bad" and when it is "good"?

It is important, then, to remember when we tell our legal, medical, and personal stories that our fears and our foibles affect what we know and how we use it.

The Medical, Legal, and Personal Compared

The other dimension is how the three epistemologies compare. Table 1.1 reviews the discussion so far by highlighting how the epistemologies used by law, medicine, and patients begin with certain features, frame the question in particular ways, draw on guiding principles, and employ certain methods. The intersections and gaps between the perspectives is apparent.

There is a marked interplay between medicine and law: they begin with the specifics of a case; term the problem as discovering the right theory to apply; work within the constraints of professional ethical standards; and employ logical, objective, and inductive reasoning. These practitioners pride themselves on their expert knowledge, their dispassioned use of information, and their application of science. They make a concerted effort to distance themselves from the personal, the emotional, and

Table 1.1 Epistemologies of the Three Perspectives

	The Medical	The Legal	The Patients'
Begins with:	physical symptoms; scientific knowledge	facts of case; textural references	the self; concrete experience
Frames the problem as:	making the right diagnosis; how to treat?	weighing competing rights; is it legal?	wanting the best treatment; what are my choices?
Guided by the principles of:	healing; duty to do no harm	universal rules, neutrality, justice	caring for the self while preserving relationships with others
Method applied is:	reasoning based on logical progression: inductive to create knowledge, deductive to apply it	reasoning based on logical progression: inductive to create knowledge, deductive to apply it	emotional, subjectivity mixed with reasoning

the intuitive. Hence, when they are faced with knowledge from these origins, they dismiss it, ignore it, or discredit it.

In stark contrast is the knowledge of the personal perspective. Patients do not regard their experiential knowledge as data to be collected and employed in theorizing. Instead, they possess their knowledge as something that is concrete, intimately known and felt, and individualized in form. Patients do not frame their situation in terms of how their conditions fit with recognized theories, but in terms of what can be done for them. The guiding principles of patients' knowledge are not the ethical standards of a profession, but the pull of relationships. Within the context of how they relate to others, patients decide what are appropriate ways to care for themselves and for others. Patients use reasoning to form knowledge by embracing, rather than distancing, the emotional and the subjective.

As so configured, the alignment between legal and medical knowledge seems inevitable—as do the consequences for patients in court. Physicians and lawyers have been trained not to trust the subjective and the emotive that constitutes patients' knowledge. Medicine and law are viewed as sources of expertise—personal experiences are not. Even patients accept this modeling of knowledge to a certain extent in recognizing and trusting the expertise of physicians and attorneys, even when to do so requires a quieting of their own doubts and a silencing of their own voices of experience. When issues like abortion and PAS go to the Court, there is a "natural" inclination for the Justices to hear legal and medical information as expert while hearing, if at all, patient's knowledge as personal stories and little more. The common epistemologies of medicine and law draw them into a discourse on how to settle medical issues, while relegating patients to the role of listeners and subjects, not participants and knowers.

Knowledge about abortion and PAS is formed, therefore, from two accounts of the story, and not from three. When the Justices of the Court assemble the facts of these cases, it frequently occurs that the knowledge of patients is discarded, and therefore, the official version of the story that will serve as the basis for the decision is composed without them. The result is that instead of being derived from three types of knowledge, the case decisions reflect the only two stories the Court really hears—those told by medicine and those told by law. It is in this way that the exclusion of patients' knowledge undermines the full accounting of the story and thereby weakens the integrity of the law.

What, then, are the consequences? In the next two chapters, I study how law and medicine converge in the Court to design a medical-legal response to these very personal of issues. Within abortion law, the result is that physicians' interests are protected at the expense of patients who seek an abortion (chapter 2). Within PAS law, physicians' interests are protected at the expense of patients who seek physician assistance in committing suicide (chapter 3). However, this alignment of legal with medical knowledge and the resulting near exclusion of patients' knowledge do not have to be the way of the law. Law can learn to value the voices of patients, to integrate the knowledge of patients, and to care for the lives of patients. The final two chapters study how listening to patients' knowledge can alter the story of what has happened to someone—and thereby transform the law. But first, the story of *Roe*.

· 2 ·

The Abortion Cases:
The Merging of
Medical and Legal Knowledge

Our task, of course, is to resolve the issue by constitutional measurement, *free of emotion* and of predilection. We seek earnestly to do this, and, because we do, we have inquired into, and in this opinion place some emphasis upon, *medical and medical-legal* history.

Justice Harry Blackmun, *Roe v. Wade* 1973 [emphasis mine]

If a list was to be constructed of the Supreme Court decisions most associated with the expansion of women's rights, surely the case of *Roe v. Wade* (1973) would appear near the top of the list. It was in this case that the Court concluded that the constitutional right of privacy was broad enough to protect from state interference a woman's decision to terminate her pregnancy during the first trimester. This was a momentous decision. In establishing the first national abortion policy, the Court's decision felled forty-six state laws,[1] and literally overnight that which was criminal became legal. The days of underground networks, secrecy, fear, and back alley abortions were over. Now, physicians could perform abortions without the fear of prosecution and women could seek abortions in a safe, professional environment. The day the Court delivered its decision, January 22, 1973, is still recognized each year—heralded by some and mourned by others—as the day on which the meaning of an unwanted pregnancy changed for women.

While it is true that *Roe* is without a doubt a case intimately connected with women—their rights, their status, and their lives—it is also a case in which women's knowledge was eclipsed by medical knowledge, and women's interests were obscured by physicians' interests. How this occurred in a case seemingly devoted to the question of women's rights can be explained by examining how three types of knowledge—medical, legal, and patients'—interacted within the environment of the Court. Justice Harry Blackmun's opening remarks in the *Roe* opinion (the epigram to this chapter) accurately described the kind of information the Court sought—medical and legal—as expertise in deciding the abortion issue, as

31

well as the kind of information the Court sought to avoid—the emotional, subjective sort most associated with the personal. In recounting the story of abortion law, then, it should come as no surprise that it is a tale constructed and shaped by the collaboration of medical and legal authorities. That patients' knowledge was not only omitted, but deliberately disregarded, is telling because it explains how it is that the abortion cases were formulated as they were and why the Court decided them as they did.

In this chapter, I analyze the abortion cases with the goal of highlighting the interplay between patients' knowledge, medical knowledge, and the legal norms of the U.S. Supreme Court. I begin with an examination of the first abortion case of *Roe* and trace how and in what form patients' knowledge and medical knowledge entered the Court. In the next section, I scrutinize the Court's opinion for evidence of how patients' and medical knowledge were used or ignored, privileged or dismissed. Finally, I study *Roe*'s progeny, that is, the twenty-four abortion cases that followed, and I suggest that there is a pattern as to which abortion restrictions the Court upheld and which they voided as unconstitutional. This pattern seems dependent not so much on patients' rights but on whether the restriction impinges on the discretion of physicians to practice. The impact of the Court's reliance on medical knowledge, then, reaches beyond the issue of what is heard to affect as well what is decided and how.

THE INTERPLAY OF KNOWLEDGE

At issue in *Roe* were Texas statutes that in effect criminalized all abortions except those performed to save the life of the mother. Texas Penal Code article 1991 read:

> If any person shall designedly administer to a pregnant woman or knowingly procure to be administered with her consent any drug or medicine, or shall use towards her any violence or means whatever externally or internally applied, and thereby procure an abortion, he shall be confined in the penitentiary not less than two nor more than five years; if it be done without her consent, the punishment shall be doubled. (Mersky and Hartman 1993, Vol. 1: 140)

The statutes were contested by the plaintiff "Roe," a pseudonym for a pregnant woman denied an abortion under Texas law, who claimed that they violated a woman's right to privacy that protected her decision as to whether or not to terminate her pregnancy. The defendant, Henry Wade, Criminal District Attorney of Dallas County, Texas, argued on behalf of the validity of the state measures, emphasizing that they were designed to protect women's health and fetal life. What the Court needed to decide this case was information. What sort of information they relied upon is the question at hand.

In deciding any case, the Court has a wide array of sources from which to draw information: lower court records; media reports; public opinion polls; political protests; congressional and executive branch actions and studies; scholarly works; and the individual knowledge or jurisprudence of the Justices themselves. However, three specific forms of information are expected to be introduced and considered as a formal part of the Court's deliberations: (1) the party briefs, the written legal arguments prepared by the attorneys for each side; (2) the *amicus curiae* briefs, information presented to the court by its "friends," i.e., interested third parties; and (3) oral argument, the live presentation to the Court of legal arguments by the attorneys for each side with questioning from the bench by the Justices. It is these three sources that I study in examining how medical knowledge and patients' knowledge were formally presented to the Court.[2] Based on this investigation of *Roe* and these informational sources, what I discover is that some types of knowledge were amplified while other forms were muted—and that legal norms provide much of the explanation as to why this was so.

Legal Norms

Legal norms set the stage for the consideration of a case by confining choices. The Court relies on a specific framework for argumentation and decision making that articulates the issue in a case in a particular way, emphasizes the importance of process over result, and applies constitutional interpretation to the case at hand. In short, legal norms define what's to be considered and how. The guiding force in the development of this legal setting is, once again, the ethic of justice and its command that decision making be objective, reasoned, and universal. Ironically, though legal norms have been adopted to further these mandates, the result is anything but unbiased. As *Roe* demonstrates, several legal norms served to privilege medical knowledge over that of patients:

The Case and Controversy Requirement. The Constitution mandates that issues brought to the Court must be real cases and controversies in order to be "justiciable" (Art. III, Sec. 2). In addition, rules of the Court require that the appellant be the one who suffered an actual, direct, and personal injury in order to have "standing" to sue. Therefore, in order to challenge the restrictive Texas abortion laws, a plaintiff had to have a real case, meaning that she had to be pregnant, had to have sought an abortion and been denied one, and had to file suit to challenge the law. At first blush, these requirements would seem to highlight patients' knowledge, however, the very nature of the abortion issue itself mitigated against this result.

Given that pregnancy runs only nine months, state abortion laws seemed impervious to legal challenge at the U.S. Supreme Court level since it takes years to bring a case through the appeals process to the Court. By that time, then, a plaintiff would no longer be pregnant when the case was finally heard, and presumably would therefore be denied standing. In order to overcome the barrier of standing, two legal fictions were created. First, was the assertion that the case was really about the woman who stood behind the pseudonym of "Jane Roe," although she had long since given birth. While such a situation would usually render a case "moot" since the issue has already been resolved, the Court chose to grant Jane Roe standing because "pregnancy often comes more than once to the same woman" and that to rule otherwise would be to allow the issue to evade review (125). A second legal fiction was the claim that Roe sued not only on her own behalf but also on behalf of other individuals similarly situated, i.e., those who were pregnant, desired a legal abortion, but could not obtain one due to the Texas laws. While such class action suits are often heard by the Court, this one was unusual in that the individuals who comprised this class of persons were not named, were not informed of the suit, nor were they directly involved in the case that proceeded in their name. Therefore, although patients were technically the litigants in this case, neither their identities, much less their personal stories, were central to the proceedings

The Shaping of the Controversy as a Federal Issue. It is only at the trial level that the individual facts of a case are most closely examined and most legally relevant. Once the record is established, the appeals process focuses on the application of the law itself rather than on the establishment of the facts of the case. Another shift takes place once a case is granted *cert* by the Court, because now it becomes quite literally a "federal issue." That is, it takes on a significance of importance no longer limited to the litigants and their individual concerns alone. Now the case has the potential of setting federal policy and so it is inevitable, as well as essential to law, that the individual facts of the case be submerged in favor of the larger constitutional issues and national concerns.

This is exactly what occurred when Jane Roe's attorneys Linda Coffee and Sarah Weddington challenged the Texas abortion statutes using the federal constitution. This approach to the case rendered irrelevant the individual circumstances surrounding Jane Roe's attempt to secure a legal abortion. Hence, as federal issues were heightened, the particulars involving the specific patient were erased.[3] Yet, this focus on the broader issues had the opposite effect on medical knowledge because its more generalizable facts, statistics, and findings regarding abortion practices made it a pertinent source of information.

The Constitution as the Reference. The Court's power of judicial review commits it to interpreting the text of the Constitution. It is this document that serves as the litmus test for those statutes that are to be upheld and those that are to be voided. The key for litigants, then, is to establish which constitutional guarantees are violated and how. Therefore, one effect of constitutionalism is that controversies are framed in terms of clashing interests or rights. For a claim to be seriously considered, it must conform to this requirement by tethering the dispute to the rights guaranteed in the document. This imperative was limiting for patients in at least two ways. First, a right must be found in the text (preferably literally but at minimum implied). Second, most of the rights listed in the Constitution and the Amendments are regarded by the Court as negative rights, i.e., that the government should not act to interfere with the right, rather than as positive rights, i.e., that the government should act in the affirmative to achieve the right.

Therefore, whatever the perceived injuries to women's lives caused by the restrictive abortion laws, the legal claim had to be made in constitutional terms. The language chosen was that of the implied right to privacy—an abstraction that proved a narrow vessel in which to pour patients' experiences. The question of how unwanted pregnancies affected women's lives appeared to be only distantly related to the question of whether they had a right to privacy. So, patients' knowledge again seemed to lack relevancy. Combined with the concept of negative rights, the best the patients could hope for was a ruling that left them alone in making the abortion decision, rather than one that responded to the barriers that blocked their access to abortion. In contrast, the focus on negative rights was more hospitable to physicians' interests and medical knowledge. Whether abortion should be a crime made medical knowledge pertinent, and the freedom offered by a negative right was sufficient to ensure physicians' interests in performing abortions without criminal penalty.

The Use of Tests. In the course of deciding Fourteenth Amendment cases, the Court chooses from among three tests in judging the constitutionality of statutes: (1) strict scrutiny, the most difficult test for a statute to meet, demands that the state show that the law was a necessary method to achieve a compelling state interest; (2) rational basis, the easiest of the tests for the statute to meet, requires only that the state show that the law is reasonably related to a legitimate state interest; and (3) the intermediate test requires that the statute be significantly related to achieving important state interests. Clearly, one of the crucial decisions facing the Court in any given challenge is the question of which test to apply, since that decision determines whether the uphill battle will be fought by the state or by the individual. Strict scrutiny is applied when a law either: (1) involves a "suspect" classification of people (i.e., it identifies people on the basis of race or national origin), or (2) when a "fundamental" right is at stake. To achieve the status of a "fundamental" right, a constitutional provision must explicitly protect the right (e.g., the right to vote), or the right must be so embedded in American culture and tradition as to warrant rigorous protection by the Court (e.g., the right to marry and to procreate).

A right to privacy or, more particularly, a right to have an abortion, lacks the explicit constitutional text to warrant the status of a fundamental right and thereby trigger application of the strict scrutiny test. However, if the Court could be persuaded that these interests are supported by historical traditions and long-standing social values, then strict scrutiny could still be applied. Otherwise, the Court would be free to apply a less stringent test in weighing the law against the individual rights at stake. Therefore, in order to gain the advantage offered by strict scrutiny, the attorneys for Roe needed to establish that the freedom to make the abortion decision is a fundamental right, and in order to prove that, they needed to trace the historical traditions and practices that demonstrated this was so. This led them quite naturally to place the history of medical practices and social mores regarding legalized abortion at the center of the case.

The Focus on Process over Result. Law's reliance on legal argumentation as logical and reasoned makes it process-oriented rather than result-oriented. Put differently, attorneys plead their case by presenting the Court with a well-reasoned argument that leads to a conclusion favorable to their clients, and not by arguing that a certain result should be achieved because it is the desirable one. The first is regarded as judicial reasoning; the second as policy making. The former is seen as a task appropriate to a court; the latter as more appropriate to a legislature.

In *Roe*, this norm resulted in the silencing of patients' voices since they argued in the personal terms of favoring a certain result, the legalization of abortion, rather than in the "objective" terms of legal reasoning. In confining the presentation of the argument to fit the requirements of legal reasoning, it was difficult to inject patients' experience into the discourse since to speak of patients' experiences is to invoke subjective evaluations of policy, not to mention emotional stories regarding consequences. Instead, abstract legal argumentation and objective scientific data like that offered by medicine were welcomed in ways that patients' knowledge based on experience were not.

Ultimately, then, while the patients of the case were participants, at least in theory, what they knew seemed largely irrelevant to judicial reasoning. It was hardly surprising, then, that when the party briefs, *amicus* briefs, and oral arguments are examined, patients' expertise appears to have been submerged within the medical-legal narrative. When abortion was described, it was framed in medical rather than in personal terms. When expertise was offered, its source was medicine, not patients. When patients were discussed, it was not their voices but the voices of others that described their experiences.

My point is not that these norms were unusually or wrongly applied in *Roe*—just the opposite—all five norms are not only usual in constitutional law cases, but are so characteristic, so inherent to judicial process that they are in fact required. And that's the point. Judicial processes and norms create an environment that makes it inherently difficult for patients to present their knowledge to the Court while making it likely that medical knowledge will be heard. *Roe* illustrates this well.

Patients' Knowledge

What becomes obvious to anyone who reads the Court documents submitted in *Roe* is that information based on patients' knowledge was for the most part missing. The three formal vehicles for introducing information to the Court, the party briefs, the *amicus* briefs, and the oral argument, rarely mentioned the significance of abortion from the patient's point of view. Instead, in the course of being presented to the Court, patients' knowledge underwent a transformation as it was translated into legalese and by attempts to fit it within the parameters of legal argumentation. The result was that it no longer sounded much like personal stories, no longer drew on personal experiences, and no longer offered personal insights.

Even the party brief filed on behalf of the appellant (Roe) constructed the case in a way that made the experiences of women of secondary concern. The brief framed the abortion issue as a medical issue, even using the subtitle "The Medical Nature of Abortion" to label the main thrust of the legal argument (18). In this section of the brief, "Roe" presented the history of medically induced abortion in the United States, described the support of the American College of Obstetricians and Gynecologists (ACOG) and the American Medical Association (AMA) for the legalization of abortion, and documented the failure rate of currently available contraceptives. In addressing the impact of pregnancy on women themselves, the brief commented in only one sentence and with a footnote referred the reader to the *amicus* brief filed by the New Women Lawyers (105). In this, Weddington and Coffee skirted the legal sin of arguing from a "result-oriented" stance. By focusing on medical evidence and legal documents rather than on the needs and lives of women, the attorneys were fitting their argumentation within the expected legal parameters and norms, thereby ensuring that their points would be taken seriously and not dismissed as inappropriate policy judgments. Therefore, the very requirements of writing a legal brief demanded that the knowledge of patients be omitted or at least relegated to a minor point like that of a footnote.

The appellee's brief (on behalf of Wade and the Texas statues) also stressed the medical nature of the issue, but did so in order to focus attention on the experience of the "patient," meaning the fetus and not the pregnant woman. In pages 29–54 of the fifty-seven-page brief, the attorneys for Texas argued "how clearly and conclusively modern science—embryology, fetology, genetics, perinatology, all of biology—establishes the humanity of the unborn child" (31). But while the appellee's brief seemed to include the viewpoint of the patient, it erased the pregnant woman in a way that even the appellant's brief had not. The appellee's brief included ten pages of photographs of the developing fetus (significantly enlarged), some emphasizing the humanness of hands and feet, and others capturing human gestures like thumb sucking. Literally invisible in the photos and the accompanying text was the person the brief referred to as the other patient—the mother—

and this invisibility culminated with the assertion that the "placenta belongs to the baby, not the mother" (47). The focus, then, of the appellee's brief included patients—but only the fetus as patient and not the pregnant woman as patient.

While the sixteen *amicus* briefs filed in *Roe* reinforced many of the legal and medical themes of the party briefs, they also included some discussion of the women patients. The main emphasis of the nine *amicus* briefs filed on behalf of Roe was the legal argument that the constitutional rights of patients (and physicians) extends to protect their right to make the abortion decision free of state interference. Closely tied to this argument was the recurring theme that abortion is a medical issue best left to the discretion of physicians and women. Some of the *amici*, however, added another dimension to the abortion issue in that they discussed the experiences of women: the brief by Women's Organizations and Named Women described the impact of an unwanted pregnancy on the life, dignity, and freedom of women; the brief by the New Women Lawyers (cited by Weddington and Coffee in their party brief) listed the impact of an unwanted pregnancy on the life of a woman and charged that a denial to abortion constitutes cruel and unusual punishment in violation of the Eighth Amendment; and the brief by Organizations and Named Women emphasized the physical invasiveness of pregnancy and argued that abortion restrictions place women in a position of involuntary servitude (i.e., slavery) in violation of the Thirteenth Amendment. A different slant was taken by the briefs of the National Legal Program on Health Problems of the Poor, the State Communities Aid Association, and the supplemental brief of Planned Parenthood Federation of America (PPFA), who argued that the Texas statutes discriminated against poor and non-white women because they lack the resources to leave the state to obtain safe, legal abortions.

Just as the party brief for Texas focused on the "fetal patients" so too did the seven *amicus* briefs filed on behalf of Wade. To support the argument that the fetus is a patient/person/legal entity, medical and legal information was highlighted in the briefs filed by Americans United for Life, the Association of Texas Diocesan Attorneys, Certain Physicians, Professors and Fellows of ACOG, the National Right to Life Committee, Robert L. Sassone, and Women for the Unborn. The two briefs that included discussion of women's experiences as patients, filed by Robert Sassone and Women for the Unborn, cited medical studies to argue that the initial negative feelings that a woman may have toward her pregnancy are common but that they will subside as the pregnancy advances and supportive care is offered.

In seeking, then, to hear the patients' voice in the *amicus* briefs, one must listen for the dissonant notes that emerge now and then behind the main themes of law and medicine. Even when they are heard, however, the listener should be aware that the sound has been dubbed: when patients' concerns and experiences are presented, they are told by others and not by patients themselves. There are no first-person accounts of what abortion means (for better or for worse) for the women who have experienced it, no stories, no telling of the horror of what it was like to undergo an illegal abortion or how it felt to lack reliable information about the procedure. Instead, this information is summarized in scholarly style in some of the appellants' briefs. As a collection, then, the *amicus* briefs added knowledge concerning some aspects of women's experience to the formal informational resources of the Court, but they did not directly challenge the dominant theme that abortion is a *medical* issue.

During the oral argument of December 13, 1991, Weddington attempted to do just that. Echoing the contents of the New Women's Lawyers' *amicus* brief, she ticked off a list of some of the consequences that pregnancy has for women and then concluded: "So a pregnancy to a woman is perhaps one of the most determinative aspects of her life. It disrupts her body, it disrupts her education, it disrupts her employment, and it often disrupts her entire family life" (Mersky and Hartman 1993, Vol. III: 460). She went on to argue that because of this impact, women should have a fundamental right to choose whether to terminate pregnancies, and physicians should be able to provide these women with appropriate medical care. In response, the next question from the bench (identified by Irons and Guitton as coming from Justice Potter Stewart, 1993: 345) indicated that Weddington had strayed from legal argument into the realm of policy making:

> Mrs. Weddington, so far, on the merits, you've told us about the important impact of this law, and you've made a very eloquent argument against it. I trust you are going to get to what provisions of the Constitution you rely on, because, of course, we'd like to, sometimes . . . leave them out here, and be involved simply with matters of policy, as you know. (Mersky and Hartman 1993, Vol. III: 460)

Thus warned against arguing from such a result-oriented perspective, Weddington shifted course to focus again on precedents and constitutional text. However, while questions from the bench steered Weddington away from discussing the consequences for women, they led Jay Floyd, attorney for Texas, toward such a discussion. When he argued that the statistics on the safety of abortion over childbirth are policy considerations, not legal issues, the Court responded,

> Certainly that's true; policy questions are for legislative and executive bodies, both in the State and Federal Government. But we have here a constitutional question, and in deciding it, assessing it, it's important to know what the asserted interest of the State is in the enactment of this legislation. (Mersky and Hartman 1993, Vol. III: 478)

Seemingly, then, the Court was willing to discuss results—but only when they were connected with the state's legal interest, not when they were connected with women's rights.

Contrary to what the legal norms and formal documents indicated, however, personal expertise could have shed some light on the abortion issue. Women who had found themselves in conflict with the law could have been an invaluable resource for helping the Court to understand abortion at the macro level—the social, relational, and economic elements that needed to be integrated in the Court's abortion decision. They also had revealing and informationally rich stories to tell the Court of abortion at the micro level: of botched illegal abortions, of sexual abuse at the hands of some abortionists, of desperate needs and realistic fears, of tattered dreams and altered lives caused by unwanted pregnancies, and of feeling trapped by conflicting personal values, cultural norms, governmental policies, and legal restrictions. But it would not be until the case of *Thornburgh v. American College of Obstetricians and Gynecologists* (1986; see the *amicus* brief filed by NARAL) that these personal stories and experiences, and the knowledge they held, would first enter the Court records. Until then, the questions of why women seek access to legal abortion, what an unwanted pregnancy means to different women, how social forces shape the issue, and what factors must be addressed if the issue is to be resolved, would be overshadowed and drowned out by the dominant refrain of whether the Texas statutes violate a woman's constitutional right to privacy, that was in turn answered by a chorus of medical experts. Ironically, it was the Court's very devotion to objectivity that prevented it from discovering both the broader cultural context of abortion and the particular experiences of women that contradicted universal assumptions. This information could have been told by the very voices that had been systematically silenced—those of patients. Quite clearly, given the legal norms and processes at play, the concrete, emotional, and experiential nature of patients' knowledge had rendered them nearly voiceless in the case of *Roe*.

Medical Knowledge

But the same was not so concerning medical knowledge. As contrasted with the ways that legal norms acted to silence patients' knowledge in the Court, the same legal norms and processes amplified the voice of medical knowledge. Instead of facing the problem of having to adapt to a conflicting epistemology, medical expertise seemed to merge seamlessly with that of the legal. Their joining, resulted in the strengthening of each as forms of expertise and enhanced their ability to dictate that the terms of the discussion fit the medical-legal design.

In particular, the legal norms of standing, federal issues, and legal reasoning had an altogether different impact on the presence of medical knowledge in the case. While an original litigant, Dr. James Hubert Hallford, was dropped from the case due to the Court's determination that he lacked standing (because he had not asserted that he was personally injured by the violation of a federal recognized right) physicians were never really dropped from the case. In particular, the legal norm of shifting the focus in an appealed case from individual to federal facts gave the medical profession the opportunity to enter the case as experts. By defining abortion as a medical issue, physicians moved to the center of the case whether they had official standing or not. Since they constituted the profession that would be primarily responsible for implementing the Court's decision, their knowledge was critical to writing a decision that made medical sense. Medical knowledge also complemented the needs of legal reasoning. Medicine could also offer the Court the "facts" about abortion—the number performed, patient mortality rates, techniques used, the biological status of the fetus, and the biological aspects of pregnancy. Offered as the result of scientific and careful study, these facts could be used by the Court to explain its decision. As Blackmun stated at the beginning of his *Roe* opinion, what the Court sought was objective information "free of emotion and predilection." Medicine could offer the Justices, in a way that patients could not, the scientific (i.e., "objective") basis they needed in developing guidelines on the legality of abortion. The party briefs, *amicus* briefs, and oral arguments attest to the authority afforded to the medical profession over the knowledge of patients.

As the discussion of the party briefs has already stated, both sides framed the case's issue in medical terms: the appellants as an issue best left to be decided within the physician-patient relationship, and the appellees as an issue that should be decided by scientific proof of the humanness, and therefore the patient status, of the fetus. The conflict, then, was not over the question of whether abortion was fundamentally a medical issue or not, but over the identification of which medical questions held the key to resolving the legal issue. Roe stressed that the state should allow doctors to serve their patients by providing safe abortions; Wade argued that the state was obligated to protect the fetus that science had proved was a person.

An interesting challenge to this consensus that abortion was a predominantly medical issue came in the *amicus* brief filed by Women for the Unborn that asserted in a footnote that "socio-economic abortions have nothing to do with medicine" (Brief of Women for the Unborn et al., 15 n.10) (a point Justice Byron White would seize on in writing his *Roe* dissent). That abortion was and is a medical procedure cannot be contested. However, it is questionable whether a healthy woman who seeks to terminate a healthy pregnancy is making a medical decision or whether she is using a medical procedure to make a decision of another sort and for reasons beyond medicine. While physicians possess the knowledge of how to safely perform abortions, abortion as an issue is shaped by much more than medical knowledge. It is shaped by social, religious, economic, ethical, and emotional forces including the status of women, social attitudes toward sexual relations, religious attitudes toward family planning, the ability to pay for raising a child, the availability of health care or maternity benefits, individual cost-benefit analysis, identification of the "right" thing to do, and the love for self or for others. Abortion, then, could be framed as an equality issue, a sexual issue, a religious issue, a family issue, a financial issue, a health care or employment issue, a utilitarian issue, a moral issue, or a caring issue. That abortion was seen primarily as a medical issue propelled to the forefront of the discussion of medical information over other types of information. Most certainly, it advantaged medical knowledge over patient's knowledge within the legal discussions.

The difference is striking when reviewing again the *amicus* briefs. Several themes emerge that illustrate how even the third parties to the case focused on medical information and the role of the physician. Five medical themes dominated these briefs:

The Sanctity of the Doctor-Patient Relationship. Several of the briefs filed on behalf of Roe argued that the physician-patient relationship was due protection from outside interferences such as restrictive abortion laws. Drawing on the sacredness of this relationship, the American College of Obstetricians and Gynecologists et al. (ACOG) offered several reasons for striking the Texas statutes: that the law was an unconstitutional interference with a physician's right to practice medicine; that the law denied women their right to secure the best of medical treatment available; and that legal liability made it in the physician's best interests to decide against abortion. In short, ACOG argued that the law was not only inconsistent with providing patients with the best medical practices available, but that it also abridged physicians' ethical pledge to work openly and honestly with patients as they work to help them.

Physician Liability and Criminal Prosecution. Under the Texas laws, anyone performing an abortion for reasons other than to save the life of the mother was subject to imprisonment for two to five years. Even physicians who believed that they had acted on behalf of "saving the life of the mother" were in danger of prosecution for how they had interpreted the mandate to save "life." Therefore, the ACOG brief, as well as the brief filed by PPFA argued that the statute should be voided for vagueness because medical judgment could differ among practitioners and, even if agreed upon by medical authorities, be second-guessed by a jury.

The Safety of Medically Induced Legal Abortions. Both the ACOG and PPFA briefs stressed the importance of allowing physicians to provide women with safe, legal abortions. In its initial brief, PPFA presented the statistics on the failure rate of contraceptives, and its supplemental brief argued that legal abortions are safer for women than is childbirth. Interestingly, allusions were made in several briefs to the horrors suffered by women who obtained illegal abortions, but no in-depth information was offered. Instead, the argument presented was that the law prohibits a safe medical procedure needed by women. This information was countered by a brief filed on behalf of Wade by Certain Physicians and Professors and Fellows of ACOG that reviewed the medical hazards of legally induced abortion for women. Faulting some medical studies for narrowly confining their observations to American female mortality rates alone, this brief included discussion of early physical complications (e.g., infections and hemorrhaging), later physical complications (e.g., ectopic pregnancies and spontaneous abortions), and psychiatric problems (ranging from self-reproach to suicide) related to abortion. The brief also pointed out that the mortality rate for the other patient, the child, is almost 100 percent.

The Official Position of Certain Medical Organizations. Two of the *amicus* briefs had the weight of medical organizations behind them: The ACOG brief was also cosponsored by the American Psychiatric Association (APA) (18,783 members), American Medical Women's Association, New York Academy of Medicine and 178 physicians as signatories; the PPFA brief (representing 190 affiliates) was also cosponsored by the American Association of Planned Parenthood Physicians (AAPPP) (650 members). These briefs cited resolutions from the APA and AAPPP maintaining that abortion is a medically acceptable procedure. The countering of this claim came not from official organizations but from a coalition of medical professionals who signed on to the brief filed by Certain Physicians and Professors and Fellows of ACOG (with signatories numbering 223).

The Beginning of Life and Fetal Personhood. This issue was addressed by briefs submitted from both sides of the case. While the briefs on behalf of Roe argued that the fetus had no constitutional rights (see, in Mersky and Hartman 1993, PPFA, American Ethical Union, and National Legal Program on Health Problems of the Poor), briefs filed on behalf of Wade argued not only that the fetus is a legal person (see Americans United for Life, Association of Texas Diocesan Attorneys, Certain Physicians et al., Robert Sassone and Women for the Unborn), but that medical evidence proved it (see Certain Physicians et al., and Robert Sassone). Offered as medical evidence are photos of fetuses at different times of gestation and the physicians' practice of treating the developing fetus as a patient.

What these five medically related concerns show is that while different approaches and even contradictory claims were made by medical authorities in *Roe*, medical information was introduced to the Court in a serious and thorough way not only by both parties to the case, but also by several *amici*. The parties as well as the *amici* seemed to understand that medical knowledge was crucial to the resolution of this case.

This was apparent in the oral arguments as well. *Roe* was argued twice before the Court, on December 13, 1971 (with seven Justices sitting), and on October 11, 1972 (with a full bench including the newly appointed Justices Lewis Powell and William Rehnquist). In both sessions there was discussion of medical knowledge, but in the second round of arguments, the time devoted to it was considerable.

During Weddington's second appearance, she emphasized the prosecution of doctors under the Texas laws, the new statistics on maternal death rates from PPFA's supplemental brief, and how the statutes posed "great, immediate, and irreparable injury" to women (Mersky and Hartman 1993, Vol. III: 488.) This was followed by exchanges on the legal dimensions of fetal personhood. Then the Court shifted gears asking Weddington whether she was familiar with the Hippocratic oath and why she failed to refer to it in her brief. In responding, she directed the Court's attention to the briefs filed by ACOG. The Court pressed on, "Tell me why you didn't discuss the Hippocratic oath?" (ibid.: 492). She then explained how she had based the case on the constitutional protection that women had and the state's failure to establish a compelling state interest, and that the oath did not pertain to that legal argument. The discussion then ended with the following exchange:

> Mrs. Weddington: It seemed to us that the fact that the medical profession at one time had adopted the Hippocratic oath does not weigh upon the fundamental constitutional rights involved. It is a guide for physicians, but the outstanding organizations of the medical profession have in fact adopted a position that says the doctor and the patient should be able to make the decision for themselves in this kind of situation.
>
> Question: Of course it's the only definitive statement of ethics of the medical profession. I take it from what you said that you didn't even footnote it because it's old. That's about really, what you're saying.
>
> Mrs. Weddington: Well, I guess it is old, and not that it's out of date, but that it seemed to us that it was not pertinent to the argument we were making. (ibid.: 492)

This signaled an interesting turn of events. Having been somewhat chastised by Justice Stewart during her first appearance for arguing policy over legal arguments, Weddington was now being challenged for not including discussion of the ethical guidelines of the medical profession. Before, when she focused on the impact of restrictive laws on women's lives, she was steered toward legal argumentation; now she was stopped from pursuing her legal argument and encouraged to discuss medical ethics and its impact on medical practice. In retrospect, it appears that medical knowledge was welcomed by the very legal norm that excluded patients' experiences as improperly result-oriented.

The Court's seeming eagerness to hear more about medical knowledge was also apparent during its exchanges with the lawyers who argued on behalf of Texas. During the 1971 oral argument, Floyd was questioned by the Court as to whether scientific data supported his contentions regarding the beginning of fetal life. This topic was picked up again in earnest at the 1972 Court session with Robert C. Flowers now representing Texas. Flowers was asked whether the concept of fetal personhood was a "legal question, a constitutional question, a medical question, a philosophical question, or a religious question" and he responded that "it could be best decided by a Legislature in view of the fact that they can bring before it the medical testimony, the actual people who do the research" (Mersky and Hartman 1993, Vol. III: 495). While their continued discussion indicated that both the Court and Flowers recognized that the question constituted a legal issue as well, Flowers suggested that the two forms of knowledge should both apply to the case: "I believe that the Court must take these, the medical research, and apply it to our Constitution the best they can" (ibid.: 502). The Court appeared to agree with this assessment, and questioned him again on fetal personhood. When Flowers described the legal argument of a lower court case, the Court interrupted him: "Now you're quoting the judge, I want you to give me a medical, recognizable medical writing of any kind that says that at the time of conception the fetus is a person" (ibid.: 503).

This brief survey of some of the exchanges at the oral arguments shows how medical knowledge was given a central role in the case. It also shows that not only were the attorneys and *amici* responsible for this casting, but that the Justices had a hand in it as well. In requesting that scientific data be provided, medical studies cited, and the Hippocratic oath discussed, the Court clearly signaled that as contrasted with patients' knowledge, medical knowledge was not only relevant but welcome in the case.

Perhaps most evident of medical knowledge's elevated status in the Court was the fact that it enjoyed at least one informal means of influence beyond the party briefs, the *amicus* briefs, and the oral arguments, and that was the interest of Justice Blackmun. Chief Justice Warren Burger had assigned Blackmun the task of writing the majority opinion for the Court in *Roe*. Once counsel to the Mayo Clinic in Rochester, Minnesota, Blackmun was well versed in medicine—its terminology, its concerns, and its practice. In the spring of 1972, he produced a first draft of an opinion that by all accounts was narrow in scope and weak in impact (see Woodward and Armstrong 1979; Craig and O'Brien 1993; Garrow 1994; Schwartz 1996). Had it come down as originally written, the Texas statutes would have been voided for vagueness with the result that other restrictive state laws would have remained untouched since the opinion did not establish a constitutional basis for a right to abortion. In light of the feedback that Blackmun received from the other Justices, including forty-eight pages of suggestions by Justice William Brennan and a draft of a dissent circulated by Justice White, Blackmun sought more time to revise and asked that the case be put over to the next term and reargued with a full Court (the first oral argument had taken place with only seven Justices on the bench). After some contentious encounters with Justice Douglas who wanted the case decided that term, the Court finally agreed to schedule *Roe* for reargument the following term. During the summer of 1972, Blackmun returned to the Mayo Clinic to conduct in private the research he needed for crafting the Court's decision. There he hoped to find the answers he sought to questions that were clearly medical, not legal:

> What was the history of the proscription in the Hippocratic oath which forbade doctors from performing abortions? What was the medical state of the art of sustaining a fetus outside the womb? When did life really begin? When was a fetus fully viable? What were the positions of the American Medical Association, the American Psychiatric Association, the American Public Health Association? (Woodward and Armstrong 1979: 218–219)

Blackmun integrated the answers to these questions within the opinion, thereby combining medical with legal knowledge. In November, Blackmun "circulated a completely revised draft of his *Roe v. Wade* opinion" (Schwartz 1996: 235). After some additional changes were incorporated and the final vote was confirmed, the case came down on January 22, 1973. Even in its final form, the decision's emphasis on medical concerns remained central to the disposition of the case.

THE COURT'S OPINION

In a nutshell, the Court in a 7–2 decision struck down the Texas statutes. It took Blackmun eighty-one pages (U.S. edition) to explain why. Blackmun divided the opinion into twelve numbered sections: the first five set the stage for the decision by introducing the statutes, the plaintiffs and allegations, examining the granting of declaratory relief, considering the factors of justiciability and standing, and stating the constitutional liberty claim; the next five sections constitute the rationale of the case; and the final two sections offer a summary of the argument and the Court's action. It is by examining the heart of the opinion, sections VI–X, that it can clearly be seen how the Court relied on medical knowledge to justify the decision. Although each section addressed a different topic of concern, all five of these substantive sections shared two common features—the framing of abortion as a medical issue and the deference given to medical expertise.

Section VI introduced the substantive discussion of the constitutionality of the Texas statutes by reviewing the medical–legal history of abortion stretching from ancient times to the present. Blackmun began this examination by turning to the ancient Hippocratic oath and its instruction: "I will neither give a deadly drug to anybody if asked for it, nor will I make a suggestion to this effect. Similarly, I will not give to a woman an abortive remedy" (quoting Edelstein's 1943 translation at 131). Since he was writing a constitutional law opinion, and not a review of medical ethical literature, this is a somewhat unusual place to begin the substantive inquiry of the case. It also treats this medical credo as central to the case while posing the problem of how to proceed in light of the prohibition. Blackmun resolved this tension by accepting Professor Ludwig Edelstein's explanation that the oath's position regarding abortion represented only the position of the Pythagoreans and not that of most Greek thinkers, thus allowing Blackmun to set aside the prohibition. The discussion then moved on to the "quickening" of the fetus (the first recognizable movement of the fetus *in utero*) as a theological, legal, and medical demarcation within pregnancy but one that did not preclude abortion. In reviewing how American law had dealt with abortion, Blackmun included three pages on the American Medical Association (AMA) and how it was at the forefront of the shifts in law: leading the states in restricting abortion after the Civil War, and then leading the effort in the early 1970s to recognize abortion as a legitimate medical procedure (410 U.S. 113, at 143). He emphasized that this trend in favor of liberalization of abortion laws had been echoed by similar resolutions passed by the American Public Health Association and the American Bar Association. Section VI of the *Roe* decision, then, told a story of the merging of medical and legal history and expertise to conclude that restrictive abortion laws "are of relatively recent vintage" (at 129).

Blackmun's reliance on medical knowledge continued in section VII where he examined the state's three reasons for prohibiting abortion. He quickly rejected the argument that the law discourages illicit sexual conduct since Texas did not argue it in this case. The second reason examined was the claim that abortion as a medical procedure is hazardous for women, and here it was that Blackmun turned to the medical community for guidance. Referring to modern advances in medical techniques and citing in a footnote current medical studies on the mortality rates of legal abortions, Blackmun argued that these rates "appear to be as low as or lower than the rates for normal childbirth" (at 149). Therefore, the state's interest in protecting women's health, while a legitimate interest, was not in fact furthered by prohibiting all abortions. In addition, the mortality rates of illegal abortions suggest that a state's interest in protecting women's health and safety could be better served by "regulating the conditions under which abortions are performed" than by prohibiting them (at 150). The third reason examined in support of the Texas laws was the state's interest "in protecting prenatal life" (at 150). Blackmun here reviewed the question of whether the prohibitions against abortion were designed to protect prenatal life alone, or whether the laws that protected the "quickened" fetus "tacitly recogniz[e] the greater health hazards inherent in late abortion and impliedly repudiat[e] the theory that life begins at conception" (at 152). While he left this question unanswered, section VII recognized that the state had two legitimate interests in prohibiting abortion: protection of the health of the woman and the protection of potential fetal life. The medical studies cited foreshadowed that the strength of women's rights vis-à-vis state's interests would be dependent on the ability of the medical profession to perform safe abortions before as well as after quickening. So far, then, it was not law but medicine that set the stage for the *Roe* decision.

In beginning section VIII, however, Blackmun left medical discourse behind in order to study the constitutional basis for the claim of a right to privacy. After considering case precedents from the First, Fourth, Fifth, Ninth, and Fourteenth Amendments as well as their "penumbras," he concluded that the right of privacy "is broad enough to encompass a woman's decision whether or not to terminate her pregnancy" (at 153). Then, he reasserted the medical nature of abortion by arguing that state prohibitions could result in "specific and direct harm medically diagnosable even in early pregnancy" as well as other detriments, and by concluding that "all these are factors the woman and her responsible physician necessarily will consider in consultation" (at 153). He then rejected the claim that the woman's right is absolute and asserted that this right "is not unqualified and must be considered against important state interests in regulation" (at 154). Section VIII, therefore, introduced a woman's privacy right as a third interest, not as a sole determinative of the abortion issue. With the two state interests and the women's right to privacy established, Blackmun again foreshadowed that this will be a decision that balances rights along the continuum of pregnancy: "at some point in pregnancy, these respective [state] interests become sufficiently compelling to sustain regulation of the factors that govern the abortion decision" (at 154).

With the resolution of the case in sight, Blackmun paused in section IX to study the thorny question of fetal personhood. First, he reviewed how the meaning of "person" as used in law suggests that it refers only to those "postnatal," i.e., born. Second, he responded to Texas's claim that their interest in the protection of fetal life is compelling from the point of conception on since life begins at conception by casting aside the issue: "We need not resolve the difficult question of when life begins" (at 159). The justification he offered for doing so is instructive. After reviewing the divisions among theologians and philosophers, Blackmun appeared to follow the position of the medical community regarding the significance of the beginning of life:

> Physicians and their scientific colleagues have regarded that event with less interest and have tended to focus either upon conception, upon live birth, or upon the interim point at which the fetus becomes "viable," that is potentially able to live outside the mother's womb, albeit with artificial aid. (160)

The significant event, then, is not the beginning of life, a point of great concern to philosophers and theologians, but viability, an event of medical interest (and defined by Blackmun, relying once again on medical sources, at about twenty-eight weeks although possible as early as twenty-four weeks). Again, the influence of the medicalization of abortion on the legal opinion is obvious.

And it is solidified in section X where the case is resolved. Finally, Blackmun laid out the sliding scale of interests and rights that was hinted at in the previous sections and thereby demonstrated how thoroughly medical knowledge and law converged in *Roe*. He proceeded by dividing pregnancy into trimesters—an approach that none of the attorneys or *amici* suggested and one that is clearly based on medical knowledge. He did not divide the pregnancy into equal increments of approximately thirteen weeks but implied that he was following the medical practice of a twelve-week first trimester, while explicitly marking the second and third trimester by medical events: a twelve- to sixteen-week second trimester whose end is "viability," and a twelve- to sixteen-week third trimester that begins with viability and ends with birth. Upon this template of a three-part pregnancy, he superimposed three interests: the woman's right to privacy, the state's interest in protecting maternal health, and the state's interest in protecting fetal life. As the fetus grows, so does the state's interests and "at a point during pregnancy, each becomes 'compelling'" (at 163).

Therefore, during the first trimester of the pregnancy, the woman, in consultation with her physician, has the right to choose an abortion. In explaining the compelling nature of the woman's liberty right during the first trimester of pregnancy, Blackmun referred to "the now-established medical fact . . . that until the end of the first trimester mortality in abortion may be less than mortality in normal childbirth" (at 163).

During the second trimester, the state's interest in protecting maternal life and health becomes strong enough to empower the state to regulate abortion to serve those ends. Therefore, Blackmun allowed the possibility of state regulations during the second trimester that are related to the preservation of maternal health. Yet he cautioned that for the period of pregnancy "prior to this 'compelling' point, the attending physician, in consultation with his patient, is free to determine, without regulation by the State, that, in his medical judgment, the patient's pregnancy should be terminated. If that decision is reached, the judgment may be effectuated by an abortion free of interference by the State" (at 163).

During the third trimester, marked by the viability of the fetus, the state's interest in promoting and protecting fetal life becomes compelling. During this period, the state may prohibit abortion except when the woman's life or health is threatened. The discretion given to the state after viability was defended by Blackmun's assertion that it is based on "both logical and biological justifications" since "the fetus then presumably has the capability of meaningful life outside the mother's womb" (at 163).

Along with Blackmun's opinion for the majority, there were three concurring opinions and two dissenting opinions. Of these, three commented on the framing of abortion as a medical issue. In the concurrence by Justice Douglas, the issue of how pregnancy can radically alter the lives and future of women was stressed more than in the other opinions of the Court (at 214–215). Yet, even given the different emphasis, Douglas still maintained his agreement with the characterization of the termination of a pregnancy as "a medical decision" (at 219). Yet another concurrence voiced some doubts about this formulation. Questioning Blackmun's reliance on medical knowledge, Chief Justice Warren Burger wrote: "I am somewhat troubled that the Court has taken notice of various scientific and medical data in reaching its conclusion" (at 208). It is, however, Justice Byron White's dissent that directly challenged the medical construction of the issue: "At the heart of the controversy in these cases are those recurring pregnancies that pose no danger whatsoever to the life or health of the mother but are, nevertheless, unwanted for any one or more of a variety of reasons—convenience, family planning, economics, dislike of children, the embarrassment of illegitimacy, etc." (at 221).

On the same day that it handed down the *Roe* decision, the Court also decided its companion case, *Doe v. Bolton* (1973), a case even more explicitly concerned with physicians and medical discretion. The Georgia statutes challenged in this case also criminalized abortion, but they were less restrictive than the Texas statutes. They had been revised in 1968 to follow provisions suggested by the American Law Institute Model Penal Code in making exceptions not only when the woman's life was threatened, but also when a physician determined, "based upon his best clinical judgment," that an abortion was necessary because maternal health was in jeopardy, the fetus was defective, or the pregnancy was the result of rape. Yet they were challenged by a twenty-two-year-old married Georgia citizen who was nine weeks pregnant with her fourth child, and by physicians who questioned the constitutionality of the additional conditions that had to be met before an abortion could be performed: a state residency requirement for the pregnant woman, the written concurrence of two physicians other than the attending physician, the required site of a licensed hospital, and the prior approval of a hospital committee. That these provisions placed physician's discretion and medical practice at the heart of the case was acknowledged by the Court's granting of standing to the physicians, even though they had not been prosecuted or threatened with prosecution under the statutes. Blackmun explained: "The physician is the one against whom these criminal statutes directly operate in the event he procures an abortion that does not meet the statutory exceptions and conditions. . . . [He] should not be required to await and undergo a criminal prosecution as the sole means of seeking relief" (at 188). Having granted them standing, Blackmun "proceeded from the doctor's point of view; a woman's right to seek and receive medical advice did not seem an issue" (Woodward and Armstrong 1979: 216).

Writing again for the Court, Justice Blackmun struck down all four conditions of the Georgia statutes. Using medical data on the safety records of abortions performed in facilities other than hospitals, he voided the requirement as not reasonably related to the protection of women's health. He voided the hospital committee requirement stating that the "woman's right to receive medical care in accordance with her licensed physician's best judgment and the physician's right to administer it are substantially limited by this statutorily imposed overview" (at 197). Arguing the state's own position that physicians use their "best clinical judgment" to decide when abortion is necessary, he struck the two-doctor confirmation requirement. Finally, he voided the state residency requirement, not as a matter of individual rights, but because it appeared unrelated to any declared state interest. When compared with *Roe*, then, *Doe* even more clearly uses medical knowledge to establish policies protective of physicians' discretion.

CONSEQUENCES

The framing of abortion as a medical issue and the use of medical information to shape the *Roe* decision itself are not without consequences—especially for patients. When Blackmun stated that "the pregnant woman cannot be isolated in her privacy," it was an understatement. While he was referring to the presence of the state's two interests, the real essence of the opinion ensured that a pregnant woman would literally never be alone in making her decision because her physician "is free to determine . . . that, in his medical judgment, the patient's pregnancy should be terminated" (at 163). By placing a pregnant woman in a physician–patient relationship, and by conferring the privacy right as a negative right against undue government interference, *Roe* clearly rejects the notion of abortion on demand, even during the first trimester or when a woman's health or life is in jeopardy. Not only is she not isolated in her privacy, she is not empowered to actualize her decision. It is one thing to say that a woman has the right to make the decision during the first trimester free of state interference and another thing to qualify this by stating that the physician has discretion over whether the pregnancy should be terminated and that the state has no obligation to help her secure that right through funding, through protecting access for minors, or through guaranteeing the availability of the abortion procedure at public facilities. In essence, *Roe* holds that while the state may not interfere with the woman's decision during the first trimester, the physician, a lack of physicians, or a lack of money may.

In contrast, when these same two qualifications of the abortion right are applied to physicians, medical control is increased. Physicians are now required participants in the abortion decision and the negative privacy right protects their use of medical discretion. Physicians who were once prohibited from using medical judgment to perform abortions may now use medical judgment to determine when not to perform abortions. What *Roe*, then, is really signaling is that physicians can now perform first-trimester abortions without the fear of criminal charges. *Roe* decriminalizes first-trimester abortions and allows physicians to use their discretion in deciding when to perform abortions.

The point, however, is that it is physicians' discretion and not women's rights that triumph in *Roe*. Gail Kellough's analysis of Blackmun's reasoning in *Roe* makes the point well: "Although this court ruling ostensibly made abortion a private decision for American women, the medical monopoly on the provision of abortion services (which also was enshrined in the ruling) meant that, in practice, a woman's right to choice was tied to a doctor's right to withhold access to medical services (1996: 71). The physician–patient relationship may look like an equal partnership but it is in fact an asymmetrical arrangement where physicians have no obligation to respond to a woman's request for an abortion and women have no means to actualize reproductive control without the cooperation of physicians (ibid.: 74). By placing the decision making within the context of the physician–patient relationship, the roles of moral agent (the person who weighs the issues and makes the abortion decision) and medical care provider (the person capable of performing the abortion) are combined. Yet, only one party is empowered under law to assume both roles—and that is the physician. By placing "choice" within the physician–patient relationship, it is physicians, not women, who emerge with reproductive control. The physician is given a choice to perform or not to perform an abortion. The pregnant woman is given an abstract right to seek an abortion, but no guarantee that her physician will agree to perform it, much less that she will have access to it if she is poor, a minor, a rural resident, or even married (see *Roe*'s progeny below for discussion of these issues). So, as physicians are reassured in *Roe* that their judgment will be respected, women receive no such assurances.

A similar result emerges from Blackmun's construction of the second-trimester limitations that a state may impose on abortion in the name of protecting maternal health. First of all, the focus on maternal health as a legitimate basis for abortion regulations places physicians once again in the role of experts while assigning to patients the passive role of object. Presumably, doctor knows best when it comes to what furthers maternal health and what does not. A related second concern, however, is how maternal health is narrowly defined to include only medical regulations. In providing examples, Blackmun offered only those restrictions that focus on medically related issues like licensing, facilities, and the qualifications of personnel, and not those restrictions involving access issues like funding or minor's rights that are also connected to the protection of women's health. After all, if a woman needs an abortion for health reasons but can't obtain one for economic reasons, isn't her health still compromised by the state restrictions? What appears to be protected during the second trimester, then, is not so much women's health as physicians' discretion. The second trimester restrictions that Blackmun does list do not threaten physician control. On the contrary, they enhance it. The state can now require that only physicians can perform abortions, that hospitals rather than clinics be the site, and that physicians have specific training to be licensed to perform abortions—all requirements that reinforce the status of physician as expert. Yet, if the state interest is truly to protect maternal health (and not paying lip service to this goal in order to justify regulations that make abortion harder or more expensive to obtain), then why no mention of non-medical regulations that promote women's health such as those guaranteeing state funding for poor women, minors' right to secure safe, legal abortions, or general access to abortion? Again, it seems that even during the discussion of the second trimester abortion, *Roe* protects physician's discretion more than it does women's rights.

Another consequence of the construction of abortion as a medical decision is that it forces women to fit their experiences into the medical model and themselves into a decision making partnership with doctors, whether the abortion decision is based on health needs or not. As Justice White points out in his dissent, abortion can be seen as a medical decision when the woman's life or health is in jeopardy, but it is questionable that abortion is a medical decision when a woman chooses to have an abortion for a non-medical reason (e.g., limiting the number of children in a family, deciding not to have any children, or economic considerations). Yet *Roe* demands that all women enter into the same physician–patient relationship regardless of their circumstances. This seems to suggest one of two things: either physicians are appropriate experts in making *all* abortion decisions or physician control is a way to ensure that abortions be obtained for medically related concerns, but not for other reasons. Either of these scenarios are problematic since the first applies medical expertise to circumstances unrelated to health concerns and the second implies a hierarchy among the reasons for procuring an abortion—a consideration without legal basis. In addition, both threaten the woman's right to decide whether or not to terminate her pregnancy. When a woman seeks a non-medically related abortion, what she seeks is a provider, not necessarily a partner in the decision, but thanks to *Roe*, what she gets is a medical partner in the decision, but not necessarily an abortion provider. Physician discretion, then, not only governs abortions that implicate maternal health, but also those unrelated to health concerns.

Finally, *Roe*'s framing of abortion as a medical issue set the terms for the future debate over abortion. First, the medical foundation of women's abortion right was subject to erosion. Restrictions on abortion were now justifiable if they could be said to promote women's health or to protect fetal life. It would not be long before measures requiring specific waiting periods and informational warnings, spousal consent or notification, parental consent or notification, or the banning of a particular abortion method were passed by the states to discourage abortion and defended under *Roe*'s mantle of protecting maternal health. Second, *Roe*'s reliance on scientific data would also threaten to be its own undoing. Since Blackmun's trimester scheme was based on the safety rates of first-term abortions that separated the first from the second trimester, and the concept of viability that separated the second from the third trimester, the framework faced collapse as medical knowledge progressed. As safety rates for abortions improved, the first-trimester demarcation could be pushed later, and as medical techniques for saving premature infants progressed, the third trimester could begin earlier. As Justice O'Connor noted in a later abortion case, *Roe* appeared to be "on a collision course with itself" (*Akron* 1983: 416, 458).

Taken together, the consequences of Blackmun's medicalization of abortion are quite significant—for women's rights, for medical practice, and for the development of abortion law. Pregnant women gained an abstract privacy right that gave them no right of access to abortion. Instead, they were placed in a relationship with their physicians during the first trimester, and with physicians and the state during the second and third trimesters. Blackmun's remark that a pregnant woman was not isolated in her privacy was an understatement since she in fact would never be alone in making the decision—only in experiencing its consequences. Physicians gained the right to practice their profession and to use their medical judgment in deciding whether to perform an abortion. The physician–patient relationship, a physician's role as counselor and provider, and the law's reliance on medical knowledge ensured that reproductive control would be in the hands of physicians. And *Roe's* influence did not stop there. All the unanswered questions that would be raised in the future cases would be influenced by *Roe's* assumption that abortion is, ultimately, a medical issue.

ROE'S PROGENY: PROTECTING PHYSICIANS' DISCRETION

That *Roe* left many unanswered questions in its wake is clearly demonstrated by the number of cases the Court heard during the next twenty-five years and the multitude of issues they raised. Even setting aside cases that were denied *cert* without comment or that were decided by *per curium* opinions (unsigned and usually short holdings by the Court), twenty-four major abortion cases followed *Roe* and *Doe* (see table 2.1). While collectively these cases would clarify, reinforce, limit, extend, challenge, and even alter various elements of *Roe*, so would *Roe* determine the framework within which these cases would be examined. As the founding

Table 2.1   The Progeny of Roe and Doe

1975	*Bigelow v. Virginia*
1976	*Planned Parenthood of Central Missouri v. Danforth*
1977	*Beal v. Doe*
1977	*Maher v. Roe*
1977	*Poelker v. Doe*
1979	*Colautti v. Franklin*
1979	*Bellotti v. Baird*
1980	*Harris v. McRae*
1980	*Williams v. Zbaraz*
1981	*H. L. v. Matheson*
1983	*Akron v. Akron Center for Reproductive Health*
1983	*Planned Parenthood of Kansas City, Missouri v. Ashcroft*
1983	*Simpoulous v. Virginia*
1986	*Thornburgh v. American College of Obstetricians and Gynecologists*
1989	*Webster v. Reproductive Health Services*
1990	*Hodgson v. Minnesota*
1990	*Ohio v. Akron Center for Reproductive Health*
1991	*Rust v. Sullivan*
1992	*Planned Parenthood of Southeastern Pennsylvania v. Casey*
1993	*Bray v. Alexandria Women's Health Clinic*
1994	*National Organization for Women v. Scheidler*
1994	*Madsen v. Women's Health Center*
1997	*Schenck v. Pro-Choice Network*
1997	*Mazurek v. Armstrong*

precedent of abortion law, it was inevitable that *Roe's* medical framework would also be applied to its progeny. In fact, when these twenty-four cases are examined what becomes apparent is that the pattern that began in *Roe* continued in earnest through 1997: the triumph of medical knowledge over patients' knowledge and the protection of physicians' discretion over women's rights.

The twenty-four post-*Roe* and *Doe* cases presented the Court with various state and federal restrictions on abortion that I have classified under four major headings: (1) funding restrictions, (2) consent restrictions, (3) medical practice restrictions, and (4) First Amendment restrictions (see table 2.2). The first category includes any government regulations regarding the use of public funds for abortions.

Table 2.2 Abortion Restrictions Imposed after *Roe* and the Court's Holdings on Them

	Funding Restrictions	
Provision	*Case(s)*	*Court's Holdings*
Denial of Medicaid for certain medically necessary abortions	*Harris* (1980) *Williams* (1980)	Federal and state governments have no constitutional obligation to subsidize abortions for indigent women
Denial of Medicaid for nontherapeutic abortions	*Maher* (1977) *Beal* (1977)	

	Consent Restrictions	
Provision	*Case(s)*	*Court's Holdings*
Parental consent	*Danforth* (1976) *Colautti* (1979) *Bellotti* (1979)	Minors may be required to obtain the consent of one parent as long as the law provides for a judicial bypass
Parental notification	*Matheson* (1981) *Akron* (1983) *Ashcroft* (1983) *Hodgson* (1990) *Casey* (1992)	Minors may be required to notify one parent as long as the law provides for a judicial bypass
Spousal consent	*Danforth* (1976) *Colautti* (1979)	Spousal consent rules are voided
Spousal notification	*Casey* (1992)	Spousal notification rule is voided
Informed consent	*Danforth* (1976) *Akron* (1983) *Thornburgh* (1986) *Casey* (1992)	Informational requirements are upheld if flexible
Waiting period	*Akron* (1983) *Casey* (1992)	First voided then upheld if not unduly burdensome

Table 2.2 Abortion Restrictions Imposed after *Roe* and the Court's Holdings on Them *(Continued)*

Provision	*Medical Practice Restrictions* Case(s)	Court's Holdings
Restrictions on site	Danforth (1976) Poelker (1977) Akron (1983) Ashcroft (1983) Simpoulous (1983) Webster (1989)	Restrictions are upheld if flexible. Voided: hospital requirement for 2nd trimester abortions; full service hospital requirements
Restrictions on who can perform abortions	Mazurek (1997)	Physicians-only requirement is upheld
Record keeping and reporting requirements	Thornburgh (1986) Webster (1989)	Voided if data is not confidential; Otherwise upheld as related to protecting maternal health
Second physician for the fetus	Ashcroft (1983) Thornburgh (1986)	Upheld if flexible; Voided if no exception is made to protect maternal health
Limits on the physician's choice of abortion procedure used	Danforth (1976) Colautti (1979)	Voided as inconsistent with protecting maternal health
Viability testing	Danforth (1976) Webster (1989)	Upheld as related to protection of women's health
Care of the fetus	Danforth (1979) Thornburgh (1986)	Voided if there's no exception to protect maternal health
Fetal disposal	Akron (1983) Ashcroft (1983)	Voided if too vague; Pathology testing for data upheld

Provision	*First Amendment Restrictions* Case(s)	Court's Holdings
Newspaper ads	Bigelow (1985)	Abortion ads are protected
Gag rule	Rust (1991)	Federal government may impose a "gag rule" on fedeally funded family planning services
Clinic blockades	Bray (1993) Scheidler (1994)	KKK Act cannot be used to prevent abortion blockades; RICO Act can be used against anti-abortion protesters

Table 2.2   Abortion Restrictions Imposed after *Roe* and the Court's Holdings on Them *(Continued)*

Buffer zones and speech restrictions on protesters	*Madsen* (1994)	Injunctions must not burden free speech more than necessary; Upheld clinic buffer zone; Voided prohibitions against uninvited approaches of persons entering clinics, and the picketing of residences of clinic staff
Protective buffer zones around clinics	*Schenck* (1997)	Upheld the 15 foot buffer zone around clinics; Voided the "floating" buffer zone around persons or vehicles seeking access to clinics

The second grouping is composed of enactments requiring the patient to meet specific mandates in giving her consent or in obtaining the consent of others (parents or spouse) or notifying others (parents or spouse). The third heading includes government actions that directly govern physicians and the practice of medicine such as those that require or prohibit certain procedures. The fourth category contains cases that are arguably not about abortion rights at all but about freedom of speech. However, while it is true that clinic protests and blockades invoke First Amendment protection, they also threaten women's access to the abortion right, physicians' ability to perform abortions, and the physical safety of patients and clinic personnel. I have therefore included these as an integral part of abortion law since they are intimately connected with the rights of both patients and physicians.

In reviewing the holdings of these twenty-four cases, what emerges is a large body of law characterized by complicated rulings and sometimes even contradictory holdings. Some restrictions were voided by the Court only to be sustained later, and some restrictions were upheld although they appear to be just as onerous to a woman's right to abortion as the ones voided. A cursory review of *Roe*'s progeny illustrates the complexity of abortion law:

- The Court has consistently upheld restrictions that the federal and state governments have imposed on the funding of abortions (whether therapeutic or nontherapeutic) for indigent women (*Maher* 1977; *Beal* 1977; *Harris* 1980; *Williams* 1980). While such restrictions can block a woman's right to abortion and ultimately harm her health or threaten her life, the Court has determined that there is no affirmative right of access to abortion.
- With regard to consent restrictions (including parental notification and consent, spousal notification and consent, substantive informational sessions, and imposed waiting periods) the results are mixed: states can require that one

parent either be notified or give consent, but the minor must have the option of securing court approval instead (*Danforth* 1976; *Colautti* 1979; *Bellotti* 1979; *Matheson* 1981; *Akron* 1983; *Ashcroft* 1983; *Hodgson* 1990; *Casey* 1992); state-imposed spousal involvement is prohibited (*Casey* 1992); state dictation of informational sessions for the woman must allow the physician a degree of flexibility to be upheld (*Danforth* 1976; *Akron* 1983; *Thornburgh* 1986; *Casey* 1992); and while at first hostile to imposed waiting periods (*Akron* 1983), the Court most recently upheld a twenty-four-hour waiting period (*Casey* 1992). Most of these restrictions on a woman's right were not viewed by the Court as undue interference.

- The Court's handling of government restrictions on medical practice also offers a mixed bag of results: strict requirements that early abortions be performed in a hospital setting are voided but more flexible restrictions are upheld (*Danforth* 1976; *Poelker* 1977; *Akron* 1983; *Ashcroft* 1983; *Simpoulous* 1983; *Webster* 1989); a requirement that physicians and not physician's assistants perform abortions is upheld (*Mazurek* 1997); record keeping and reporting of data are sustained when women's confidentiality is maintained (*Thornburgh* 1986; *Webster* 1989); viability testing is upheld as related to the state's interest in protecting fetal life (*Danforth* 1976; *Webster* 1989) but statutes that require the presence of a second physician (*Ashcroft* 1983; *Thornburgh* 1986) or that require certain care of fetal life (*Danforth* 1976; *Thornburgh* 1986) are voided if they do not protect maternal health; and requirements that limit the physician's choice of abortion procedures are struck as inconsistent with maternal health (*Danforth* 1976; *Colautti* 1979), while fetal disposal restrictions are upheld unless they are vague (*Akron* 1983; *Ashcroft* 1983).
- Finally, decisions concerning First Amendment restrictions have produced different results: newspaper ads for abortion services are protected speech (*Bigelow* 1975); federally funded family planning services must limit their speech in counseling pregnant women to conform to federal guidelines (*Rust* 1991); and abortion blockades cannot be prevented by the KKK Act but can be challenged by the RICO Act as well as local ordinances (*Bray* 1993; *Scheidler* 1994). Courts can order protesters to stay out of a fixed protective zone encircling a clinic, but they cannot offer individuals and vehicles "floating" bubbles of protection as they attempt to enter a clinic area (*Madsen* 1994; *Schenck* 1997).

If these twenty-four cases are studied from the vantage point of how they affect women's right to privacy and to abortion, the law appears to follow a serpentine path. A woman's right to abortion is recognized and afforded constitutional status but is limited by both state interests as well as medical interests; the state must not place significant obstacles in her way that negate her right, but it can deny her funding or access if she is a minor; the abortion decision is hers to make (that is, with her physician), but the state can force her to hear specific counseling information, or make her wait twenty-four hours to act on her decision; her spouse may not interfere with her decision, but clinic protesters can; the state cannot demand that her physician perform one abortion procedure rather than another, but she can first be required to submit to invasive tests to determine fetal viability; her health is a primary concern of the state, unless she is poor.

However, what looks like a haphazard and improvisational course of law is in fact a coherent strategy united by a common principle. Remembering that abortion was constructed by the Court primarily as a medical issue, the cases seem to form a coherent pattern when the perspective of physicians is adopted. The question then becomes: what effect did *Roe*'s progeny have on physicians? Viewed from this vantage point the seemingly disparate abortion cases are unified by some very particular medical-legal themes:

When government regulations impede or restrict physicians' discretion in the practice of medicine, they are consistently struck down by the Court. This can be seen in the cases in which a second physician was required (pitting one doctor's role against another's); certain abortion procedures were proscribed (thereby not allowing the doctors to use their medical judgment); particular care of a fetus was dictated (requiring the doctor to focus on the fetus rather than the woman patient); and fetal disposal requirements were imposed (making doctors liable even if following their best medical judgments). In voiding the first three of these regulations the Court explained that they were contrary to *Roe*'s requirement that maternal health be protected. Yet, given the uneven application of this principle, another factor seems to be at work. All four of these restrictions contained a similarly fatal flaw—that of inflexibility. They did not allow physicians to make their own best medical judgments, and therefore, the Court struck them down as undue interferences with medical practice.

When government regulations are connected to the advancement of scientific knowledge, they are upheld, and when they are contradicted by scientific knowledge, they are struck down. Since fetal viability is the determining point after which the state can proscribe abortions, regulations that impose viability testing are sustained as using scientific knowledge to identify the legal status of the abortion. Regulations allowing for the collection of data, in the form of recordkeeping, or of fetal pathology tests are allowed in the name of furthering medical knowledge (and thereby, the Court claims, advancing once again women's health). In contrast, the Court voided regulations requiring that early abortions be performed in hospitals because the regulation could not be defended by data that instead showed that abortions performed in clinics posed no greater health risk to women.

When government regulations adversely affect the physician–patient relationship they are struck down, but when they are consistent with medical practices, they are upheld. The medical profession has long held as sacrosanct the relationship between physicians and their patients. For this trusting relationship to occur, there must be an honest exchange of information, and patients must be informed as well as competent to give consent. Spousal control over the abortion decision is a breach of this relationship and the Court struck it down. In contrast, minors have traditionally entered into this physician–patient relationship with an adult acting as guardian, and the Court has protected this arrangement by upholding consent and notification laws, but also by protecting minors' rights to appeal to courts as substitute guardians. The counseling sessions between physician and patients can be regulated by the state—but only if they offer guidance and flexibility so as not to unduly interfere. Finally, the twenty-four-hour waiting period is upheld as a way of making sure the patient's consent has been well considered.

When government regulations have no legal bearing on physicians, they are likely to be upheld. The negative right founded in *Roe* worked well to protect physicians' discretion, since all they really wanted was to be left alone to practice medicine, but it offered little protection to those women who depended on governmental help to secure access to an abortion. Within this context, then, the Court could uphold restrictions on the government funding of abortions for indigent women. It could also offer First Amendment protection to abortion clinic protesters. Without attempting to reconcile the six First Amendment cases whose decisions are more the result of the technicalities of free speech law than to abortion law, what these cases again indicate are the limitations inherent in the conferring of a negative right of protection against government interference that offers no affirmative obligation on the part of the government to protect against the interference of others.

Together, these four themes constitute a consistent and rather clear pattern that abortion law follows. *Roe's* progeny protects physicians not from government prosecution alone, but also from government interference in making medical decisions, in advancing medical knowledge, and in consulting with patients. However, and even more importantly, the pattern also suggests that while the Court is able to both recognize and safeguard physicians from most forms of interference, the same is not true concerning patients. Physicians are afforded flexibility in their practice of medicine, and are protected from state measures that challenge their judgments. The same cannot be said of patients and their judgments. Instead, state measures that second-guess the decision, that attempt to dissuade women from the abortion decision, that allow parents, the state, and physicians to exert influence, and that delay the abortion procedure demonstrate that patients' judgments can be challenged in a way that physicians' judgments cannot.

In addition, while seemingly sensitive to the harms suffered by physicians, *Roe's* progeny appear callous to the harms suffered by patients. The *Casey* (1992) decision and the clinic protest cases are illustrative.

Both the decision as well as the tone of the opinions in *Casey* took many court watchers by surprise. Given the fact that recent appointments had created a conservative majority of 7–2 on the Court, many anticipated that *Casey* would result in the overturning of *Roe*. Instead, Justices O'Connor, Kennedy, and Souter defied expectations and issued a plurality opinion that not only preserved women's right to abortion, but also spoke eloquently of women's experiences: "The mother who carries a child to full term is subject to anxieties, to physical constraints, to pain that only she must bear. . . . Her suffering is too intimate and personal for the State to insist, without more, upon its own vision of the woman' role" (505 U.S. 833 at 852). Yet, while the language used by this trio of Justices seemed to recognize the cultural context of the abortion issue, their actual decision demonstrated a lack of appreciation for the particulars. The Court replaced the strict scrutiny test with the "undue burden" test that allows state regulations to stand unless they constitute a "substantial obstacle" to the abortion right. In applying this test, the Court sustained measures that resulted in an increase in the cost of abortion, a delay in the procedure, and mandatory physician–patient informational sessions designed to dissuade the woman from having an abortion. While the plurality opinion does recognize the consequences that unwanted pregnancies have for women in the abstract, it failed to apply this knowledge to the specifics of the Pennsylvania statute and to particular women. In this, the Court appeared to be especially insensitive to the circumstances of poor women, minors, and women who did not want the physician to participate in the decision making process.

The clinic protest cases are particularly instructive as to how the Court can disregard or diminish the harm experienced by patients. For example, in *Schenck* (1997), Chief Justice Rehnquist described the combative situations that often erupted outside of the western New York clinics involved in the case: "Unfortunately, if the women continued toward the clinics and did not respond positively to the counselors, such peaceful efforts at persuasion often devolved into 'in your face' yelling, and sometimes into pushing, shoving, and grabbing" (13). Yet Rehnquist's next comment focuses not on the patients and their experiences but those who escorted them: "*Men* who accompanied women attempting to enter the clinics often became upset by the aggressive sidewalk counseling and sometimes had to be restrained (not always successfully) from fighting with counselors" (13, emphasis mine). But what was the harm suffered by the *women* who tried to enter the clinic or by those who did not even dare to try? The Court did not ask but instead focused on the harm that the "floating" buffer zone had on the First Amendment rights of the protesters, and ruled to void it—leaving the harm done to patients unaddressed. One wonders if the Court would have had the same reaction to similar protests and physical struggles held outside of voting sites located in mostly minority precincts. Would the targeting of a class of people with the intent of intimidating them from acting on a constitutional right be seen as equally benign and equally protected under the First Amendment? In the school desegregation case of *Cooper v. Aaron* (1958), federal troops were sent in to protect the black children as they acted upon their right to integrate a public school. Should pregnant women who act upon their right to access an abortion expect any less? The Court answered this clearly but less than persuasively in *Bray* (1993) when it ruled that pregnant women are not a protected class.[4]

The First Amendment cases, however, also pose a threat to physicians. In assigning the abortion right to medical hands, the Court made physicians the primary targets for the opposition. Indeed, the anti-abortion movement has found the weak link in the chain of events necessary for women to actualize the right—abortion providers. If physicians could be discouraged or prevented from practicing, the right becomes a mere abstraction. As abortion politics has moved from protest to harassment, threats, violence, and even assassination, physicians, patients, and the abortion right are in real jeopardy (see O'Connor 1996: 158–173). The Court's rulings that protected the abortion right against governmental restrictions are of little use when the restrictions come from private individuals and organizations invoking their own set of constitutional rights.

In sum, based on this study I find that *Roe*'s progeny does in fact form a discernible pattern of decision making. Not only is medical knowledge used by the Court, medical practice is protected. Physicians' discretion is protected in ways that women's rights are not. The Justices recognize the ways in which government restrictions harm the right of physicians to practice, while they allow women's rights to be burdened to the point of constituting a "significant" obstacle—a concept of harm for which the Court seems to have a high threshold. Rather than unpredictable, then, abortion law follows a consistent design that is repeated over and over again. Upon seeing this design it is clear that it was physicians, and not their female patients, who gained the most from *Roe* and its progeny.

CONCLUSION

Medical knowledge over patients' knowledge. Physicians' discretion over patients' rights. These are the legacies of the Court's decisions in the abortion cases. While the physicians and patients who served as litigants in these cases were not at odds, but appeared on the same side of the case (i.e., the pro-choice side), their interests were not always the same. This is reflected in how the Court's decisions not only treated the knowledge they offered as different in kind, but also by how the results affected them in different ways.

The abortion decisions, then, demonstrate how medical knowledge converged seamlessly with the law. Excluded from this merger of medical and legal knowledge was the knowledge of patients, even though the decision was depicted as being made on their behalf. In truth, the abortion cases were about patients, but the determinative knowledge did not come from them and the resulting decisions were not for them. Just as Justice Blackmun had promised, the emphasis was on medicine and law—not on the emotional, the subjective, or the personal.

Yet, the cost of "objectivity" was a lack of care. In relying on medical and legal knowledge and purposely excluding the knowledge of patients, the Court sabotaged its ability to understand the complexities of the abortion issue and to respond to the issues, needs, and rights of the female patients. The Court was not wrong to include medical knowledge in its decision making—indeed, it was a necessary component of the case. Where the Court erred was in assuming that it had to disregard the knowledge of patients. In the name of justice, medical knowledge was given a legal forum while patients were denied recognition as knowers.

Such an established pattern has power. It pulls the Court to follow it and it constrains the choices available. Twenty-four years after *Roe*, the Justices were asked to settle another issue involving patients, physicians, and the law. The cases of *Glucksberg* and *Quill* and the issue of physician-assisted suicide presented the Court with another opportunity to hear the voices of patients. This time, the knowledge of patients would challenge the medical–legal discourse, but the pull of *Roe* and its progeny would be too powerful to resist. Sadly, one legacy of the abortion cases would be that medical–legal knowledge would overwhelm patients' knowledge in yet another area of biomedical law.

• *3* •

The Physician-Assisted Suicide Cases: The Triumph of Medical Knowledge over Patients' Knowledge

> There can be no objectivity in any decision involving the end of life. It is so emotional, it is almost instinctual so; whether one is a Supreme Court Justice or not, that person cannot help but be influenced by personal experiences involving death.
>
> Dr. Sherwin B. Nuland, author of *How We Die*

There was a sense of deja vu on January 8, 1997, when the attorneys in the *Washington v. Glucksberg* and *Vacco v. Quill* cases presented their oral arguments before the U.S. Supreme Court. While this was the first time the Court entertained arguments concerning the constitutionality of state bans on physician-assisted suicide (PAS), there was a striking sense of having covered this ground before:

Chief Justice William Rehnquist: What precisely is the liberty interest that you urge us to recognize?
Justice Anthony Kennedy: You're asking us in effect to declare unconstitutional the law of fifty states.
Justice Sandra Day O'Connor: There is no doubt that . . . if we upheld your position, it would result in a flow of cases through the court system for heaven knows how long.
("Excerpts from the Supreme Court" 1997)

References to substantive due process, ordered liberty, state police powers, personal choice, and the value of life rang familiar. Attorneys were peppered with predictable questions from the bench: the wisdom of asking the Court to decide such a case, whether ethical and moral questions are best left to the legislature, how to set limits to the liberty right, and by what criteria the case should be judged. Yet, it was not just the legalese that seemed familiar. References to scientific information, to statistics, and to the practice, norms, and opinions of medicine, placed physicians once again squarely in the center of an emerging legal controversy.

All of this was reminiscent of another set of oral arguments twenty-five years earlier when the Justices first scrutinized the attorneys who argued the landmark abortion case of *Roe v. Wade*. The story of an emotionally charged life and death issue involving patients and the medical community, litigants' claims to constitutional rights, appeals to morality and higher law, differing responses from state governments, and intervention by the U.S. Supreme Court describes equally as well the abortion saga and the emerging issues associated with euthanasia. Yet the controversies share much more than just intellectual linkages. It is hard to imagine two issues more personally compelling, more emotionally charged, or more touched by human suffering than the decision to terminate a pregnancy or to end one's own life.

The Court's consent to hear the PAS cases of *Glucksberg* and *Quill* presented the Justices with a challenge as well as an opportunity. Once again they were faced with the dilemma of weighing competing claims concerning a life and death issue. If they resisted the option of deciding the case on a technicality and chose instead to address the issue head-on, they would have to decide whether terminally ill, competent adult patients had a constitutionally protected right to secure the aid of a physician in committing suicide. But the granting of *certiorari* also presented the Justices with an opportunity to develop a distinctively different approach in addressing the cases, their issues, and their resolutions than they had employed in the abortion cases. Here was a chance to fashion a new approach—one that regarded PAS as more than just a medical issue, that was capable of hearing and incorporating patients' knowledge, and that appreciated the central role played by human relationships. In short, the Court of 1997 did not have to follow the script penned by the Court of 1973. Several factors gave the Court the flexibility to create anew.

First, for all their similarities, PAS is not the same issue as abortion. In fact, they are separated in many ways. While abortion involves the fate of one life situated within the body of another life, PAS involves singular lives. Abortion terminates life before birth, PAS terminates life before natural death claims it. An unwanted pregnancy is a "temporary" physical condition in that it will end with birth (although social, emotional, and financial obligations may remain), but dying is a "permanent" physical condition from which a patient is only released by death. While a pregnant woman makes the decision (with her physician) to abort the fetus, the terminally ill patient ends his or her own life with medication prescribed by a physician. Only women experience first-hand the abortion decision, but the prospect of dying from an illness is something we all face. The rights afforded to the fetus are limited since it is not considered a legal person, but the terminally ill, whether competent or incompetent, are endowed with full rights and legal protections. In sum, many of the complexities central to the abortion controversy, like the questions concerning who is the patient, the ethics of terminating a developing human life at the request of the mother, the most obvious gender implications, and the legal status of personhood are not usually pivotal points in the PAS debate. The Court, then, was free to focus on different questions and concerns in the PAS cases.

A second factor that presented the Court with an opportunity to shape a new area of law without relying on *Roe*, was that another, and perhaps more relevant, precedent existed. The Court had already ventured into the field of euthanasia and the "right to die" in the 1990 case of *Cruzan v. Director, Missouri Department of Health*, and had decided that case without drawing on *Roe* as precedent. *Cruzan*, therefore, freed the Court from tying PAS to the abortion precedents. Yet, *Cruzan* was also narrowly confined to the issue of withdrawing nutrition and hydration support, thus leaving unanswered other euthanasia issues and opening the possibility of constructing a broader ruling.

Third, the *Glucksberg* and *Quill* cases showcased patients' knowledge and their experiences in ways that *Roe* had not. From the party briefs to oral arguments, Court documents provided the Court with first-hand information concerning the pros and cons of legalized PAS. Some of the information offered by patients directly contradicted the information provided by the American Medical Association (AMA), while other patient accounts challenged any attempt to define PAS as a mostly medical issue. Unlike the marginalized voices of patients in *Roe*, then, the patients involved in the PAS litigation trumpeted their experiences as knowledge. This prominent display of patients' knowledge demanded that the Court deal with their concerns.

A final factor that presented the Court with an opportunity to depart from the patterns set in *Roe* was that the PAS cases involved a fracture between the medical community and the general public that had not been present in the abortion cases. Granted, although abortion was a highly politicized issue before the *Roe* decision, it became even more polarized after 1973, and continues to be highly charged, since 1972 both the official position of mainstream medical organizations and the opinion of the general public have consistently supported one side of the issue— the pro-choice side. Organizations like the AMA and the American College of Obstetricians and Gynecologists (ACOG) became pro-choice advocates several years before the *Roe* decision and vocally supported efforts by state legislatures to reform restrictive abortion laws (Luker 1984; Petchesky 1984; Brief of ACOG 1971; Brief of 281 American Historians 1988). Similarly, public opinion polls continue to document a public supportive of abortion rights, although not necessarily in favor of absolute choice (see Cook et al. 1992; Rosenblatt 1992; Craig and O'Brien 1993). This is not to ignore the fact that the pro-life/anti-abortion position is held by some physicians, some medical organizations, as well as many members of the general public, but these remain dissents in the face of general agreement among representative organizations of physicians and the majority of the general public that abortion should be legal. Such consensus, however, was not the case concerning PAS. Instead, while the AMA and other representative medical organizations supported the efforts of states to ban PAS, early polls indicated a public in favor of the legalization of PAS (Gallup 1996).[1] Even though the litigants who challenged the PAS state bans in Washington and New York included seven physicians, it was obvious from the start that these physicians were outside of the medical fold in regard to this issue. With the fracture, then, between most of the official organizations of the medical community and the public at large, there was little reason for the Court to conflate physician's concerns with patients' concerns. With such distinct positions, patients' voices would be audible in ways that they were not in the abortion cases.

With these forces at play, the Court was free to escape the confines of *Roe*. While abortion had been defined as a medical issue, PAS need not be. While physicians became the central characters in abortion, the same need not happen in PAS. While medical knowledge trumped patients' voices in the abortion cases, the PAS cases presented patients' knowledge to the Justices as expertise.

This chapter explores whether these opportunities to frame PAS in nonmedical terms, to focus on the concerns of patients rather than physicians, and to incorporate the knowledge of patients, were actually taken by the Court. To study this question, I employ the same strategy that I used in the previous chapter concerning *Roe* and its progeny. Once again, I examine the party briefs, the *amicus curiae* briefs, and the oral arguments to determine what knowledge was presented to the Court, how, and by whom. Next, I shift to the Court's decisions in *Glucksberg* and *Quill* to explore how the Court used the information. What I find is that while these cases are distinctively different from the abortion cases, the Court with the exception of one Justice applied the same worn template it had used in the abortion cases to the PAS cases. Rather than seizing the opportunities to develop a new approach in resolving this new issue, the Court approached PAS as a medical issue involving physicians and their role as healers, and viewed patients collectively as objects needing protection from themselves, not as moral agents deserving of a particularized legal response.

THE PAS CASES AND KNOWLEDGE

The *Glucksberg* and *Quill* cases began on opposite coasts, emphasized different constitutional concerns, and emerged as challenges to different state laws. In the end, however, they shared: a similar start, in that the highest state courts found the state bans on PAS to be unconstitutional; a similar response, in that the appeals from the states to the U.S. Supreme Court were granted *cert*; and a similar fate, in that the Court overturned the lower courts and upheld the state bans on PAS.

At issue in *Glucksberg* was a Washington state statute that declared, "A person is guilty of promoting a suicide attempt when he knowingly causes or aids another person to attempt suicide" and that established violations as class C felonies (Wash. Rev. code S 9A.36.060). The law was challenged in the lower court by three competent, terminally ill adult patients (using the pseudonyms of "Jane Roe," "John Doe," and "John Poe"), four physicians (Harold Glucksberg, M.D.; Abigail Halperin, M.D.; Thomas A. Preston, M.D.; and Peter Shalit, M.D., Ph.D.) suing on their own behalf and on behalf of their patients, and a non-profit organization (Compassion in Dying). By the time the case arrived at the U.S. Supreme Court, only the physician-plaintiffs remained since the patient-plaintiffs had died and the claims of Compassion in Dying had not been addressed by the district court. The four physicians argued that the Washington statute infringed on the Fourteenth Amendment liberty interest of competent, terminally ill adults to make end-of-life decisions free of undue government interference, and that it denied Fourteenth Amendment Equal Protection to competent, terminally ill adults who are not on life support (Respondents Brief). The case followed a tumultuous route to the U.S. Supreme Court: the district court for the Western District of Washington struck down the law on the basis of the Fourteenth Amendment's liberty interest (*Compassion in Dying v. Washington*, 850 F. Supp. 1454 W.D. Wash. 1994); a three-judge panel of the U.S. Court of Appeals for the Ninth Circuit reversed, upholding the state law (49 F.3d 586 9th Cir. 1995); a limited *en banc* panel (composed of eleven judges) of the U.S. Court of Appeals for the Ninth Circuit reversed the three-judge panel and affirmed the district court, invalidating the statute (79 F.3d 790 1996); and a request to rehear the case before the full Ninth Circuit Court was denied (85 F.3d 1440 9th Cir. 1996). The U.S. Supreme Court granted *cert* on October 1, 1996 (*Washington v. Glucksberg*, 135 L.Ed. 2d 1128) and oral arguments were scheduled for January 1997.

At issue in *Quill* were two sections of New York State Penal Law S 125.15 (3): "A person is guilty of manslaughter in the second degree when . . . (3) He intentionally causes or aids another person to commit suicide. Manslaughter in the second degree is a class C felony" and S 120.30 "A person is guilty of promoting a suicide attempt when he intentionally causes or aids another person to attempt suicide. Promoting a suicide attempt is a class E felony." The original suit was brought by three competent, terminally ill adult patient-plaintiffs ("Jane Doe," George Kingsley, and William A. Barth), who all died before the district court rendered its opinion, and three physician-plaintiffs (Timothy E. Quill, M.D.; Samuel G. Klagsbrun, M.D.; and Howard A. Grossman, M.D.) who sued both on their own behalf and on behalf of their competent, terminally ill adult patients. The District Court granted summary judgment for the plaintiffs (*Quill v. Koppell*, 870 F.Supp. 78 S.D.N.Y. 1994); the Second Circuit reversed (*Quill v. Vacco*, 80 F.3d 716 2d Cir) stating that it could not recognize a constitutionally protected liberty interest in this case. However, the Second Circuit Court voided the law on the basis of the equal protection claim that while the terminally ill who are on life-support systems are allowed to hasten their deaths by being removed from these systems, the similarly situated terminally ill who are not on life-support are not allowed to hasten their deaths by self-administering prescribed drugs (Respondents Brief). The U.S. Supreme Court granted *cert* on October 1, 1996 (135 L.Ed. 2d 1127), and scheduled the case to be argued jointly with *Washington v. Glucksberg* in January 1997.

The story of these cases became no less complicated when they arrived at the U.S. Supreme Court. Telling of the perceived importance of these cases as well as their complexity was the sheer amount of information filed with the Court. The two cases produced not only four party briefs and two reply briefs, but also a 238-page Joint Appendix and fifty-nine *amicus curiae* briefs. Composed by the parties, the Joint Appendix contained twenty-two documents including declarations of the plaintiff patients and physicians, excerpts from two *amicus* briefs that had been filed in the abortion case of *Webster v. Reproductive Health Services* (1989), a report on PAS and a Model Penal Code, and legal motions, answers, stipulations, and orders. The fifty-nine *amicus curiae* briefs were filed by individuals, states, and approximately 138 organizations. When laid flat and stacked on each other, they measured almost a foot high. Clearly, the Court was not at a loss for resources as they prepared for and heard the case.

The question, then, is how knowledge was constructed and presented to the Court. To answer this, I offer a brief review of legal norms and how these set the context for what was presented and argued in the Court records. Next, I examine in turn the party briefs, the *amicus* briefs and the oral arguments, highlighting the presence and influence of legal, medical, and patients' knowledge. In referring to the two sides of the cases, I break with the usual practice of labeling these according to the identities of the litigants because to do so would be confusing. Depicting the cases in terms of states versus physicians would be misleading since most of the mainstream medical organizations supported the other side of the cases. Therefore, in order to avoid confusion, I refer to the position taken by the Respondents Drs. Glucksberg and Quill as the pro-PAS or the PAS advocates' side and the position taken by the Petitioners Washington and New York as either the anti-PAS side or the states' side.[2] The final section examines how the opinions in the *Glucksberg* and *Quill* cases reflect the choices made by each of the Justices in deciding which thread of knowledge to follow—that of medicine or that of patients.

Setting Up the Framework

Because the PAS controversy was no longer destined to be resolved in the privacy of a household, the institutional constraints of a hospital room, or the political arena of a state legislature but instead in the setting of a courtroom, it was legal norms rather than other constraints that dominated how the issues would be articulated, addressed, and adjudicated. The construction of the definitions, facts, anecdotes, arguments, and attempts at persuasion took aim at a specialized audience—the judges of the lower courts and the Justices of the highest court. Within this legal context, the focus of the cases, the points of contention, and the structure for resolving them were equally as specialized: constitutional text, judicial tests, and legal precedents would provide the framework within which all the litigants, all the knowledge, and all the arguments would be woven together.

Constitutional text would serve as the basis for the claims and would set the parameters for the clashing of rights and interests. The patients and their physicians would find textual footing for their grievance in the clauses of the Fourteenth Amendment. In particular, the right of terminally ill patients to determine the manner of their death could be bolstered by the liberty interests of the Due Process Clause, and the claim that they were entitled to the same right of self-determination as that afforded to those patients on life support could find support in the Equal Protection Clause. The Constitution, then, set the framework for interpreting the controversy presented by the PAS cases as a clashing of individual rights versus state interests.

The Court's selection of *judicial tests* would also help to shape the PAS dilemma into a legal case. A right to die, or more specifically, a right to have medical assistance in committing suicide, does not involve a "suspect" classification of people and neither does it have the explicit constitutional textual basis to warrant the status of a fundamental right, thereby triggering application of the strict scrutiny test. However, if the Court could be persuaded that these interests are supported by historical traditions and long-standing social values, then strict scrutiny could still be applied. Otherwise, the Court would be free to apply a less stringent test in weighing the law against the individual rights at stake. Therefore, the legal question of which test to apply in evaluating these cases highlighted the history of medical practices and social mores regarding treatment and suicide. In this, the Court practice of employing certain judicial tests to resolve liberty and equal protection claims directed litigants to include in their arguments the history of assisted suicide in American culture.

Precedents would add more detail to this framework and would further dictate the content of the litigants' arguments. Two cases in particular promised to be influential: *Cruzan v. Director, Missouri Department of Health* (1990), a "right to die" case, and *Planned Parenthood of Southeastern Pennsylvania v. Casey* (1992), the most influential of the recent abortion cases. Both of these cases offered the plaintiff patients and physicians a foundation on which to build their claims. *Cruzan* represented the Court's first foray into the field of euthanasia and it sent a mixed message regarding how to unravel the tangle of individual rights and states interests. The case revolved around a patient, Nancy Beth Cruzan, who as the result of injuries suffered in an automobile accident was in a persistent vegetative state (PVS). After six years in this condition, her family sought a court order to have her artificial nutrition and hydration terminated so that she could die. Missouri insisted that before the request could be honored, the family had to meet the state's requirement that "clear and convincing" evidence be presented as to the incompetent person's wish regarding the withdrawal of life-sustaining treatment. Judging that the Cruzans had failed to produce such evidence, the State Supreme Court denied the Cruzans' petition. The U.S. Supreme Court agreed with this assessment in regard to the level of evidence required, but also recognized a common law right for patients, whether competent or not, to refuse medical treatment. Therefore, based on its connection to euthanasia, *Cruzan*'s relevance as precedent in the PAS cases seemed assured.

The same was not immediately apparent regarding *Casey*. When rendered in 1992, the importance of the *Casey* decision was due to its unexpected reaffirmation of the central premise of *Roe*—that a woman has a constitutional right to choose to have an abortion before fetal viability. While seemingly part of a separate, and possibly even an unrelated, area of law than PAS, *Casey* was potentially relevant for the PAS cases in at least two ways. First, the plurality opinion by Justices Sandra Day O'Connor, Anthony Kennedy, and David Souter offered an impassioned defense of the liberty right as protecting personal autonomy, bodily integrity, and human dignity: "At the heart of liberty is the right to define one's own concept of existence, of meaning, of the universe, and of the mystery of human life" (at 851). Second, in reconciling the state's interests in promoting maternal health and fetal life with the woman's liberty interests, the plurality replaced *Roe*'s strict scrutiny test (i.e., that a state regulation could only be upheld if it was necessary to achieve a compelling state interest) with a less stringent "undue burden" test that allowed the state to regulate abortions unless the restriction had "the purpose or effect of placing a substantial obstacle in the path of a woman seeking an abortion of a nonviable fetus" (at 877). Clearly, both the Court's rendering of liberty and its strategy for recognizing both state and individual interests could prove useful to the pro-PAS side in *Glucksberg* and *Quill*. Both sides to the cases would therefore be compelled to address the applicability of these cases or to distinguish the PAS cases from these precedents.

One ramification of these legal parameters for the PAS cases was that they appeared to give an initial advantage to the states of Washington and New York over the pro-PAS side. One reason for this was that the conflict over rights enabled the states to stand on the bulwark of democracy in arguing that by banning assisted suicide they represented the will of the majority of the people. In addition, while the state interests in regulating this practice appeared obvious, the rights claimed by the plaintiffs were less so—exactly what was the right claimed, its constitutional source, its legal force? A second advantage enjoyed by the states was that the history of suicide was a story of legal, religious, medical, and community objections to the practice. Clearly, assisted suicide seemed to run against the grain of legal and social norms. PAS advocates would have to struggle to shift the focus to the harmful role that technology played in changing the meaning and the experience of death. A third state advantage was that adherence to precedents highlighted the slippery slope[3] argument by demonstrating how each case pushed individual rights farther and farther along. In this struggle over holding the line against the downhill slide to legalized murder, the states were cast as protectors of the sanctity of life. A significant disadvantage for the pro-PAS position was that there was no information by which to counteract the charges of the dangers of sanctioned suicide because there was at the time no state in the country that had actually legalized PAS.[4]

However, the major consequence of these legal norms, was that the multifaceted nature of PAS as an issue would be ground down until it fit the mold of a constitutional i.w case. The purpose here was not legislative in nature—finding the "best" response to the issue or offering compromises or alternatives that could lessen the conflict. In fact, if this had indeed been the objective then the Court might have studied how dehydration is an option that answers many of the concerns of dying patients without provoking the legal conflicts of PAS (see Hoefler 1997). Instead, in shaping this problem into the particularized form of a legal controversy, certain aspects of the issue would be pared away so as to heighten others. Naming the conflict as a clashing of individual rights versus state interests threatened to sharpen points of disagreement into dichotomous claims while ignoring the mutual concerns of the parties. Focusing on the history of suicide within American legal, social, and medical culture implicated the behavior of patients rather than the medicalized approach to death followed in the United States. Looking to form a line of precedent extending from *Cruzan* to *Casey* to *Glucksberg* and *Quill* risked reigniting the abstract slippery slope debate at the expense of the particular concerns of these plaintiffs. But despite the varied consequences, the framework was set. *Glucksberg* and *Quill* were now constitutional law cases, and it was within this legal context that knowledge would be accumulated, arguments composed, and documents submitted to the Court.

The Conflicting Knowledge of the Party Briefs

As foreshadowed by the legal norms discussed above, certain arguments dominated the party briefs. The constitutional rights invoked by the PAS advocates were countered by claims of state interests; a debate ensued as to whether terminally ill patients were similarly situated to patients dependent on artificial life support; the two states urged use of the rational basis test while the pro-PAS side called upon the Court to use a higher standard such as the undue burden test; and the relevancy of *Casey* and *Cruzan* to these cases was batted back and forth. Yet, even amid these predictable lines of argumentation, another pattern emerged—different types of knowledge dominated each side of the cases. The arguments of the two states relied heavily on both legal and medical knowledge while the briefs of the PAS advocates prominently presented patients' knowledge.

This division was highlighted from the start by the different ways that the sides understood the issues. The state of Washington asked the Court to consider the following questions:

1. Is there a constitutionally protected liberty interest under the Due Process Clause of the Fourteenth Amendment in *committing suicide*, and if so, does that interest include assistance in so doing?
2. If the answer to the foregoing question is in the affirmative, is a State statute that infringes on the protected liberty interest by prohibiting one *person* from assisting *another* to commit suicide nonetheless valid under the Due Process Clause because it furthers *legitimate State interests*?
3. Is there a *rational basis* for distinguishing between refusing life-sustaining medical treatment and requesting life-ending medical intervention, so that a State whose law allows the former but not the latter does not violate the Equal Protection Clause of the Fourteenth Amendment? (Brief for Petitioners, *Glucksberg*, emphasis mine)

The Glucksberg brief countered with the questions of

Whether the Fourteenth Amendment's guarantee of liberty protects the decision of a *mentally competent, terminally ill adult* to bring about *impending death* in a certain, humane, and dignified manner?

Whether a state denies equal protection when it permits terminally ill patients who are on life support to choose a humane death with medical assistance but prohibits terminally ill patients who are not on life support from *exercising the same right* by self-administering medication prescribed for that purpose? (Brief for Respondents, *Glucksberg*, emphasis mine)

Similar approaches were adopted by New York and Quill in their briefs. While the state put the questions in terms of generic "persons," suicide, and states interests, the PAS advocates framed it in the more specific terms of terminally ill competent adults facing impending death, and the right of these patients to control it. Indeed, a significant point of contention in the briefs was whether these cases were really about suicide at all. The states maintained that persons desiring to kill themselves clearly fit the definition of suicide, while the patients' advocates countered that these cases did not involve people who *wanted* to die, but terminally ill people whose only choice was *how* to die.

Yet the differences in the presentation of the issues was only the start for the disparate ways in which the sides evaluated and used knowledge. The breach began early, as the sides chose different places from which to begin their arguments. Both Washington and New York launched into analyses of the legal doctrines involved—liberty and equal protection. The PAS advocates chose a very different point at which to begin—the people at the heart of the disputes, the terminally ill patients and the plaintiff physicians representing them. The Quill brief, in particular, made it clear that it was no accident that the presentation began in this way: "An understanding of the intolerable pain and suffering that confronts such patients is the appropriate starting point for consideration of this case" (Brief for Respondents, *Quill*). But patients' knowledge would serve as more than just a starting point for the briefs—it was also used to challenge the "conventional wisdom" regarding PAS. This strategy was put into practice at several points in the briefs submitted by the pro-PAS side.

First, the anecdotes were necessary to assert the concreteness of the class of people affected by this issue. Washington's claim that this class of people was "hypothetical" had to be contested (Brief for Petitioners, *Glucksberg*, p. 25). The lower court records (i.e., the briefs, the Joint Appendix of the briefs, and the *amicus* briefs) were replete with stories of how the terminally ill and their loved ones suffer as they are denied assistance in hastening death. Told by real people concerning their real experiences, the testimony of these patients injected a human element into what could have been abstract argumentation. In addition, the patients who were represented by the stories were carefully confined to an identifiable class of people—mentally competent, terminally ill adults. The stories, then, were intended to clarify and heighten the legal issues by illustrating that these were real cases and controversies involving a specific group of people.

Second, patients' stories were told to challenge the validity of the medical claim made in some of the *amicus* briefs filed on behalf of the two states that physical pain could be effectively managed through palliative care. Each of the plaintiff patients and physicians told of experiences to the contrary. Jane Roe declared that despite having received "good" treatment, "the pain associated with this cancer is unrelenting. It is a constant, dull pain, interspersed with sharp, severe pain provoked by movement" (Joint Appendix, *Glucksberg*, p. 24). John Poe cited his "extreme leg pain" and the "terror associated with the sensation of suffocation" (Joint Appendix, *Glucksberg*, p. 30). John Doe challenged the notion that pain control alone was the issue. He told of how his loss of vision "is fatal to my ability to paint," how his ability to care for himself was diminishing, and how, having seen his longtime partner die of AIDS, he feared "the pain, suffering, anguish, and loss of dignity of dying from AIDS" (Joint Appendix, *Glucksberg*, p. 28). The plaintiff physicians declared that the law prevented them from helping their suffering patients and that it in fact caused additional suffering. Dr. Glucksberg told of one dying patient who had committed suicide by leaping off a bridge; Dr. Halperin told of a terminally ill patient who suffocated herself with a plastic bag; and Drs. Preston and

Shalit described how the statute resulted in their patients "dying tortured deaths" (Joint Appendix, *Glucksberg*, pp. 36, 51, 56, 74). Together, the declarations and their summaries in the briefs told not only of pain, but physical suffering, emotional suffering, and the assault to personal dignity and autonomy caused not only by the illnesses but by the state statutes in question.

Third, patients' knowledge was used in the briefs to contest the claim of the two states that assisted suicide had always been an illegal and a shunned, medical practice. The PAS advocates' briefs drew the Court's attention to how the states employed the "direct effects" argument to obscure current practices. The Quill brief charged that "acts of euthanasia take place in New York and throughout the United States *every day*" (Brief for Respondents, *Quill*, p. 21, emphasis in original). Quill explained:

> The law of New York evinces no blanket policy against a physician assisting such a terminally ill person in dying. Once a person reaches the final states of life, New York always allows (as it sometimes does not for those whose conditions are reversible) the physician's termination of life-sustaining procedures, including the provision of food and water, even when the patient seeks such termination for the specific purpose of bringing about a merciful death. And for those dying patients willing to endure it, the State permits a procedure known as "terminal sedation" in which doctors induce a state of continuing unconsciousness (a "barbiturate coma") wherein the patient is denied nutrition and hydration until he is dead. (Brief for Respondents, *Quill*, p. 1)

This attack on medicine as duplicitous in its actual practices was cranked up another notch later in the brief when Quill charged that the attempt to distinguish terminal sedation from PAS amounted to a state interest in preserving appearances over a commitment to protecting either the value of life or constitutional rights:

> But surely the Constitution does not permit the State to sacrifice the rights of the dying on the altar of appearances. However well-tailored the State's ban is to the achievement of this goal, it cannot be doubted, in a nation committed not to regulation by winks and nods but to the rule of law . . . that a state's interest in *appearing* to protect life in a way that it does not actually protect it is neither sufficiently "substantial" nor sufficiently "important" to outweigh a terminal patient's liberty to avoid a horrific death. (ibid: 21, emphasis in original)

The questions, then, of what was really practiced and what was really the state's interests were challenged by what the plaintiff patients and physicians knew from their own experiences.

While clearly setting the course for the briefs and at times offering them fuel, it is also important to note that personal experiences were not the sole basis for the arguments in the pro-PAS briefs. As in any constitutional law case, this specialized knowledge had to be integrated into legal arguments involving text, tests, and precedents—and the PAS advocates' briefs did exactly that. This was particularly evident in the Joint Appendix filed in *Glucksberg* in which the declarations of the patients were highly technical descriptions of their medical conditions as well as legalistic statements of their soundness of mind, but not descriptive at all of their emotional turmoil, the impact the issue had on their relationships with others, or how they felt about their condition and circumstances. Yet, even with these points said, it was still evident that at the core of the pro-PAS briefs was the belief that patients' knowledge contained instructive and compelling information. Clearly, the PAS advocates were intent on reminding the Court of the real people and the real suffering that led to these cases.

While the states' briefs did not contest the reality or degree of the suffering involved in these cases, they did contest the value of the anecdotal information submitted to the Court. The states challenged the value of this form of knowledge in a number of ways. First, stories were used to counter stories. While acknowledging the truth of patients' personal suffering, Washington challenged whether it "would be alleviated by finding a constitutional right to assisted suicide" (Brief for Petitioner, *Glucksberg*, p. 15). Suggesting that the result might be otherwise, the brief countered, "there are, of course, stories that make a different point" and then described three stories illustrative of the dangers of allowing PAS (ibid.). Second, the necessity of this suffering was challenged. The states produced information regarding palliative care that suggested that the source of patients' suffering was not the ban against PAS, but problems regarding the delivery of medical treatment.

Third, lest the Justices become distracted by the personal dimension, Washington cautioned of the emotional impact of the personal stories, and reminded the Court of the primary role that judicial reasoning should play in judicial decision making. As to the stories, the state commented, "these accounts cannot be read without evoking at least two strong emotional reactions—sympathy for those afflicted, and apprehensiveness that some day a similar fate may befall the reader or a loved one" (Brief for Petitioner, *Glucksberg*, p. 15). Then, after introducing the stories "that make a different point," the state concluded: "But this Court's jurisprudence has not been and should not be determined on the basis of anecdotes, no matter what points they make or how compellingly they make them. This Court must focus on the needs of our society as a whole and its role in responding to those needs, and it must do so in a principled manner that builds upon, but does not distort, its prior jurisprudence" (ibid.: 15–16).

In this, the state also posed a fourth challenge to patients' knowledge by suggesting that the Court weigh the good of the whole community against the needs of a few patients. This concern was articulated more pointedly in references to the dangers of the slippery slope. Washington maintained that "there is no principled basis on which the asserted right to assisted suicide can be limited to physician prescription of medication for mentally competent, terminally ill patients to administer to themselves" (Brief for Petitioner, *Glucksberg*, p. 27). If this class of people received such a right, Washington contended, it could not be limited to the terminally ill, the mentally competent, or to passive and not active euthanasia. New York echoed this concern that the right "is not so readily contained and could be employed to extend a right of assisted suicide to patients who are not terminally ill and to those who are not ill at all" (Brief for Petitioner, *Quill*, p. 7). Citing a study of the New York State Task Force, New York added to this slippery slope argument by suggesting that "those who will be most vulnerable to abuse . . . are the poor, minorities, and those who are least educated and least empowered" (ibid.: 28).

Fifth, the patients' perspective was countered by logic. While the Quill brief emphasized how the experiences of the terminally ill patients and those on life-support were essentially similar, New York argued that "these legal and medical distinctions are rooted in *logical* differences between refusal or termination of treatment and assisted suicide" (Brief for Petitioner, *Quill*, p. 7 emphasis mine). A discussion then followed as to how distinctions can be supported through study of the philosophical dimensions of intent, action and inaction, and causation.

A final challenge to patients' knowledge came in the form of legal and medical expertise. The state briefs introduced a survey of the history of legal and medical practices to make their case that suicide, no less assisted suicide, was never understood as a legally protected right. The New York brief traced the legal history to show that even though the states have traditionally recognized the right of patients to consent to medical treatment they have at the same time refused to legalize assisted suicide. Likewise, Washington contended that the lower court's decision was a departure from the Court's substantive due process jurisprudence and that the PAS advocates' historical analysis was misleading: "This selective and incomplete analysis glossed over the fact that throughout our legal traditions from English common law to colonial times to the present, suicide and attempted suicide have been disfavored and have resulted in adverse legal consequences" (Brief for Petitioner, *Glucksberg*, p. 17). A parallel argument was made in regard to the medical community by once again introducing expert opinion: "The American Medical Association, the American College of Physicians, and the American Geriatrics Society all 'consistently distinguish assisted suicide and euthanasia from the withdrawing or withholding of treatment'" (Brief for Petitioner, quoting the New York State Task Force on Life and the Law, *Quill*, p. 14). Added to this was the pronouncement, "the rank and file of the medical profession likewise observes the distinction" (Brief for Petitioner, *Quill*, p. 15).

A particularly powerful example of using experts to counter patients' knowledge (and one that would prove influential among the Justices) came in the form of a report of the New York State Task Force on Life and the Law. Composed of twenty-four experts from public service, law, academics, medicine, and organized religion, the Task Force had studied the clinical, legal, and ethical context of PAS, and published their findings and recommendations under the title *When Death Is*

Sought: Assisted Suicide and Euthanasia in the Medical Context (1994). The report made it clear that the heartrending anecdotes of the patients had been considered. However, equally clear was that the Task Force had reinterpreted the meaning of their stories and cast doubt on the applicability of their knowledge. While for patients, their very real pain and suffering was reason enough to support the legalization of PAS, the Task Force maintained that the possibility of improving health care delivery to alleviate most patients' pain and suffering justified opposition to the legalization of PAS. In adopting this stance, the Task Force succeeded in shifting the ethical question away from that of addressing actual suffering to that of assessing potential solutions and potential social harms. So, while expressing "deep compassion" (xiv) for patients whose pain was not in fact relieved, and while acknowledging the numerous barriers that contribute to the "pervasive inadequacy of pain relief and palliative care" (xi), the Task Force unanimously recommended that "New York laws prohibiting assisted suicide and euthanasia should not be changed" (vii). In this, expert knowledge recast the meaning of patients' knowledge.

These six challenges to the value of the anecdotal information offered by patients and their physicians exemplified several of the characteristics of legal and medical knowledge studied in chapter 1. Law's emphasis on textual references, competing rights, universal rules, and logical reasoning resonated throughout the briefs of the states. So too did medicine's emphasis that physicians heal and not harm their patients, and that scientific knowledge can produce the answer for the problem of patient suffering. The states' briefs used the very nature of patients' knowledge to undermine its value: its lack of schooling, its particularity, and its emotional, subjective nature. In issuing this challenge to patients' experiences, however, the states attempted to strike a balance between admitting that the suffering was real while also maintaining that this fact should not determine the outcome of the PAS cases.

Unlike the briefs submitted in *Roe*, then, the party briefs in *Glucksberg* and *Quill* did not focus on medical and legal information to the exclusion of patients' knowledge. In fact, it was the clashing of patients' knowledge from the one side with legal and medical knowledge on the other that animated the controversy. If the Court in the end chose one form of knowledge over the other, it was not because the knowledge presented to them was limited, but that one was not as highly regarded as the other.

The Contributions of the Amicus Curiae Briefs

If the number of *amicus curiae* briefs filed is any barometer of the social importance attributed to a case, then the fifty-nine submitted once the cases of *Glucksberg* and *Quill* were granted *cert* indicated that PAS was emerging as one of the most anticipated constitutional issues since *Roe*. Put into perspective, the most *amici* briefs ever filed in one case were the seventy-eight of *Webster* (1989), the first abortion case that forecasters predicted would overturn *Roe*, followed by the fifty-seven submitted in *University of California at Davis v. Bakke*, the Court's first foray into the affirmative action issue in 1978. The *Glucksberg* and *Quill amicus* briefs demonstrated just how wide-ranging the impact of the case was anticipated to be. A broad scope of interested parties were represented in the briefs: state and national legislators; prosecutors; scholars; religious groups; advocacy groups (e.g., pro-life associations, legal institutes, senior citizen organizations, gay men's groups, women's organizations); medical organizations representing hospitals, hospices, doctors, and nurses; and coalitions of patients, patient organizations, and family members of patients (see table 3.1). Clearly, the PAS cases possessed an incredible power to mobilize from diverse populations.

The information offered by the *amici* was equally as expansive. In order to demonstrate the presence of legal, medical, and patients' knowledge in the *amicus* briefs filed on both sides, I have constructed three tables that summarize some of the most prominent (i.e., thoroughly discussed or recurring) arguments offered to the Court by its "friends." Also named is at least one *amicus* who advanced a particular argument. These tables, then, are not exhaustive lists of every point made or every *amicus* who made a particular point, but are instead illustrations as to how the three bases of knowledge—the legal, medical, and patients'—produced different types of arguments. These tables are also visual renderings of how arguments made on one side of the cases were countered by *amici* who supported the other side.

Table 3.2 summarizes how *legal* knowledge was used in the *amicus* briefs. Four themes shaped the legal arguments: the use of text, the judicial tests to be used, the precedents to follow, and the Court's obligations in reviewing these cases. That these themes animated some of the argumentation reiterates the point made earlier concerning the power of legal norms to shape a case. Since these briefs focused on presenting the Court with legal knowledge, it is hardly surprising that constitutional text, judicial tests, and legal precedents dominated the substance of the *amici*'s legal arguments as they had the party briefs. Yet, while reinforcing the party briefs, the *amici* also added to the legal arguments by emphasizing different points (e.g., the religion clauses as text supportive of respondents), attacking the other side (e.g., the claim that there is no fundamental right at stake in these cases), and inviting the Court to reconsider prior holdings (e.g., *Cruzan*). In addition, *amici* on both sides urged the Court to act "responsibly." According to the Petitioners' *amici*, this meant respecting the determination of the states, while for Respondents' *amici* this required protecting constitutional rights even in the face of majority will. In sum, these briefs spoke the language of the Court, used legal reasoning to persuade them, and relied on sources well known to the Court.

Table 3.1 List of *Amici* who filed briefs in *Glucksberg* and *Quill*

On Behalf of Petitioners (41)

Agudeth Israel	Evangelical Lutheran Church	National Right to Life Comm.
American Assn. of Homes & Services for the Aging	Family Research Council	National Spinal Cord Injury Assn.
	Sen. Orrin Hatch, Rep. Henry Hyde, et al.	New Jersey
American Center for Law & Justice	Institute for Public Affairs of the Union of	Not Dead Yet & American Disabled for
American Geriatrics Society	Orthodox Jews, et al.	Attendant Programs
American Hospital Assn.	Int'l Anti-Euthanasia Task Force	Oregon
American Life League	Gary Lee, M.D. & others & nursing homes	Project on Death in America
American Medical Assn., American	Legal Center for Defense of Life &	Rutherford Institute
Nurses Assn., American Psych. Assn.	Pro-Life Legal Defense Fund	Schiller Institute
American Suicide Foundation	Members of WA & NY Legislatures	Southern Center for Law & Ethics
Bioethics Professors	National Association of Pro-Life Nurses, et al.	States of CA, AL, and 17 others
Carendon Foundation	National Catholic Office for Persons with	Richard Thompson, Oakland Prosecutor
Catholic Health Association	Disabilities & Knights of Columbus	U.S. Catholic Conference, et al.
Catholic Medical Association	National Hospice Assn.	United States (2 briefs)
Christian Legal Society	National Legal Center for the Medically	Wayne Co., Michigan
D. A. of Milwaukee Co.	Dependent & Disabled, et al.	

On Behalf of Respondents (17)

American Civil Liberties Union, Gray	Coalition of Hospice Professionals	State Legislators
Panthers, Hemlock Society, et al.	Council for Secular Humanism	Surviving Family Members
American College of Legal Medicine	Ronald Dworkin, Nagel, Noszick, Rawls,	36 Religious Organizations
American Medical Student Assn.	Scanlon, Thomson	WA State Psych. Assn., et al.
Americans for Death with Dignity	Gay Men's Health Crisis, Lambda, et al.	Julian Whitaker, M.D.
Bioethicists	Law Professors	
Center for Reproductive Law	National Women's Health Network	

Non-Aligned (1)

Choice in Dying, Inc.

Table 3.2 Examples of Contrasting Legal Knowledge Introduced by the *Glucksberg* and *Quill* Amicus Briefs

	On Behalf of Petitioners	On Behalf of Respondents
Text:	There is no constitutionally protected liberty interest to PAS. (American Hospital Assn.) Legalized PAS for the terminally ill will constitute invidious discrimination since they would be protected less than others. (Nat'l Catholic Office for Persons with Disabilities, et al.) Health care professionals with religious convictions opposed to PAS will be affected. (Christian Legal Society) Legalized PAS for the terminally ill violates the Americans with Disabilities Act. (Nat'l Center for the Medically Dependent & Disabled)	The liberty interest is deeply rooted in history and tradition and it encompasses a right to PAS for terminally ill competent adult patients. (ACLU) Terminally ill patients are similarly situated on life support. Different recognition of the liberty to end one's life violates the Equal Protection guarantee. (ACLU) The religion clauses of the 1st Amendment support the choice of PAS. (36 Religious Organizations)
Tests:	States interests in protecting life are compelling. (Catholic Medical Assn.) There is no fundamental right at stake. (American Assn. of Homes & Services for the Aging) There is an unalienable right to live. (Nat'l Catholic Office for Persons with Disabilities, et al.) State interests are legitimate. (Clarendon Foundation)	The state laws fail strict scrutiny. (Gay Men's Health Crisis) The state laws constitute an undue burden on patients' rights. (Americans for Death with Dignity) The state laws are irrational. (Law Professors) State interests cannot justify the ban. (Ronald Dworkin, et al.)
Precedents:	Misreadings of *Cruzan* and *Casey* have led to the recognition of a right to die. (Institute for Public Affairs of the Union of Orthodox Jews, et al.) Should reconsider *Cruzan*. (American Life League)	Both *Casey* and *Cruzan* support PAS. (Ronald Dworkin, et al.) *Casey* does not apply. *Cruzan* does. (Center for Reproductive Law)
Judicial Responsibility:	Judiciary is ill-suited to resolve this issue. (Sen. Hatch, et al.) It is the role of the states in the federal system to serve as laboratories for policy making. (State of CA, et al.)	When constitutional rights outweigh state interests, the Court must strike the law. (Americans for Death with Dignity)

The same cannot be said of the briefs that used *medical* knowledge to ground their arguments. Yet while serving in the capacity as technical advisers in a field in which the Court did not share expertise, these *amici* still appealed to the Court's sense of the type of information that constitutes valuable knowledge. Granted, medical knowledge employs a different language, but it is still a language of facts, and it still employs reason and expertise to persuade. That medical knowledge was repeatedly used in the briefs is evidenced by the range of topics covered. Table 3.3 summarizes the points presented by the *amici* who acted as technical advisers concerning medical knowledge (it excludes from consideration other forms of "technical" knowledge such as religious or philosophical discussions). Collectively these briefs introduced six topics connected to medical practice: whether medical ethics condemned or allowed PAS; the extent to which PAS is currently in practice; whether abuses can be controlled through regulations; whether the distinction drawn between terminally ill patients desiring PAS and patients on life support requesting withdrawal of medical intervention is justified; whether the pain and suffering of terminally ill patients can be relieved; and whether the competency of patients can be reliably determined.

Of the forty-one *amicus* briefs filed on behalf of the Petitioners, thirteen of them emphasized medical information, and of the seventeen filed on behalf of the Respondents five focused on medical information. In addition the one non-aligned brief also emphasized medical knowledge bringing the total to nineteen of the fifty-nine briefs. What emerged was a clash of the medical titans—bioethicists, medical associations, hospice professionals, and advocacy groups—but it was not an even battle. The *amicus* briefs clearly tipped the scales in favor of the states. While the prestige or authority of an organization is a difficult concept to measure, their membership figures are at least a rough indicator of the support they enjoy. When applied to the line-up of organizations on each side of the cases, these numbers indicate a striking imbalance. The PAS advocates drew support from organizations like the American College of Legal Medicine (1,300 professionals in law and medicine), the American Medical Student Association (nearly 30,000 physicians-in-training), the Washington State Psychological Association (900 doctoral level psychologists and other related mental health practitioners), Bioethicists (42 professors, lawyers, and medical doctors), the Coalition of Hospice Professionals (22 individuals), and Law Professors (18 individuals). In stark contrast, weighing in on the states' behalf in *a single brief alone* were the American Medical Association (290,000 members), American Nurses Association (180,000 members), the American Association of Critical Care Nurses (76,000 members), the American Society of Clinical Pathologists (75,000 members), the American Psychiatric Association (42,000 members), the American Osteopathic Association (40,000 members), seventeen other medical organizations, and twenty-three state medical associations. In addition to this one brief, the states were supported by other technical briefs including those filed

Table 3.3 Examples of Contrasting Medical Knowledge Introduced by the *Glucksberg* and *Quill Amicus* Briefs

	On Behalf of Petitioners	*On Behalf of Respondents*
Medical Ethics:	Medical ethical codes (see Hippocratic oath) do not countenance PAS. This is suicide. (Medical Society of New Jersey)	The AMA does not speak for all doctors. The Hippocratic oath has been updated and must be seen in context. This is not really suicide; they're dying. (Bioethicists)
Current Practices:	The Court should not rely on the unsubstantiated reports that PAS is currently practiced. This would involve collusion on a large scale. (American Geriatrics Society)	PAS is already practiced but without the sanction of law and without regulations. (Coalition of Hospice Professionals)
Regulation:	Regulations will be too subjective. (American Geriatrics Society) PAS is at odds with nursing ethics. (Nat'l Assn. of Pro-Life Nurses, et al.) The Netherlands euthanasia policy has resulted in abuses. (American Suicide Foundation) Economic pressures and managed care will imperil patients. (Int'l Anti-Euthanasia Task Force)	Medical protocols are already in place; PAS is consistent with medical treatment. (American College of Legal Medicine) Claims of abuses in the Netherlands are "empirically false and grossly distorted." (Bioethicists)
Distinction between patients:	The legal distinctions made between the terminally ill and those on life support are widely accepted. (Medical Society of New Jersey)	The clinical realities do not justify the legal distinctions between the terminally ill and those on life support. (American Medical Student Assn.)
Pain and Suffering:	Pain can be controlled through medical care and suffering eased through counseling. (AMA) Depression plays a major role in patients who desire suicide. (American Suicide Foundation) The standard of care could be improved. (American Geriatrics Society)	All pain and suffering cannot be relieved; suffering is not merely physical. (Coalition of Hospice Professionals)
Competency:	Determining competency is problematic since there's a slow slide to incompetency. (American Geriatrics Society)	Mental health professionals can assess the competency of patients. (WA State Psych. Assn., et al.)

by: the American Association of Homes & Services for the Aging (representing over 5,000 not-for-profit facilities and organizations), the American Geriatrics Society (6,000 professional health care providers in geriatrics), the National Hospice Association (representing 2,200 hospice programs, 47 state hospice organizations, and over 4,000 hospice professionals and supporters), the National Spinal Cord Injury Association (its members are "among the more than 250,000 Americans paralyzed as a result of injury and disease to the spinal cord"), and Bioethics Professors (49 individuals). Therefore, although the briefs presented disagreement concerning the medical facts of PAS, they also made it abundantly clear that an overwhelming majority of the medical experts/practitioners involved in this issue stood on one side of the case—unified in support of state bans. While the *amici* who supported the pro-PAS side offered arguments countering each of the medical points made by the Petitioner's *amici*, the PAS advocates had to overcome not only an informational divide but a credibility gap. There was no denying that the uphill battle they fought in favor of legalized PAS was being waged without the support of the majority of their medical colleagues. This fact would surely not be lost on the Justices when they considered and weighed the conflicting medical knowledge presented to them in the briefs.

In contrast to the very visible roles that legal and medical knowledge played in shaping the *amicus* briefs, patients' knowledge, though present, was far less apparent. Of the forty-one briefs filed on behalf of the Petitioners, five were sponsored by "patients" broadly defined (i.e., anyone acting as a signatory of a brief who claimed patient's status whether terminally ill or not). Of the seventeen briefs filed on behalf of Respondents, one came from "patients." However, the fact that patients were filing the brief did not guarantee that patients' knowledge, rather than legal or medical knowledge, would inform the argument. This was demonstrated by the fact that of these six briefs, only one drew predominantly on patients' knowledge in constructing its argument. Of the five patient-sponsored *amicus* briefs in support of the petitioners, none emphasized patients' knowledge. Instead, they relied either on legal arguments (Brief of Gary Lee, M.D., et al.; Brief of Not Dead Yet and American Disabled for Attendant Programs Today; and Brief of the National Legal Center for the Medically Dependent & Disabled, et al.), or on technical medical information (Brief of the American Suicide Foundation and Brief of the National Spinal Cord Injury Association). These patients, therefore, drew on their personal authority but spoke in the language of law or of medicine, and not in the language of the personal. The one patient-sponsored brief filed on behalf of the respondents, the Brief of Gay Men's Health Crisis et al., drew on the authority of personal knowledge in speaking for their membership but presented a highly legalistic account. The result, therefore, was that no patient-sponsored brief truly related to the Court the experiential knowledge of patients.

Table 3.4 Examples of Contrasting Patients' Knowledge Introduced by the *Glucksberg* and *Quill* Amicus Briefs

	On Behalf of Petitioners	On Behalf of Respondents
Concern for others:	[Persons with disabilities argue that safeguards will not protect the vulnerable. (Gary Lee, M.D., et al.)]*	[Persons with disabilities argue that they will not be harmed by legalized PAS. (Gay Men's Health Crisis)]
Particularity:	[Plaintiff patients are not representative of what happens to dying persons in general. (American Geriatrics Society)]	Individual cases illustrate the degree of pain and suffering experienced in a medicalized dying environment where PAS is banned. (Surviving Family Members)
Dangers:	[Organizations recall the atrocities of Nazi Germany and, in the name of patients, warn of similar consequences. (Agudeth Israel; Shiller Institute; Family Research Council)]	Family members tell of the harms imposed on patients and families by denying patients access to PAS. (Surviving Family Members)

*Brackets indicate that the argument was presented in briefs that relied predominately on legal or medical knowledge, not patients' knowledge.

The single brief that did present patients' knowledge to the Court was the one filed by Surviving Family Members. This brief told of personal stories that illustrated the consequences that the PAS bans had not only for terminally ill patients but also for their loved ones. It relied on the personal rather than medical or legal arguments. It therefore took a gamble in that it presented the Court with a type of information of which legal reasoning is highly suspicious—personal knowledge that is colored by emotions, feelings, relationships, and particular experiences. Such a brief risks being ignored by the Court, antagonizing the Court, or even undermining the more "serious" arguments of the party. Those patients who filed the other briefs seemed to appreciate these risks and therefore avoided them by framing their personal viewpoints within the context of either legal or medical knowledge. Yet, the Surviving Family Members' brief offered the Court a rare opportunity to hear about PAS in nonlegalistic and nonmedical terms. Personal feelings and relationships were recorded rather than medical conditions, and the cultural context of dying was emphasized over claims to constitutional rights. In this brief, the call for a right to die with dignity reached beyond the sloganistic to offer an examination of the roots, meaning, and potential impact of PAS.

Therefore, in summarizing the arguments stemming from patients' knowledge, table 3.4 is unlike the other tables in that it includes arguments found in briefs that advanced legal or medical knowledge (these being indicated by brackets). While the personal experiences of patients supported respondents' positions that PAS does not threaten the disabled, that the terminally ill suffer extensively from the PAS ban, and that family members share the consequences, the counterpoints came from briefs that rejected the authority of this highly personalized voice. Instead, the Petitioners' *amici* adopted a medical or legal voice in offering the refutations that: safeguards cannot protect vulnerable patients from the abuses that will result from legalized PAS, that the depictions of personal suffering are not typical of what happens to most dying people, and that the atrocities resulting from Nazi Germany's euthanasia policies should not be forgotten. While the three briefs that invoked the horror of the Nazi medical policies spoke in the name of the patients who suffered and died under that regime, the knowledge they drew on was that of history, law, or ethics, and not that of patients themselves. Therefore, table 3.4 illustrates that while patients' knowledge was recognized by some of the *amici*, only a limited amount of this knowledge found its way into the briefs.

As a collection, the fifty-nine *Glucksberg* and *Quill amicus* briefs added a richness to the store of knowledge presented to the Court. The legalistic briefs documented in classic terms the polarities between positions over how text, tests, and precedents should be interpreted and applied. The medically inspired briefs conveyed in point and counterpoint fashion disputes over the meaning of medical knowledge, even as they depicted a medical community largely in favor of state bans on PAS. The one brief that thoroughly incorporated patients' knowledge brought the haunting voices of the dead and dying to the Court and pleaded with the Justices to allow patients to end their pain and suffering through legalized PAS. Again, these voices were countered by other briefs that warned of the calamity ahead if PAS were legalized. Together, the fifty-nine briefs formed a kaleidoscope of facts, arguments, and concerns that offered varying, but related pictures of PAS. The question ahead was whether the Court would turn their gaze this way or that way in assembling these pieces into a whole.

The Knowledge Surfacing at Oral Arguments

The cases were argued before the Court during a two-hour session on January 8, 1997, notable for the interplay between legal, medical, and personal knowledge. Reporters covering the session for the New York *Times* and Washington *Post* commented:

> Although the doctrinal jargon of due process and equal protection was sprinkled throughout the argument, this was a Supreme Court session notable for the proportion of plain English that was spoken. The Justices wanted theory, but they were also hungry for the facts. They sat as judges but appeared to feel themselves very much participants, on a human level, in a far reaching societal debate. (Greenhouse 1997)
>
> During the solemn two-hour hearing, the justices pursued not just legal questions, but evolving societal attitudes, the role of modern medicine, their own personal experiences and moral considerations that thread through the emotional issue. (Biskupic 1997)

All of the five attorneys who participated in the oral arguments addressed medical knowledge. William Williams, senior assistant attorney general of Washington argued that among the state interests at stake was that of regulating the medical profession: "Precisely because physicians have the capacity to injure or perhaps cause the death of their patients, the state has an important interest in maintaining a clear line between physicians as healers and curers and physicians as instruments of death of their patients" ("Excerpts from the Supreme Court" 1997: A16). Questioned by Justice Stephen Breyer concerning statistics of the number of people who die in pain, Walter Dellinger, acting solicitor general of the United States, responded, "The fact that 25 percent unnecessarily die in pain shows the task awaiting the medical profession, but it's not a task that calls for the cheap and easy expedient of lethal medication rather than the more expensive pain palliative" (ibid.). Kathryn L. Tucker, the attorney on behalf of Dr. Glucksberg and the other litigants from Washington, emphasized the critical gatekeeping role played by physicians in this issue: "These patients want a humane death and they want a dignified death. And in order to access that kind of death they need the assistance of their physician" (ibid.). Dennis Vacco, attorney general of New York State was pressed by Justice Ruth Bader Ginsburg on the difference between terminally ill patients and those patients who chose to withdraw life support. Emphasizing that these individuals are not similarly situated, Vacco responded that the act of exercising one's right to refuse treatment was "clearly distinguishable" from that of having a physician kill oneself ("Vacco Argues for Reinstatement" 1997: A10). Finally, on behalf of Dr. Quill and the other New York litigants, Laurence Tribe refuted Vacco's attempt to draw lines between these types of patients and argued that the distinction is based on a "fantasy" of a sharp demarcation in medical terms (Greenhouse 1997). He reminded the Court of the difference between abstractions and what is actually practiced:

> I don't think so much the issue is how many people violate the law. Charlatans, doctors of death . . . they operate in the dark and we don't know. The winks and nods, I think, affect the capacity of the system to respond humanely and rationally to what is actually going on rather than just to bright-line hypotheticals. ("Vacco Argues for Reinstatement" 1997)

Yet, even amid the legal and medical arguments, patients' knowledge was asserted, questioned, and evaluated. The strategy adopted by the attorneys arguing on behalf of the states seemed to be to downplay these considerations. Williams argued that as described by the physicians, the individual right asserted "is limited to a very few of our citizens" ("Excerpts from the Supreme Court" 1997). Dellinger acknowledged the power of the personal anecdote but reminded the Court of the risks involved in recognizing a right to PAS: "While the individual stories are heartrending . . . it's important for this court to recognize that, if you were to affirm the judgments below, lethal medication could be proposed as a treatment, not just to those in severe pain, but to every competent terminally ill personal [*sic*] in the country" (ibid.). Vacco opened his arguments by recasting the personal nature of the issue in terms of states interests: "The question in this case is whether the state must remain neutral in the face of a decision of one of its citizens to help another kill herself" ("Vacco Argues for Reinstatement" 1997).

In contrast, attorneys on the other side used patients' knowledge to counter the states' position. In two instances, this attempt ignited a response from Justice Scalia. In describing why the right to PAS would be limited to the terminally ill alone, Tucker explained, "This individual does not have a choice between living and dying. This dying patient whose dying process has begun and is underway, this individual has only the choice of how to die," to which Scalia replied, "I hate to tell you, but the dying process of all of us has begun and is underway" ("Excerpts from the Supreme Court" 1997). In contrast to Vacco's description, Tribe's rendering of the issue downplayed the legal aspects in favor of the personal: "I think the liberty interest in this case is . . . when facing imminent and inevitable death, not to be forced by the government to endure a degree of pain and suffering that one can relieve only by being completely unconscious" ("Vacco Argues for Reinstatement" 1997). His assertion that a person has a right "not to be forced to be a creature of the state" and to "have some voice" in the way the "final chapter of life" unfolds was met with a measure of derision by Scalia, who responded, "This is lovely philosophy. Where is it in the Constitution?" (Greenhouse 1997). Yet there were signs that some of the other Justices were more comfortable with the role that personal dimensions played in the cases. Justice O'Connor noted, "This is an issue every one of us faces, young and old, male and female, whatever it might be" (ibid.). On a similar note, Justice Ginsburg acknowledged, "Most of us have parents and other loved ones who have been through the dying process, and we've thought about these things" (ibid.).

Outside the Court was yet another reminder of the personal dimensions of the cases—demonstrators. More than 200 protesters from the disability rights group Not Dead Yet gathered outside the Court. Some carried signs declaring "Hitler Would Be Proud," "Your Mercy Is Killing Us," and "Euthanasia Is a Bummer." One disability-rights advocate explained his own reaction to the personal nature of the issue: "You can come up with lots of those heart-wrenching stories about terminally ill people in tremendous pain who really want aid in dying, but they have to understand: This isn't just about them" ("Demonstrators Take Opposing Sides of Issue" 1997). Representing the pro-PAS side were about two dozen protesters marching under the banner of the Hemlock Society. As depicted by one reporter, when these groups engaged with each other and the media, the lines drawn between their positions began to blur:

> "There's no point when I'm half dead making me stay alive," says Roy R. Torcaso, a white bearded, withered man from the right-to-die Hemlock Society. "The government has no right to tell me I have to live and suffer."
> "People should make their own choices when they live or die," says Richard St. Denis, 42, a Not Dead Yet activist who uses a wheelchair.
> "Exactly," says Torcaso.
> "Exactly," says St. Denis. And they look at each other funny.
> Nearby, a chorus is singing: "We are strong and gentle people, and we are singing for our lives." It is impossible to tell by the lyrics which side of the case they're boosting. (Blumenfeld 1997)

The exchange stood as a reminder that the disagreement among patients might not be quite as dichotomous as the legal arguments inside the Court seemed to insist they were.

Collectively, the party briefs, *amicus* briefs, and oral arguments highlighted a clash between medical and patients' knowledge. Most pronounced were the disagreements over the appropriate response to "suffering," whether the doctor–patient relationship or a patient's private relationships were most due protection; and who among patients was to be sacrificed—the terminally ill who demanded access to PAS or other patients who demanded protection from legalized PAS. But beneath these three contested areas lurked a greater issue—one that appeared to enjoy consensus but that remained largely unarticulated throughout: there is something wrong with how we die. Kathryn Tucker alluded to this issue during oral arguments when she stated that "ours is a death denying culture" ("Excerpts from the Supreme Court" 1997). American culture's fear of death, the medical fight against it, the marginalization of the dying, the loneliness of the process, and the search for rituals and meaning were as intertwined in the PAS cases as were the liberty and equal protection clauses (see Anderson 1996). While the Court was asked to address the legal issues alone, in the course of reading the legal records, deliberating over the cases, and writing their opinions, they could not help entering as well the larger debate over the meaning of life and the meaning of death.

THE COURT'S OPINIONS

While the Court had been presented with a richness of information, when it came time to construct its decisions in the *Glucksberg* and *Quill* cases, the majority did so by a selective use of the knowledge. In the end, it was the legal and medical knowledge that informed the majority opinions while patients' knowledge was cast aside. This knowledge was rescued from oblivion by a single Justice who integrated it in his concurrence opinion.

The Court's decisions were announced on June 26, 1997. By a vote of 9–0, the Court rejected the constitutional challenges to the Washington and New York laws and upheld the bans on assisted suicide as rationally related to legitimate state interests. However, the unanimous ruling obscured a fracture among the Justices— only four Justices (Sandra Day O'Connor, Antonin Scalia, Anthony Kennedy, and Clarence Thomas) joined the primary opinion authored by Chief Justice William Rehnquist. However, even this five-member coalition was fragile. A concurrence authored by Justice O'Connor stated that while she agreed that there was no generalized right to suicide, she believed the narrower question of "whether a mentally competent person who is experiencing great suffering has a constitutionally cognizable interest in controlling the circumstances of his or her imminent death" had not been decided here. Four other Justices (John Paul Stevens, David Souter, Ruth Bader Ginsburg, and Stephen Breyer) concurred in the judgment alone (i.e., although they voted with Chief Justice Rehnquist to uphold the state laws, they did not join his rationale as to why). Therefore, behind the 9–0 facade was a Court divided—four Justices willing to settle for now the constitutional questions posed by the PAS issue and five Justices hesitant to close the door to future constitutional claims.

In tracing what the Court decided in this pair of PAS cases, my focus is once again on identifying the type of knowledge they used to shape their opinions. Not surprisingly, all the Justices drew heavily on legal knowledge in their opinions, and they all to some extent included references to medical knowledge. A difference emerged, however, concerning the use of patients' knowledge. To illustrate the variety of ways that the individual Justices drew on and used particular forms of knowledge, I have organized the discussion of the opinions in such a way that a continuum is formed moving from arguments that excluded patients' knowledge at one end to arguments that integrate patients' knowledge at the other end. Therefore, I begin with Rehnquist's majority opinion that relies on medical and legal knowledge, then I move to Souter's highly legalistic discussion that opens the possibility of formulating some form of a liberty right to PAS, to O'Connor's inclusion of empathetic statements concerning the patients' perspective, to Breyer's seeming acceptance of a "right to die with dignity," and finally to Stevens's complete incorporation of patients' knowledge.

The Rehnquist opinions in both the *Glucksberg* and *Quill* cases took an approach that integrated medical with legal knowledge but that excluded from consideration the knowledge of terminally ill patients. He began his analysis in the Washington case by "examining our Nation's history, legal traditions, and practices" (at 781) and concluded that

> our laws have consistently condemned, and continue to prohibit, assisting suicide. Despite changes in medical technology and not withstanding an increased emphasis on the importance of end-of-life decision-making, we have not retreated from this prohibition. Against this backdrop of history, tradition, and practice, we now turn to respondents' constitutional claim. (at 787)

On the basis of this historical reading, Rehnquist rejected respondents' claim that there exists a fundamental liberty interest that includes a right to suicide and assistance in committing suicide, since the right is not deeply rooted in the nation's history. Rehnquist added that neither did the claim meet the judicial requirement of offering a "careful description" of an asserted liberty interest since there appeared to be some confusion as to what exactly the claimed right was (e.g., a "right to die," or a "liberty to choose how to die" or a right to "control of one's final days," or "the right to choose a humane, dignified death," or "the liberty interest to shape death") (at 789). Therefore, history, tradition, and practice did not support respondents' position that a fundamental right was at stake.

Neither did precedent. Rehnquist argued that while *Cruzan* established the right to refuse medical treatment, this right was supported by both common law and long-standing legal tradition, making it quite distinct from the right to suicide and therefore inapplicable in *Glucksberg*. Likewise, he found respondents' reliance on *Casey* unconvincing when they argued that personal decisions regarding the meaning of life were protected decisions. Rehnquist countered, "That many of the rights and liberties protected by the Due Process Clause sound in personal autonomy does not warrant the sweeping conclusion that any and all important, intimate, and personal decisions are so protected, and *Casey* did not suggest otherwise" (at 792). Therefore, since the right to suicide was not a fundamental right, the appropriate test for evaluating challenges to the Washington law was whether the ban was rationally related to legitimate government interests.

In explaining how that requirement was "unquestionably met here" (at 792), Rehnquist not only referred to the medical knowledge offered by Washington and its *amici* (including the oft-cited report by the New York State Task Force on Life and the Law), but also accepted as valid the mainstream medical position regarding several contentious points:

- That the ban furthered respect for the sanctity of life (at 793);
- That those who desire suicide "often suffer from depression or other mental disorders" (citing the New York Task Force and others) (at 794);
- That PAS "is fundamentally incompatible with the physician's role as healer" (quoting the AMA, Code of Ethics) (ibid.);
- That the lives of the vulnerable (i.e., the terminally ill, the disabled and the elderly) would be valued less if PAS were legalized (citing the New York Task Force) (at 795); and
- The slippery slope argument: that if a total prohibition was lifted, the right could not be contained (citing the Briefs of the United States, Not Dead Yet et al., Bioethics Professors, the New York Task Force, and others) (at 796).

While each of these points had been challenged by medical expertise presented by the pro-PAS side, it was clear that the Court neither regarded this contrary information as representative of the medical profession nor as factual. Accepting instead the assertions listed above as true, there was no need to evaluate the exact weight of these state interests. Medical fact had joined with legal norms to demonstrate that the rational basis test had been met—so, end of case. His final paragraph summarized his belief that while the Court now closed the door to the constitutional debate, the policy debate over the moral, legal, and practical aspects of PAS should continue in the states.

A similar orientation influenced Rehnquist's *Quill* opinion. Serving again as the author of the primary Court opinion (the line-up of Justices in both cases being identical), the Chief Justice quickly turned his attention to the equal protection claim: were the terminally ill patients similarly situated to those on life-support systems? Again, Rehnquist wove together medical knowledge with legal knowledge to settle the issue: "we think the distinction between assisting suicide and withdrawing life-sustaining treatment, a distinction widely recognized and endorsed in the medical profession and in our legal traditions, is both important and logi-cal; it is certainly rational" (at 842). A footnote backed the assertion that the med-ical profession disapproves it by citing two publications of the AMA's Council on Ethical and Judicial Affairs, the Brief of the AMA et al., and the New York State Task Force Report (at 842). This distinction drawn by physicians was then bol-stered by a review of how "the distinction comports with fundamental legal prin-ciples of causation and intent" (ibid.). Numerous precedents and state laws were then listed to affirm how New York State's distinction between "killing" and "let-ting die" is consistent with legal norms. Rehnquist then reiterated the state's in-terests in enacting the ban on PAS. Echoing the *Glucksberg* opinion, he listed the reasons as "prohibiting intentional killing and preserving life; preventing suicide; maintaining physicians' role as their patients' healers; protecting vulnerable people from indifferences, prejudice, and psychological and financial pressure to end their lives; and avoiding a possible slide towards euthanasia" (at 847).

Distancing himself from the Rehnquist opinion, Justice Souter focused on the fact that respondents had posed a *facial challenge*[5] to the state laws, and therefore, that it was their burden to prove that the laws were "arbitrary impositions" or "purposeless restraints" (at 808). His *Glucksberg* concurrence, a lengthy legalistic analysis of the substantive due process claim that challenged some of the reason-ing of the Rehnquist opinion, expressed both the plausibility of constructing a lib-erty right to suicide as well as his doubts about its strength and durability. While indicating that experimentation is better suited to legislative bodies than to judi-cial, Souter did not foreclose the possibility of viable future claims: "While I do not decide for all time that respondents' claim should not be recognized, I ac-knowledge the legislative competence as the better one to deal with that claim at this time" (at 831).

Justice O'Connor's concurrence in the twin cases (joined by Justices Breyer and Ginsburg except insofar as it joined the Rehnquist opinion) began rather differ-ently in that she seemed to adopt, at least momentarily, the patient's point of view: "Death will be different for each of us. For many, the last days will be spent in physical pain and perhaps the despair that accompanies physical deterioration and a loss of control of basic bodily and mental functions" (at 797). O'Connor then described her point of disagreement with the Rehnquist opinion: since the case posed a facial challenge to the law, she maintained that the Court had not reached the narrower question urged by respondents as to whether a mentally competent terminally ill patient had a right to control the circumstances of his or her death. The concurrence indicated that her votes to uphold the Washington and New York laws were dependent on the fact that the states allowed terminally ill patients to obtain medication to alleviate suffering even when it hastened their death. This qualification seemed to invite future constitutional claims by patients who were denied such palliative care.

These efforts to narrow the holding at hand and to leave room for future adjudication were emphasized for a third time by Justice Breyer. Stating that he "would not reject the respondents' claim without considering a different formulation, for which our legal tradition may provide greater support," Breyer suggested that perhaps a "right to die with dignity" would be a more accurate description than the Court's description of the claim as a "right to commit suicide with another's assistance" (at 832). Continuing, he stated, "But irrespective of the exact words used, at its core would lie personal control over the manner of death, professional medical assistance, and the avoidance of unnecessary and severe physical suffering—combined" (ibid.). Echoing O'Connor's point that the state laws at issue in these cases did not prevent physicians from prescribing pain-relieving drugs that may cause or accelerate death, Breyer advised,

> Were the legal circumstances different—for example, were state law to prevent the provision of palliative care, including the administration of drugs as needed to avoid pain at the end of life—then the law's impact upon serious and otherwise unavoidable physical pain (accompanying death) would be more directly at issue. And as Justice O'Connor suggests, the Court might have to revisit its conclusions in these cases. (at 833)

Before turning to Justice Stevens's concurrence, an opinion strikingly different in tone than that of the majority or of the other concurrences, it might be useful to summarize some of the similarities among the concurrences as to how they approached knowledge. While open to future constitutional claims, Justices Souter, O'Connor, Ginsburg, and Breyer all seemed to accept the mainstream medical profession's claim that physicians are free to give palliative care even if it causes death, that pain can be controlled (albeit sometimes only by induced coma), and that the law does not block patients' access to such care. Interestingly, these assertions were challenged by the testimony of the physicians on the other side of the cases, who claimed that physicians hesitate to give such care because of fear of legal repercussions, as well as by the patients' sworn statements that their pain was unrelieved even when receiving "good" care. Still, the Justices accepted as true the mainstream medical claims. As Justice Breyer put it, "Medical technology, we are repeatedly told, makes the administration of pain-relieving drugs sufficient, except for a very few individuals for whom the ineffectiveness of pain control medicines can mean, not pain, but the need for sedation which can end in a coma" (at 833). Seemingly, then, terminally ill patients and their physician advocates were "wrong" in their claim that medicine could not adequately respond to their suffering. In fact, however, the suffering noted by the concurring Justices was limited to a medicalized notion of "pain" as *physical* pain. Never addressed was the claim of patients that their suffering was not only physical but psychological, emotional, relational, and spiritual as well.

It was Justice Stevens alone who seemed to hear, really hear, what the dying patients and their physicians were telling the Court. In his concurrence, patients' claims were not only seriously considered but their knowledge about dying was actually integrated with legal knowledge to suggest how the Court could protect their interests. Although voting with the majority, Stevens emphasized that what was being rejected here were facial challenges to the Washington and New York laws, and that the holdings did not "foreclose the possibility that some applications of the statute[s] might well be invalid" (at 799). While this position connected him with Justices Souter, O'Connor, Ginsburg, and Breyer, his approach to forming knowledge separated him from all of his colleagues on the Court.

Most distinctive, and perhaps even most remarkable, was that Stevens rejected the medicalized perspective that death is essentially a physical event involving the body. Instead, he adopted the stance urged by the dying patients that for them, death was the process by which they lost themselves—their identity, their essence, and their existence. Dying, then, was more than merely a physical event, it was a time period in which people had the final opportunity to define their life, bring relationships to a close, construct the final memories by which they would live on, and ready themselves for whatever they believed would follow. Within this perspective, the physicality of "death" and what was happening to the body was secondary to the spiritual and social dimensions of what was happening to the whole person. Called by many names, this focus placed personhood, identity, life force, *chi, ahamkara*, soul, spirit, or self at the center of the dying process (see Anderson 1996). This approach to death explained why the medical treatments for pain and suffering were seen not only as insufficient but actually assaultive. If dying is a spiritual and social as well as a physical process, then medicalized death becomes an insult, an interference, and an injury. While unassuaged pain makes the process unbearable, terminal sedation makes meaningful death unattainable. Treatments aimed at saving the body interfered with patients' efforts to face and participate in their death. A "good death" meant more than a painless release from life—it required that patients die through a process connected to who they were. While the medical community focused on protecting medicalized deaths, the dying patients and their physicians reminded the Court that there was another way to approach the end of life.

Stevens heard and understood the distinction. After announcing in the first section of his opinion that he was "convinced that there are times when [an interest in hastening death] is entitled to constitutional protection" (at 801), he proceeded in the next section to reexamine the liberty interest recognized by the Court in *Cruzan*. His understanding of this right insisted that it was both broad and firmly based: "This freedom embraces, not merely a person's right to refuse a particular kind of unwanted treatment, but also her interest in dignity, and in determining the character of the memories that will survive long after her death" (at 802). At the end of this sentence was a footnote in which Stevens quoted from his *Cruzan* dissent:

> Nancy Cruzan's interest in life, no less than that of any other person, includes an interest in how she will be thought of after her death by those whose opinions mattered to her. There can be no doubt that her life made her dear to her family and to others. How she dies will affect how that life is remembered. . . .
>
> Each of us has an interest in the kind of memories that will survive after death. To that end, individual decisions are often motivated by their impact on others. A member of the kind of family identified in the trial court's findings in this case would likely have not only a normal interest in minimizing the burden that her own illness imposes on others, but also an interest in having their memories of her filled predominantly with thoughts about her past vitality rather than her current condition. (Footnote 11 at 802; citations omitted)

In applying this right to the Washington and New York cases, Stevens contended that "the now deceased plaintiffs in this action may in fact have had a liberty interest even stronger than Nancy Cruzan's because, not only were they terminally ill, they were suffering constant and severe pain" (at 803). While a unique argument among the Justices, this reference also marked the first time that any of the Court's opinions even mentioned the dying patients who initiated these cases. Drawing on their perspective, Stevens then summarized the right at stake as "an interest in deciding how, rather than whether, a critical threshold shall be crossed" (at 804).

In the third section of his concurrence, Stevens drew on patients' knowledge to reexamine the interests the states claimed in banning PAS. While agreeing that the state has an interest in preserving life, he qualified its force: "Properly viewed . . . this interest is not a collective interest that should always outweigh the interests of a person who because of pain, incapacity, or sedation finds her life intolerable, but rather, an aspect of individual freedom" (ibid.). Recognizing the unique circumstances of terminally ill patients, Stevens focused on their particular interests by again quoting from *Cruzan*:

> Allowing the individual, rather than the State, to make judgments "about the 'quality' of life that a particular individual may enjoy" does not mean that the lives of terminally ill, disabled people have less value than the lives of those who are healthy. Rather, it gives proper recognition to the individual's interest in choosing a final chapter that accords with her life story, rather than one that demeans her values and poisons memories of her. (ibid.; citations omitted)

In using the metaphor of a "final chapter," Stevens used the very words employed by Laurence Tribe during oral arguments. While accepting, then, the respondents'

view of death as a meaningful process, Stevens rejected the state's argument that
the ban on PAS is necessary to protect the vulnerable from abuses:

> I agree that the State has a compelling interest in preventing persons from commit-
> ting suicide because of depression, or coercion by third parties. But the State's legiti-
> mate interest in preventing abuse does not apply to any individual who is not
> victimized by abuse, who is not suffering from depression, and who makes a rational
> and voluntary decision to seek assistance in dying. (at 805)

A discussion then followed in which Stevens rejected two medical claims, favoring instead the knowledge offered by patients. First, he refused to equate a desire
for PAS with mental illness. Instead, he contended that while it is difficult to assess a patient's mental health, mental health professionals can help patients in coping with depression and pain and in assessing their options. Second, accepting
again the information offered by terminally ill patients, he asserted that "palliative
care . . . cannot alleviate all pain and suffering" (ibid.). Indeed, he referred in several instances to the decision for assisted suicide as being a "rational" choice (ibid.).

The last state interest examined by Stevens was that of preserving the integrity
of the medical profession. Again, adopting the vantage point of the dying patients
and their physicians, Stevens argued that the healing role can include giving a
dying patient assistance in suicide. In fact, to do otherwise may signal to patients
that the physician has abandoned, rejected, or exerted paternalistic authority over
them. Citing an article by Dr. Quill, Stevens contended:

> For doctors who have long-standing relationships with their patients, who have given
> their patients advice on alternative treatments, who are attentive to their patient's in-
> dividualized needs, and who are knowledgeable about pain symptom management
> and palliative care options, heeding a patient's desire to assist in her suicide would not
> serve to harm the physician–patient relationship. (ibid.)

In the final section of the opinion, Stevens addressed the equal protection issues
raised in the New York case and again accepted patients' knowledge over medical
knowledge. He approached the question of whether there is a distinction between
the terminally ill patient seeking PAS and the patient on life support seeking to
remove it, by focusing on what the patient desired rather than what the physician
did. Stevens concluded: "There may be little distinction between the intent of a
terminally ill patient who decides to remove her life support and one who seeks
the assistance of a doctor in ending her life; in both situations, the patient is seeking to hasten a certain, impending death" (at 807). He then explicitly rejected the
AMA's position that there is a difference between intent and causation. Charac-
terizing this distinction as "illusory," Stevens offered as evidence the fact that the
AMA "unequivocally endorses the practice of terminal sedation" even as it fights
the legalization of PAS (ibid.). In a footnote he explained that the physician's in-

tent in removing a patient from life support may be similar to the intent in providing a patient with a means to commit suicide in that it is not "at all clear that
the physician's intent is that the patient 'be made dead'" (ibid, n. 15). Instead, patients may seek such medication and physicians prescribe them in order to alleviate patients' fears and to help them to acquire "some sense of control in the
process of dying" (ibid.). He ended by suggesting that while the debate over PAS
will continue, future cases may be decided according to their particular facts:

> In my judgment, however, it is clear that the so-called "unqualified interest in the
> preservation of human life" [quoting *Cruzan* and the *Glucksberg* majority] is not itself
> sufficient to outweigh the interest in liberty that may justify the only possible means
> of preserving a dying patient's dignity and alleviating her intolerable suffering. (at
> 807–808)

From beginning to end, then, Stevens was attuned to the knowledge of the terminally ill patients. He heard their plea for dignity as more than just buzz words,
he drew on their experiences to refute medical claims, and he understood dying
as something more than merely a physical process. Using the knowledge of patients that had been discounted by the other Justices, Stevens painted a picture of
the PAS issue that was at once general and particular—a portrait of a culture in
which death was denied and medicalized, and in which individual patients were
condemned to suffer so that the slide down the slippery slope could be stayed.
Demonstrating how patients' knowledge could be integrated within the law,
Stevens moored patients' concerns on the footing of the Constitution's liberty interest and argued on behalf of their right to judicial protection. In so doing, he illustrated not only how patients' knowledge could be heard at the Court, but also
how such inclusion can alter the nature of judicial decision making. Here, then,
was a hint as to how transformative patients' knowledge could be if only it was
heard.

CONCLUSION

Twenty-four years after *Roe*, the PAS cases of *Glucksberg* and *Quill* reaffirmed how
knowledge that draws on the objective, the impartial, the reasoned, and the universal trumps knowledge founded on the subjective, the involved, the emotional,
and the particular. Medical knowledge was assumed to have the former attributes
while patients' knowledge was assumed to have the latter. Yet, to hear patients'
knowledge as it was represented in the party briefs, *amicus* briefs, and Justice
Stevens's concurrence, challenged the validity of these dichotomies. How was the
medical community's stance toward PAS any more "objective" or "impartial" than
that of the terminal patients? Both seemed to bring values and judgments to the

issue that appeared self-serving. How well "reasoned" was the medical position that interpreted the motives of physicians who withdrew patients from life-support as lacking any intent to kill? Certainly, the terminally ill patients who wanted access to PAS could also make the claim that they did not intend to kill themselves but to end their suffering. Just how "universal" were the medical claims that pain could be alleviated when medical experts also admitted that in reality such care was not available to all? It seemed to be the terminally ill patients, and not the medical profession, who posed a logical challenge to the validity of the rule by referring to the exceptions. Ultimately, the very fact that some terminally ill patients would be left to really suffer in order that *other* future patients would be protected from *possible* abuses cast doubt as to the significance of objectivity, impartiality, reasonableness, and universality in the law. The perils of the slippery slope would be avoided but only by sacrificing the terminally ill patients to their suffering.

In this the PAS decisions seemed to be uncaring decisions—a charge not usually made in reference to Supreme Court decisions since justice, not caring, is the presumed goal. Yet, it was hard not to notice how the result of the cases seemed unresponsive to the issues brought to the Court by the original litigants. The circumstances that led patients and their advocates to challenge the state bans were left unchanged: the legal options remained limited; patients' pleas for help were left unanswered; and the suffering promised to continue. One terminally ill patient who was hopeful of a Court decision that recognized a right to PAS now discussed instead how she might "go down the road to a motel" to end her life so that no one else might be implicated in the illegal act. She described her disappointment at the decisions: "The court has failed me utterly" ("Patient" 1997). Indeed it appeared that patients had been forgotten by the majority of the Court who had instead concerned themselves with protecting the integrity of the medical profession. While providing medical organizations and states with the ruling they requested, the Court offered little, if anything, to the terminally ill patients who had told the Justices that the state bans were injuring them, the medical profession failing them, and the suffering swallowing them. In light of these pleas for help, Chief Justice Rehnquist's assurances to them rang hollow: that the state bans were reasonably related to legitimate state interests, and that the ruling "permits this debate to continue, as it should in a democratic society" (at 797). Left unsaid was what would happen in the meantime to the terminally ill patients who were currently suffering. For them, there was no time to wait for a democratically formed consensus to emerge that would allow them to define their own lives by controlling the circumstances of their own deaths. Instead, their worst fears had been realized in that the Court had sacrificed them on the altar of the slippery slope and then justified its decision by referring to the constraints imposed by law—their role was to dispense justice, not caring.

Yet, seemingly all was not lost—one Justice in the PAS cases did succeed in finding a way to incorporate patients' knowledge within law, and four others seemed to look for a way not only to hear their voices but to respond to their needs. Opening, as they did, an opportunity for the terminally ill patients and their physicians to "try again" in a future case, the PAS decisions posed a challenge and an invitation to develop a jurisprudence capable of integrating patients' knowledge within the law. Such is the task of the next chapter.

· 4 ·

A Jurisprudence of Justice and Care: Enabling the Court to Hear the Knowledge of Patients

The quality of mercy is not strained,
It droppeth as the gentle rain from heaven
Upon the place beneath. It is twice blest;
It blesseth him that gives and him that takes.
'Tis mightiest in the mightiest. It becomes
The throned monarch better than his crown.
His scepter shows the force of temporal power,
The attribute to awe and majesty
Wherein doth sit the dread and fear of kings.
But mercy is above this sceptered sway,
It is enthroned in the hearts of kings,
It is an attribute to God himself,
And earthly power doth then show likest God's
When mercy seasons justice . . .

Portia, in Shakespeare's *Merchant of Venice*

$\mathcal{O}$n the campus of Samford University in Birmingham, Alabama, in the plaza bordering the Lucille Stewart Beeson Law Library, there is a striking sculpture. Lady Justice, though sitting, is captured in a familiar pose: in her left hand she holds aloft the scales of justice, in her right hand she wields the sword of authority, and encircling her head is a blindfold that ensures her impartiality. But unlike most depictions of Justice, here she is not alone, for standing behind her and leaning over her right shoulder is the Angel of Mercy. With wings spread wide enough to envelop them both, the angel's right hand reaches out to stay the sword as she seems to whisper in the ear of Lady Justice. Sculpted by Glynn Acree, the statue was inspired by words etched in granite in the foyer of the Law Library; a phrase that expressed Mrs. Beeson's philosophy of legal education: "Seek wisdom to temper justice with compassion."

While the classical rendering of a blindfolded and solitary Lady Justice stills dominates our image of this concept, it is not without its challengers. From Portia to

Mrs. Beeson, from New Testament passages to feminist legal scholarship, Justice has been reenvisioned to enable her both to see and to feel. Whether called "mercy" or "compassion," "love" or "caring," the concerns raised are similar—that Justice should not be too quick to wield her sword, should not act in isolation of other principles, and should not be so blinded that she cannot see. This is, of course, to challenge the mainstream understanding of Justice that personifies the American legal system. Within that tradition, the sword of Justice symbolizes her authority, her right, her power, to decide and resolve as swiftly as possible the dispute brought before her. Her scales admit of only two sets of interests and only one of two possible outcomes because in the balancing, one party will win and the other will lose. Justice's signature feature, her blindfold, is essential to guarantee her impartiality and to ensure that "equal justice before the law" be delivered.

Therefore, to seek a way to temper Justice with caring is to challenge mainstream understandings of law (see, e.g., Rawls 1971). In essence, it is to question the wisdom and the rightness of law's impartiality, universality, and logic. The Samford statue of Lady Justice with the Angel of Mercy illustrates this well. Mercy not only stays the sword, she whispers to Justice as well. But whispers what? Perhaps she reveals to Justice an aspect of the case that she cannot see, thereby rendering Justice partial. Or perhaps she implores Justice to hesitate and consider again whether application of this rule in this case is really the fair thing to do, thereby asking the law to make an exception. Or perhaps her words aim at the heart of Lady Justice, trying to evoke in her a particular feeling to inform her decision making, thereby checking reason with emotion. But listening to Mercy exacts a price. Justice can no longer defend her decision as the product of a process that is impartial, universal, and reasoned. Her noticing of the particulars opens her to charges of favoritism or prejudice, her uneven application of rules to complaints of unfairness, and her use of emotion as evidence of irrationality or caprice.

Is it inevitable then, that law be either impartial, universal, and reasoned, or involved, particular, and emotional? Is Justice separated from Mercy still just? Is it possible or even desirable to integrate justice and compassion?

These questions have been in the background throughout the first three chapters of this book, and so it makes sense to retrace the argument thus far and to connect it to the present inquiry before moving on. Throughout the earlier discussion, my concern has been how, in deciding cases involving questions framed as medical issues, the U.S. Supreme Court regards the knowledge of patients. What we have seen is that legal norms and practices erect barriers that impede the integration of patients' knowledge in judicial deliberations. However, these same norms and practices serve to highlight medical knowledge and to elevate its role in the Court.

Chapter 1 explored the basis for law's preference for medical over patients' knowledge by contrasting how law, medicine, and patients construct knowledge.

Both law and medicine share a common epistemology that constructs knowledge through an impartial, universal, and reasoned process. Because of this similar orientation, medical knowledge can converge with legal knowledge—the Justices regard it as expert and as reliable, and can use it as the basis for their own decisions. This convergence of legal and medical expertise has a different effect on the voices of patients—it silences them. Because the Court operates under the assumption that justice demands that involved, particular, and emotional knowledge be disregarded, patients' expertise is undermined and at times even disregarded as not offering knowledge at all. Therefore, legal norms aimed at preserving justice have set in motion a dynamic whereby the Court hears physicians over patients, and isolates justice from caring.

Chapters 2 and 3 explored the ramifications of these legal norms for two particular sets of cases—those concerning abortion and those concerning physician-assisted suicide (PAS). In both sets of cases, the issues were framed as primarily *medical* issues even though they were formed by intimate personal relationships and contextualized by social, cultural, psychological, political, ethical, and economic considerations. The result of this orientation was the amplification of medical knowledge and the muting of patients' knowledge. Within the abortion decisions, the harms suffered by the pregnant women and the cultural contexts within which they made their decision were repeatedly ignored in favor of the interests of physicians. Ultimately, *Roe v. Wade* and its progeny came to symbolize the Court's concern with protecting physicians from legal prosecution rather than with responding to the pleas of pregnant women for access to safe and legal abortions. Justice's blindfold prevented her from seeing the personal nature of the abortion issue, the distinctive circumstances of different women, and in whose interests she was ruling. That the women litigants faded to the periphery of the case was hardly noticed at all.

In the PAS cases, the Court once again followed the path suggested by the majority of the medical profession—even to the extent of rejecting patients' experiences regarding their suffering and pain in favor of guarding against harms that supposedly will befall future patients. Following the expert testimony of medical organizations and scholars, the Court determined that patients' pain could largely be controlled and that any wish to commit suicide was so inherently irrational that it only proved that more medical care, and not less, was needed. Despite patients' accounts describing the importance of their ties to family and friends, and the meaning that certain activities and practices gave their lives, the Court determined that the physician–patient relationship was the primary association implicated by PAS, and thus chose to protect it (as defined by the physicians) over other personal connections. Once again, the Court turned a blind eye to the particular litigants who initiated the *Glucksberg* and *Quill* cases, and the experiential and deeply personal knowledge that they offered the Court. Just as they had in the abortion decisions, legal norms had constructed the facts, formulated the issues, and set the framework by which personal knowledge would come to be devoid of influence.

So far, then, I have used the abortion and PAS cases to illustrate two crucial points—that the law is willfully blind to patients' knowledge and that this blindness causes it to be uncaring. That is, the Court operates under the assumption that justice demands that involved, particular, and emotional knowledge be disregarded—and therefore it deliberately excludes patients' knowledge. But as Justice John Paul Stevens demonstrated in his concurring opinions in the PAS cases, this assumption may not be valid. In drawing on patients' knowledge to inform his judgment, Stevens showed not only that it is possible to integrate patients' knowledge with medical and legal knowledge, but that to do so enhances justice. While this is instructive in that it suggests that patients' knowledge can inform law, the impact of Stevens's approach is limited in two crucial ways: first, because he was unable to convince even one other member of the Court to join him, and second because he did not articulate the theoretical framework that he employed in writing his opinion. It therefore might be tempting to dismiss Stevens's patient-centered approach as lacking a principled framework, but I believe that such a conclusion is ill founded. There are in fact principled ways to incorporate patients' knowledge in legal decision making. That Stevens did not explicate such a jurisprudence in his concurrence neither means that he lacked one nor that one cannot be developed. Therefore, in this chapter I suggest one jurisprudential, principled approach that enables the Court to hear patients' knowledge. It is an approach that is informed by both the ethic of justice and the ethic of care.

First, I argue that by excluding patients' knowledge and focusing only on impartial, universal, and reasoned knowledge, the Court fails to achieve the justice it seeks. Second, I argue that a key to achieving justice is to temper it with caring. Within a jurisprudence that values both justice and care, and in which they serve to check each other, the inclusion of patients' knowledge becomes a necessary feature of the Court's deliberations. The model that I propose rejects using the ethics of justice and care as diametrical forces that pull the law in opposite directions, and instead suggests how the contending forces of justice and care can work together as the warp and weft of the fabric of law. My goal in this chapter, then, is to develop and defend a judicial approach that integrates an ethic of justice and an ethic of care, and that thereby recognizes the knowledge that patients have to offer. I call this approach a "caring jurisprudence."

For the better part of two decades, many feminist scholars have considered the possibilities born of shifting from an ethic of justice to an ethic of care. I therefore begin with a brief examination of why feminism is particularly well suited to the inquiry at hand. The questions that feminists raise concerning the societal division of labor, the privileging of knowledge, and the dynamics of oppression shed light as to why patients' knowledge and concerns for caring are diminished by the

Court. I use this discussion as a context for the next section that explores feminist reenvisionings of the relationship between justice and care. In particular, the theories and approaches used in Carol Gilligan's *In a Different Voice*, feminist philosophy, and feminist jurisprudence all suggest methods for challenging mainstream legal norms. In the final section, I propose as an alternative judicial approach a model for a "caring jurisprudence" that integrates justice and care. Again, my ultimate goal is to develop a way to overcome the constraints of legal norms so that patients' knowledge can be integrated within the Court. In this, I hope not only to enable Lady Justice to see, but also to hear.

FEMINISM

Feminism—that is, the commitment to identify and eradicate the many ways that women are oppressed—holds many lessons for the inquiry at hand. Feminist scholarship is particularly relevant in addressing why it is that patients' knowledge has been relegated to the fringes of Supreme Court cases since certain themes within feminist inquiries also resonate for patients. These themes include the analysis of: the impact of the public/private dichotomy; the privileging of certain types of knowledge; and the dynamics of oppression.

Separation of the Public/Private Spheres

The dominant paradigm for understanding Western industrial societies has been to split the world into two realms—that of the public (including employment, governance, and organized activities) and that of the private (defined by life within the family). Feminist analyses have challenged this dichotomy in several ways. First, they have revealed how this view of the world is deeply gendered in that the work associated with the public life has been dominated by men while that of the private life has been left to the care of women. The public/private split, therefore, suggests separate spheres of work based on gender. Second, they have refuted the assumption that this division in labor is caused by the natural differences between men and women and have maintained instead that a gender-based division of labor has been socially constructed from stereotypes about the appropriate roles for each sex. Third, they have identified how the split in work has also resulted in differences regarding the behaviors expected and the values ascribed to the public versus the private realms. Public work, the forum where careers are built, politics is done, and culture is shaped, is valued in terms of individual accomplishments and afforded wages, power, and prestige. The public realm is therefore an individualistic, competitive, and rights-oriented arena. In contrast, private work, the realm where children are raised, families are nurtured, meals cooked, and homes tended, is seen as relational work that is unpaid and that goes mostly unrecognized. The private realm is therefore characterized by connections, relations, love, and self-sacrifice. Fourth, while such service and care by women has been deemed as admirable, feminists have argued that it has also contributed to women's subordinate position in society. Hence, the public/private dichotomy has within it a politics of sexism. Finally, they have argued that the split implies that political concepts like justice are applicable to the public realm alone, while an emotion like caring is more suitable to private life. In challenging this dichotomy, feminist scholars argue that families can indeed be held to the ethic of justice and that public policy be accountable to the ethic of care.

However, feminist challenges to the public/private split are not only based on the argument that it is harmful to women, but also on the grounds that the dichotomy itself is untrue. Perhaps best expressed by the feminist slogan "the personal is political," feminists challenge the notion that the world can be neatly separated into two distinct realms. They argue instead that politics is not confined to the public realm alone. Tracing how patriarchy in the public world becomes patriarchy at home, and demonstrating how public policies like those regarding rape, incest, domestic violence, health care, and education affect the personal lives of family members, feminists reject the public/private dichotomy as an inaccurate description of the world, especially how it is experienced by women.

Feminist critiques of the public/private dichotomy, then, have at least two implications for this study. First, the assignment of justice and care to particular realms and thereby to particular sexes is open to question. Justice as a public pursuit undertaken by men, and care as a private act of women can be challenged as an inaccurate dichotomy that limits human behavior and social possibilities. The claim that law, as a part of the public realm, be guided by justice and not by caring also calls for further examination. Second, feminist critiques of the public/private dichotomy also suggest that attention be paid as to how disputes are characterized within the legal system. Since the public sphere focuses on actors and their rights, it is no surprise that seemingly private issues like abortion and PAS are reconfigured when they become public. While a private orientation would view the issues in terms of the relationships they involve and how best to care for the people involved, a public rendering of the cases depicts them as matters of individual rights calling for public justice. The feminist critiques of the public/private split serve, then, to question the limits imposed on our conceptions of justice and of care.

The Privileging of Knowledge

The traditional model of knowledge as formed through an objective, universal, and reasoned process has also been challenged by feminists. Given that much knowledge about the world was constructed by men and about men, the exclusion of the truths concerning women's lives have rendered suspect the claims of objectivity, universality, and reason. Yet, feminists not only challenge traditional knowledge as offering at best partial truth but at worst supporting a system of oppression known as sexism. The basis for this charge is the history of how most disciplines have formed their knowledge: medicine studied the male body and treated the female body as an aberration; history focused on the battles, campaigns, and accomplishments of upper-class men and rendered women invisible; literature preserved the stories of male writers while women fought for the right to become literate, to write, and to publish; political philosophy espoused the natural rights of men and the merits of democracy even while denying women the basic right to vote. The list could go on to include almost every discipline. Therefore, one of the major contributions of Second Wave feminism (i.e., from about 1965 on) has been the reconstruction of knowledge so that it is inclusive of women (and other people marginalized by various combinations of social characteristics including gender, race/ethnicity, class, sexual orientation, age, and disability). The purpose behind this inclusivity is not only to broaden and enrich knowledge but to challenge and change the effects of patriarchy.

Feminism offers not only the prescription of developing inclusive knowledge, but a method for creating it as well—the concrete experiences of individuals must serve as the starting point of all inquiries. For the women's movement, the only way to challenge the veracity of mainstream knowledge was to draw on personal experiences to the contrary. In order to do this, women first had to find their "voice," that is, the courage to articulate and to believe what they knew to be true. "Consciousness raising" became the tool by which women learned to trust their own knowledge and to join with others to offer and to act on a different view of the world (see Sarachild 1995).

There are three particular concerns that these feminist critiques suggest for this study. First, knowledge can be formed in a variety of ways. Following the scientific method is not *the* path to knowledge, but only *a* path to *some* knowledge. Another way to knowledge is through personal experiences—even though this source is based on a process that can be subjective, involved, and emotional. Second, this alternative vision of knowledge is particularly important for patients since it empowers their voices and recognizes them as bearers of information. For people like patients who have been excluded from the formation of knowledge that claims to speak for them or about them, knowledge drawn from personal experiences is crucial since it enables them to challenge and question other authoritative voices. Third, there is a politics to knowledge in that those who control it are thereby empowered to influence and even to control others. Feminism encourages a healthy skepticism toward any professionals who claim to know what is best for their "uninformed," "uneducated," or "emotional" clientele. Paternalism, a son of patriarchy, should be questioned whether it is found within medicine, the law, or any discipline whose practitioners claim to objectively know what is best for other people. Feminism, therefore, offers a strong reminder as to how knowledge can be recognized or denied, limited or expanded, and used or abused to achieve particular results.

The Dynamics of Oppression

That power can be used by some to control and to subjugate others is well accepted. That it has been so used by men to control and to subjugate women is still contested. Thus, a goal of feminism has been to name oppression in order to begin to dismantle it. This has been an inherently difficult undertaking because gender oppression was neither evident to many of those who oppressed nor to many of those who were oppressed. In fact, the oppressors and the oppressed often shared outwardly loving relationships as sexual partners, spouses, family members, colleagues, and friends, even though they lived within a patriarchal system. This was not, then, the type of oppression easily discerned—of one people conquered by another, of one race or ethnicity subjugated by another, or of a minority controlled by a majority. This was oppression hidden by assumed biological differences, long-accepted social customs, deeply held religious beliefs, democratic political processes, seemingly neutral legal reasoning, and unexamined personal habits. The difficulty, then, lay in this—how to mobilize people against an oppression that even many of the oppressed did not see. Not so incidentally, the public/private dichotomy and the privileging of certain forms of knowledge made this task all the more difficult. Gender differences appeared to be natural and neutral—thus spake social institutions, cultural history, and every academic discipline. Therefore, before strategies for combating sexism could even be considered, feminists had to create a way for people to see oppression and to name it as such. In short, they first had to come themselves to understand the dynamics of oppression, and only then to begin to develop ways to make it visible to others.

A key in this effort was to expose how hidden categories and assumptions are implicated in distinguishing among people in order to control them. For feminists, the concept of "gender," i.e., the construction of feminine and masculine roles, is a vantage point from which to view, evaluate, and reinterpret the world. A gender analysis inquires as to how "feminine" and "masculine" have been defined, how these concepts interact to exploit, limit, or injure people, and what changes must be made to eliminate these harms. Within mainstream American culture, masculinity implies strength, power, and reason while femininity implies weakness, nurturance, and emotions. Again, feminists are skeptical of such dichotomies especially when they are defended as natural and when the result is that those in one category enjoy rights, opportunities, and status not afforded to those in the other category. Another concern is raised when the use of gender is hidden from view. For instance, even when public policies are expressed using generic or universal pronouns, women are not really included if masculine behavior or needs serve as the reference point for everyone. (For example, think about how women versus men are affected by the consequences of the following: an inflexible work schedule of nine to five, five days a week; the standards of appropriate dress and mannerisms in various professions; the use of adult male crash test dummies to test the safety of air bags in cars; the willingness of health insurance companies to cover Viagra and not birth control pills; and so on.) In addition, feminists are deeply concerned with how gender combines with other socially significant characteristics to oppress people. It is, therefore, not enough to contrast women's experiences with those of men, but to ask: which women? which men? These questions lead to the study of how gender intersects with other social indicators such as race, ethnicity, class, sexual orientation, age, and disability. They thereby question how these factors combine to oppress different people in different ways.

   This focus on oppression is relevant to this study although the category under scrutiny is that of "patients" rather than that of "women." As surely as gender oppression can be invisible but still very much real, so can the pervasive acceptance of attitudes toward patients render us blind to their subjugation. Like the socially constructed category of gender, the "patient" designation can be used to disempower one group of people while empowering others. Dichotomous categories such as physician-patient and lawyer-client require scrutiny since oppression is not only a social phenomenon but can exist within personal relationships as well. While oppression may take many possible forms, there are some disturbing similarities in the ways that women as permanent members of a class and patients as (sometimes temporary) members of a category have been subjugated: both groups have traditionally been disparaged as knowers, sometimes for lacking expertise and other times for being too emotional; "facts" have been constructed without consideration of their knowledge, and at times contrary to it, and yet they will be the ones subject to governance by these "truths"; and finally, membership in these categories erases the differences among people, thus allowing assumptions of universality to be made when there is none. Feminism's commitment to the ending of all types of oppression suggests that the inquiry extend to all categories that may disempower people—including that of "patient."

   Feminism's agenda, then, is "to question everything" (Wishik 1986). World views, knowledge, and power are approached critically. Assumptions are challenged, dichotomies dismantled, new knowledge founded, and oppression named. But the task, of course is more than mere analysis—it entails nothing more and nothing less than an effort to change the world.

FEMINIST REENVISIONINGS OF JUSTICE AND CARE

Within feminism's tradition of valuing that which had been devalued, of challenging that which was held to be true, and of naming as oppression that which others did not see, came Carol Gilligan's *In a Different Voice* (1982), a book that studied how gender affects moral reasoning. Claiming that men tend to follow an ethic of justice whereas women tend to speak with a "different voice" drawn from an ethic of care, Gilligan launched a debate that has yet to subside. It is hard to overestimate the impact that this work and the scholarship that responded to it have had not only on feminist thought, but also on academics in general, and public perceptions regarding gender differences in particular. Indeed, entire academic forums have been devoted to examining Gilligan's claims, and her ideas have served as the basis for blockbuster books like Deborah Tannen's *You Just Don't Understand* (1990) and John Gray's *Men Are from Mars, Women Are from Venus* (1992). My intent in examining some of this scholarship, however, is not to exhaustively review the literature but to paint with broad stokes a picture of the discourse in order to suggest how to construct a jurisprudence capable of both justice and care.

Gilligan's "Different Voice"

In a sense what Gilligan, a developmental psychologist, began in this work was a feminist effort to rehabilitate the concept of "care." That this concept was even in need of rehabilitation is in itself revealing both of cultural attitudes regarding gender as well as the need for feminist inquiries. In particular, Gilligan was responding to studies by one of her mentors, Lawrence Kohlberg, that she saw as adopting the male model of moral reasoning as the norm by which all people were measured. Based on the study of male subjects, Kohlberg proposed that from childhood to adulthood, moral judgment develops through six hierarchical stages (see Kohlberg 1981). In applying his scale to both males and females, Kohlberg found that females were overly represented among the most developmentally deficient. They appeared to be stalled at stage three. As described by Gilligan, "At this stage morality is conceived in interpersonal terms and goodness is equated with helping and pleasing others" (1982: 18). Gilligan went on to read Kohlberg and Kramer (1969) as implying that if women entered the male world of employment, they would progress to stage four, where relationships become subordinated to rules, and stages five and six where rules are replaced by universal principles of justice. She then took aim and fired:

> Yet herein lies a paradox, for the very traits that traditionally have defined the "goodness" of women, their care for and sensitivity to the needs of others, are those that

mark them as deficient in moral development. In this version of moral development, however, the conception of maturity is derived from the study of men's lives and reflects the importance of individuation in their development. (Gilligan 1982: 18)

Gilligan stood the conventional wisdom on its head. Standing squarely within a feminist orientation, her method was to begin with the study of women and of the experiences drawn from their lives. In particular, she conducted three studies: the college student study, the abortion decision study, and the rights and responsibilities studies whereby female subjects were interviewed about the moral conflicts they experience in their lives. From this information she developed a theory regarding women's moral reasoning whereby care was no longer an emotion that stalled women's moral development, but was in fact an ethic that could guide moral development. Women, then, were not morally deficient when they resolved moral dilemmas by reference to relationships and responsibilities; they were instead employing a "different voice" stemming from a feminine ethic of care rather than from a masculine voice of justice. Whereas the masculine ethic applied rules and logic, the feminine ethic approached problems "contextually rather than categorically" (ibid.: 38). Where a justice orientation viewed human beings as separate bearers of rights, a care perspective assumed human connection and responsibilities.

Gilligan's theory is not without controversy. Besides opening an old wound within the body of feminism by reintroducing the seemingly sexist assertion that women *were* in fact different from men, Gilligan was also faulted on the basis of a number of issues, including empirical problems that raised questions concerning the validity of her work,[1] the assumptions she made regarding gender,[2] her lack of appreciation for how care may not be a choice for women but a tactic for surviving in a misogynist culture,[3] and her disregard for the role that race and class play in positioning people within a culture.[4]

Still, Gilligan remains helpful to my inquiry. Even though her research focused on developing a theory of moral reasoning, some of the findings may also be applied to legal reasoning (as illustrated below in the section on feminist jurisprudence). Two aspects of her research are of particular interest here: first, her analysis of the ethics of justice and care as gendered ethics, and second, her argument as to how the ethic of justice has been used to denigrate women as moral reasoners. Drawing on Gilligan's comparison of the ethics of justice and care, a theory can be constructed as to why the legal system does not "hear" subjective, involved, and particular knowledge as knowledge. Driven by an ethic of justice, judicial decision making adopts a "masculine" approach to resolving dilemmas by seeking knowledge that is impartial, universal, and reasoned, and by viewing litigants as bearers of rights. In contrast, patients' knowledge, like the feminine "different voice" of moral reasoning, is shaped by an ethic of care that draws on the subjective, particular, and emotional and that views people as connected to one another through responsibilities. Therefore, just as the feminine voice was devalued in Kohlberg's study concerning moral reasoning, so Gilligan's theory can be used to suggest that patients' knowledge is devalued before the Court because it resembles the "feminine" form of knowledge derivative of an ethic of care.[5] In continuing this line of reasoning, it then becomes apparent that one way to change the way the Court regards patients' knowledge would be to introduce the ethic of care into the legal system. Within this framework, then, the introduction of an ethic of care can challenge and change legal norms and practices by serving as a counterweight or balance to the ethic of justice.

In light of Gilligan's claim of a "different voice," the classical rendering of Lady Justice seems most appropriate. Depicted as a woman, Justice needs to be blind-folded, weighed down with a sword, and limited by balancing scales in order to achieve justice over caring. Given her different orientation, the Lady would be in-clined to see the particularities of the case, use her arms to embrace those who come before her, and seek a resolution not suggested by the duality of the scales. But legal norms based on the ethic of justice have stripped Lady Justice of her abil-ity to draw on her "different voice" of an ethic of care. Instead, the blindfold has forced her to be impartial, the sword severs her relationship with the litigants, and the scales confine her choices. Gilligan's theory suggests that, though female, Lady Justice has been masculinized to serve the law.

Justice and Care

Gilligan's theory of the contrasting nature of the ethics of justice and care has been utilized and extended by many other scholars. So much has been written from so many different disciplines that to survey it all would pull me off the point of this study—that is, how to draw on this scholarship to develop a caring jurisprudence capable of hearing the knowledge of patients. The approach I take here, therefore, is not a thorough literature review that moves from scholar to scholar (see Clemont 1996 for a good summary or anthologies like Larrabee 1993 or Held 1995), but a more thematic approach that highlights concepts relevant to the study at hand. My focus is on what the scholarship suggests concerning the relationship between the ethic of justice and the ethic of care.

Feminist scholars who take up Gilligan's theory of a distinctive voice are re-markably similar in how they define and contrast the ethic of justice versus the ethic of care. Marilyn Friedman's description, which explicitly draws on Gilligan (even citing the pages from *A Different Voice*), provides an excellent summary of the contrasts:

> According to Gilligan, the standard (or "male") moral voice articulated in moral psy-chology derives moral judgments about particular cases from abstract, universalized

moral rules and principles which are substantively concerned with justice and rights. For justice reasoners: the major moral imperative enjoins respects for the rights of others (100); the concept of duty is limited to reciprocal noninterference (147); the motivating vision is one of the equal worth of self and other (63); and one important underlying presupposition is a highly individualed conception of person.

By contrast, the other (or "female") moral voice which Gilligan heard in her studies eschews abstract rules and principles. This moral voice derives moral judgments from the contextual detail of situations grasped as specific and unique (100). The substantive concern for this moral voice is care and responsibility, particularly as these arise in the context of interpersonal relationships (19). Moral judgments, for care reasoners, are tied to feelings of empathy and compassion (69); the major moral imperatives center around caring, not hurting others, and avoiding selfishness (90); and the motivating vision of this ethic is "that everyone will be responded to and included, that no one will be left alone or hurt" (63). (1995: 61–62)

These distinctions are echoed by others. Joan Tronto offers the following summary: "From the perspective of caring, what is important is not arriving at the fair decision, understood as how the abstract individual in this situation would want to be treated, but at meeting the needs of particular others or preserving the relationships of care that exist" (1995: 105). Alison Jaggar states that "justice thinking is portrayed as appealing to rational and universalizable moral principles, applied impartially, whereas accounts of care thinking emphasize its responsiveness whose morally salient features are perceived with an acuteness thought to be made possible by the carer's emotional posture of empathy, openness, and receptiveness" (1995: 180). Grace Clemont contrasts justice and caring as the differences between focusing on the abstract vs. the detailed concrete; emphasizing human separateness vs. connectedness, and prioritizing equality vs. relationships (1996).

There also seems to be general appreciation of the limitations inherent in applying each of these ethics alone. The dangers of employing an ethic of justice are well known and constitute much of the feminist critique of mainstream reasoning. A focus on justice tends to ignore the particular person, experiences, and circumstances at hand, is tied to dualities, and is lacking in compassion. Because general rules are employed, this approach may not be capable of responding to people's specific needs. Yet, the negative implications of employing only an ethic of care have been traced by feminists as well: the danger of nepotism and favoritism (Friedman 1995: 69); the inclination to care only for those like ourselves (Tronto 1993b: 249); particularity that invites an unleashing of sexism, racism, etc. (Tong 1993: 126); and the opportunity for paternalism and codependency (Jaggar 1995: 189, 192). The limitations of each of these ethics, then, partly explain why the ethic of justice has been applied most often in the public realm while the ethic of care has been reserved for situations in the private realm. Care seems most appropriate for responding to personal situations involving people who know each other and who have genuine emotional ties to each other, while justice seems more appropriate for resolving fairly the issues that arise among strangers. John Broughton explains that justice is intended as public caring and reiterates Kohlberg's claim that "love is a local form of justice" (1993: 123). Yet, even when applied in their usual sphere, each ethic appears limited. Care's micro focus seems to miss the larger picture of the social and cultural forces that shape personal relationships. Justice's macro focus seems to miss the smaller portrait of the specific people involved and how they depart from the abstract. Clearly, then, the ethics of justice and care have usually been regarded as opposites in need of some sort of reconciliation.

Feminist Jurisprudence

In that law is a discipline founded on justice, directed by knowledge, and practiced by and for people, it is clear as to why Gilligan's "different voice" theory and the scholarship focusing justice and care have found a home within the field of law. That home has been constructed by feminist legal theorists/practitioners who draw on feminism to challenge as well as to reshape how law is understood and practiced. Gilligan's work seems particularly relevant to law because her major criticism of the field of psychology can be stated with equal force concerning the field of law—that while claiming universal applicability, in reality the discipline constructs knowledge on the basis of male experience alone and is therefore less than neutral in its assessment of "truth." With the introduction of Gilligan's theory of a "feminine" voice to the field of law, further fuel was added to the feminist-inspired changes that were already sweeping three areas of law: legal epistemology, legal practice, and legal education.

One goal among feminist legal scholars is to challenge the common belief that law neutrally creates knowledge (see Law 1984; Minow 1987; Finley 1989; Hawkesworth 1989; Bartlett 1990). Seemingly "neutral" laws are revealed to be as biased as the knowledge on which they are based. Katharine Bartlett suggests corrective measures that include expanding the lens of legal relevance to include women's knowledge, and making social and political factors more visible instead of hiding them behind the mask of objectivity (1990). The transformative power of integrating women's experiences is evident in many areas of law: in rape law the definitions of "coercion," "force," and "consent" are reevaluated (MacKinnon 1989; Estrich 1987; Olsen 1984); in domestic violence law, the victim's point of view supports a broader interpretation of self-defense and state intervention (Walker 1984); in abortion law, the consequences of an unwanted pregnancy highlights the inadequacy of the constitutional right to privacy (see Baer 1990; Colker 1992; McDonagh 1996); in laws governing death and dying, attention is drawn to the communal nature of the process (Bender 1992; Harmon 1998); in criminal law, women's unique experiences challenge assumptions regarding due process

(Daly 1989); in equal protection law, the question of how race intersects with sex illuminates the different ways that women of color experience oppression (Crenshaw 1989; Harris 1991; P. Williams 1991); and in employment law, the perpetual problem of sexual harassment in the workplace was finally named and then challenged as a form of sex discrimination (Farley 1978; MacKinnon 1979). While the argument for inclusion of various experiences and viewpoints has been mocked largely by conservative commentators with the tag "political correctness," the point for feminists is not of inclusion for its own sake, but that without inclusivity, knowledge is at best partial, and at worst is not knowledge at all. Gilligan's scholarship on the previously neglected experiences of women served to reinforce this point.

A second focus of feminist legal scholars is to incorporate theoretical changes in legal practice (see Dalton 1991; Bender 1988; Scales 1986; Sherry 1986; Littleton 1987; Resnik 1988; Talarico 1988; Bartlett 1990; Rhode 1990). The conviction that law can be practiced in ways different from the norm opens new possibilities: legal questions can be framed in terms of relationships and responsibilities rather than in terms of individualistic entreaties to rights (Nedelsky 1993); emotions can play an informational role within the reasoning process (Nussbaum 1990, 1995); and conflict resolution can be prized over adversariness (Menkel-Meadow 1985; Resnik 1988). To use Gilligan's terminology, the ethic of justice need not dominate the practice of law—legal practice can be caring.

On a third level, the infusion of feminism within law schools dramatically alters how law is taught (see Pickard 1983; Menkel-Meadow 1985, 1988, 1997; Scales 1986; Cain 1988; Crenshaw 1989; Harris 1991; P. Williams 1991). The introduction of new knowledge is accomplished through the inclusion of experiential information in the form of storytelling, anecdotes, and literature. Learning strategies are employed that eschew the Socratic method in favor of feminist and other student-centered pedagogies so that cooperation rather than adversarialism is practiced. In addition, the importance of the results of judicial decision making becomes a measure of legal practice rather than only the mechanics of the process employed. Therefore, Gilligan's emphasis on the feminine voice of care can be integrated within law school pedagogies to radically reshape how law is learned.

While Gilligan's scholarship appears to reinforce these feminist efforts to alter law, it has also reinflamed a recurring controversy within feminist legal studies— the sameness/difference debate. In light of Gilligan's claim of a different voice and a number of legal changes made in the name of gender equality, the debate took on a renewed sense of urgency. What does it mean for women if a "different voice" is embraced by the law? The feminist legal community has split on the answer. Kenneth Karst (1984), Carrie Menkel-Meadow (1985, 1997), and Robin West (1988; 1997), advocates of applying "relational" or "cultural" feminism to law, argue that feminist legal theory should support laws that acknowledge the differences between men and women, particularly concerning reproduction. Critics of difference theory like Wendy Williams (1985), Cynthia Fuchs Epstein (1988), and Joan Williams (1992) warn that difference theory could prove a double-edged sword whereby special protections translate into gender limitations. Others like Catharine MacKinnon (1987) and Mary Joe Frug (1992) point out the futility of this debate. They argue that not only do both the difference and sameness advocates use men as the reference point, but that the debate cannot analyze the deeper cultural and institutional issues behind the problem of inequality.

This debate within feminist legal theory makes it clear that the development of feminist approaches to law is not dependent on whether there is acceptance of a "feminine" ethic of care. In fact, some feminist scholars have drawn a distinction between feminine and feminist approaches to legal studies by arguing that a "different voice" is not enough—a feminist consciousness is required (see MacKinnon's comments in "Feminist Discourse" 1985: 27), otherwise, there is a risk of essentializing women so that we expect that by mere inclusion of a woman (like the appointing of Justice Sandra Day O'Connor to the U.S. Supreme Court), we would expect her "different voice" to be a feminist voice (Behuniak-Long 1992). The radical potential for change comes, therefore, not from the feminine voice speaking "in a higher register" (MacKinnon 1987: 39), but from infusing these voices with feminist values.

Two distinctive elements of feminist jurisprudence inform my effort to create a caring jurisprudence. First, I begin with the understanding that law is not neutral terrain. Indeed, its epistemology, practice, and ideology are conservative in that they support the status quo and disadvantage those who would change it. Janet Rifkin summarizes this well:

> The power of law is that by framing the issues as questions of law, claims of right, precedents and problems of constitutional interpretation, the effect is to divert potential public consciousness from an awareness of the deeper roots of the expressed dissatisfaction and anger. The ideology of law serves to mask the real social and political questions underlying these problem of law. (1980: 87)

Rifkin's insistence that the male power paradigm of law be challenged is applicable to the abortion and PAS cases as well. Rather than assume that the process that created these decisions are neutral ones, feminist jurisprudence encourages skepticism of, if not outright cynicism toward, the cultural and political forces that shape the law.

Second, I adopt the goal of feminist legal studies that theoretical challenges to mainstream law will eventually lead to practical changes. The lesson of feminist legal critiques has been that legal norms are not in fact immutable. We have already witnessed examples of how feminist inquiries can alter legal practices. This is particularly evident in how feminist analyses have resulted in changes in how the law:

defines, prosecutes, and punishes the crime of rape; the meaning of and assumptions behind the "reasonable man" standard, the measurement of "equality," and the notion of "consent." Again, the lesson is that conceptual changes lead to practical changes. Such transformative work has already begun in the area of constitutional law—a field seemingly immune to change because it relies so heavily on static knowledge such as text, history, and Founder's intent. Yet, feminist legal scholars have created openings within which to work. Questioning how rights are defined, how text is interpreted, how knowledge is used, and how politics shapes law has opened the way for even the practice of constitutional law to change (see Law 1984; Binion 1991; Baer 1992; Becker 1992; Nedelsky 1993).

In summary, feminist scholarship on the ethic of justice and the ethic of care has opened many possibilities in the name of change. I apply and build on much of this analysis in creating below a model for changing how the Court addresses patients' knowledge. In particular, I employ a feminist methodology that is built on the following principles: (1) begin with personal experiences and use these to question abstract knowledge; (2) challenge the validity of dichotomies; (3) analyze the politics that support an ethic of justice over an ethic of care, i.e., who and what is served by the law's focus on competing rights, universal rules, impartiality, and reasoning; and (4) explore the possibilities for change by shifting the axis of law away from justice and toward care in order to integrate them. Again, my central concern is what such an approach can mean for patients. Can legal norms be reformed so that patients' knowledge is integrated within the Court's decision making process? Feminist scholarship and methodology tell us that the answer is yes.

A MODEL FOR A CARING JURISPRUDENCE

In constructing my model for a caring jurisprudence, I am inspired by the words and sentiments of several feminists who appeal to the use of imagination and creative license. Catharine MacKinnon reminds us that we must "remember where we are going—and, in Monique Wittig's words, 'failing that, invent'" (1987: 348). Heather Ruth Wishik expands on this thought by stating, "since we have never experienced any reality but patriarchy, to remember where we are going is necessarily an act of invention" (1986: 72). When confronted with doctrinal traps in the law, Judith Baer urges us to "employ the mind's intuitive and imaginative faculties" (1992: 165).

What follows, then, is an imagining. What if law incorporated justice and care? What would such a caring jurisprudence look like and how would it change the way the Court treats the knowledge of patients? My usage of the term "jurisprudence" is not meant to indicate the development of a concrete theory of principles by which law is measured, but a way of approaching law so as to engage in an analysis. Here, the analysis is decidedly feminist, and the concern is clearly that the knowledge of patients be integrated in the biomedical cases that involve them. Therefore, in developing a caring jurisprudence I do not offer a "grand" theory of law (indeed, most feminists would say such an effort emulates patriarchal rather than feminist aspirations), but an attempt to incorporate patients' knowledge in law through a jurisprudence as caring as it is just. I leave to others the question of whether and how such an approach could inform or apply to other areas of law.

An Integrationist Approach

How then to reconcile the ethics of justice and of care? There are several possibilities: one is to subordinate one ethic to the other (see Noddings 1984; Okin 1989; Ruddick 1989, 1995); another is to blend the two perspectives to create a new unified theory (see Gilligan 1982: 174; Brabeck 1993: 48; Baier 1995: 57); and finally, a third approach, the one most consistent with my goal of fusing patients' knowledge to legal reasoning, is to integrate the two ethics. As Jaggar notes:

> Most proponents of the ethics of care now dispute the possibility of any easy synthesis of care with justice. . . . Rather than seeking to include care and justice in a unified account of moral reasoning, most contemporary advocates of an ethics of care are committed to exploring care's strength as an independent style or practice or moral thinking. . . . In this view, care and justice both involve distinctive ontological, epistemological, and practical commitments, though this is not to deny that the concepts, themes, and priorities associated with both orientations are often loosely defined, permitting considerable disagreement between them. (1995: 187)

Another scholar who resists the impulse of reconciling the two ethics through a blending process is Grace Clemont. She argues that most attempts to assimilate care into justice result in the subordination of care to justice, reinforcing cultural norms whereby "that which is coded as masculine is regarded as more important than that which is coded as feminine" (1996: 5). Instead, she argues in favor of preserving the distinctiveness of the ethic of justice and the ethic of care as strengths that can then be used to check each other.

What, then, would such an integration of justice and care look like? To visualize the possibility, begin by imagining a weaving loom on which a tapestry will be made:

> *Weaving* is the interlacing of two sets of threads to form a fabric. The yarn or threads that are wound on the loom before weaving begins are called the *warp*. The warp forms the foundation of the tapestry; to make a smooth, even fabric, the warp must be threaded on the loom at even *tension*, or tightness. One of our main structural objectives in tapestry is to control the tension of both warp and weft to achieve a flat, smooth woven piece with straight edges. . . . The thread that goes over and under across the warp is called the *weft*. (Harvey 1991: 12)

The art of weaving is instructive in several ways for the art of law. First, weaving can only be accomplished by having two distinct threads that play different but connected roles. As is true of the ethics of justice and care, the resulting tension between the threads is not due to their being pulled in opposite directions, but to their perpendicular placement. The point is that justice and care are distinctive, but they are not in fact dichotomous concepts posing an either/or dilemma. Second, a weaver must take care that a consistent tension be maintained by the counter-vailing threads, less the fabric become twisted. Likewise, overemphasis on either the ethic of justice or the ethic of care will contort the law. Third, the foundation thread of the warp, disappears from view as the weaving progresses, but it remains the essential component on which the fabric is constructed. That we do not in fact "see" it, does not mean that it is not there. The ethic of care serves in a similar vein as the warp in the fabric of law. While the legal system appears to be defined by justice alone, there exists even now an interdependency between justice and care, though it is mostly hidden from view. Similarly, Katharine Bartlett argues that legal reasoning actually combines techniques usually associated with either the justice or care ethics: "This process unfolds, not in a linear, sequential, or strictly logical manner, but rather in a pragmatic and interactive manner. Facts determine which rules are appropriate, and rules determine which facts are relevant" (Bartlett 1990: 836). The weaving metaphor, then, invites us to look below the surface and to examine what forces are assumed in the structure of law.

Keeping these observations in mind, I argue that the tensions between the ethic of justice and the ethic of care can be addressed through the adoption of an integrationist approach. This approach accepts the fact that the two ethics are different though not dichotomous and that the tension between them calls for balance. It also suggests that the ethic of care is not absent from the foundational understandings of the obligations of the judicial system, but it does need to be revitalized through recognition of the role it plays in supporting the structure of law. Through integrating justice and care, law can be seen to be living rather than static, malleable not immutable, and humanistic not scientific.

Robin West, a relational feminist legal scholar, incorporates all these elements in her book, *Caring for Justice*. Her eloquent rendering of the relationship between the two ethics is powerful not only in its persuasiveness and use of poetic imagery, but also because it identifies the ways in which justice and caring are distinct but intimately connected. West responds to the visual descriptions of justice suggested by William Byron, S.J. in *Quadrangle Considerations* (1989). In attempting to elucidate the components of justice, Byron uses three images: (1) the plumb-line that connotes a sense of being on the level, fair and square, of uprightness and integrity; (2) cupped hands that symbolize the need to consistently hold and protect the internalized waters of justice; and (3) the trays of the balancing scale, usually held by a blindfolded figure, representing the impartiality of the law. According to Byron, then, justice requires integrity, consistency, and impartiality in order to be just. With these three components of justice in mind, West offers three corresponding images of care: (1) the protective "O" shape of a maternal embrace symbolizing an interdependent circle of care; (2) the free-flowing compassion symbolized by the extension of an outreached hand and the flowing water of tears; and (3) the focused, intent, loving gaze. According to West, then, caring requires nurturance, compassion, and commitment. Seemingly, these qualities of justice and care appear to be oppositional: integrity vs. nurturance, consistency vs. compassion, and impartiality vs. commitment. However, West argues "against the continuation of the traditional segregation of these two virtues" (36) and in favor of their integration. She contends that "justice must be caring if it is to be just, and that caring must be just if it is to be caring" (24). As an example of how these two ethics can work together within a case, she offers the example of *Brown v. Board of Education* (1954), the landmark case that ended the use of the "separate but equal" doctrine in public schools. While recognizing that the case has been criticized as an unprincipled reach into policy making, she argues that *Brown's* greatness was due to its demand "that we attend to the pain and hurt caused by societal racial relationships, and by so doing it brought into being not only a new understanding of the equal protection guaranteed by the constitution, but a new understanding of racial justice" (93).

West's approach can also be applied to the cases of abortion and PAS—two legal issues that demonstrate the interconnectedness of justice and care. What I want to argue here is two points. First, that the lack of caring in these decisions (already discussed in chapters 2 and 3) is in itself a serious judicial failing. And second, that this lack of attention to the ethic of care also cause these decisions to be unjust.[6]

The abortion and PAS decisions were uncaring in that they did not seriously address the injuries that the patients petitioned the Court to relieve. While it may be tempting to dismiss this concern as irrelevant to judicial decision making because it is result-oriented, I want to argue that the ethic of care is already assumed to be an obligation of the legal system although most times this fact is ignored by legal practitioners. John Broughton reminds us that justice is a public form of caring: "while justice requires abstraction, it is intended as the abstract form that caring takes when respect is maintained and responsibility assumed for people whom one does not know personally and may never come to know" (1993: 123). I use this quote not to argue that justice and caring are at root the same, but as a reminder that among the goals of the judicial system are the care of human beings and the righting of wrongs. Severing care from legal deliberations places both of these goals in jeopardy. A vision of judicial decision making devoid of particulars, compassion, and commitment is a threatening, mechanical, and even sinister image. It seems to require a blind respect for law in that it equates justice with the following of rules while exempting the rules from moral scrutiny (see Lyons

1993). If justice directs process alone, then care is needed as a way to assess what the system has produced. To this end, the ethic of care that is assumed in the very foundation of the judicial system needs to be invigorated so it can play a role along side the ethic of justice.

Therefore, my argument is not that the ethic of care be *added* to judicial decision making but that its role be *heightened*. To draw again on Robin West, it is precisely because of the different orientations of the ethics of justice and care that they can temper each other. Within this context, caring is not limited to serving as a private ethic used by patients as they make their medical choices—caring can also serve as a public ethic that can temper, check, and ultimately guide the administration of justice. By recognizing the integral role that the ethic of care plays in supporting the moral authority of the judicial system, it can be deliberately used to promote justice.

This leads to my second point, that the abortion and PAS decisions were unjust. True, the Court followed procedural requirements and strove for objectivity, reasoning, and universality, but these are hardly the only requirements of justice (see Lebacqz 1986). In particular, the Court's decisions failed to achieve justice on three other levels. First, they were dismissive of the "truth" contained in patients' knowledge. In the abortion cases, the pregnant women, their voices barely audible in the Court documents, had poignant stories to tell about how unwanted pregnancies dramatically affected their lives. There were concrete details to be known. In the PAS cases, the terminally ill, competent adults also had harrowing stories to tell of pain, suffering, and the importance of preserving meaning as they lived out their final days. Dismissing as absurd the claim to a "right to die," a majority of the Court disregarded the realities of the patients. Testimony that they were suffering and in pain despite medical treatment was disregarded by a Court that focused instead on whether such pain could hypothetically be controlled. While an argument can be made that justice should remain blind to certain things, the truth of each situation should not be one of them.

Second, the Court failed to focus on the injuries alleged. Certainly at minimum justice requires that the specific complaint of the litigants bringing the case be the focus of the deliberations and that the Court respond directly to this complaint. Instead, in both the abortion and PAS cases, the complaints of the litigants were reshaped under legal norms so that the needs of others became the focus, patients' knowledge was dismissed, and their petition for help left unanswered. In fact, by the time the decisions were rendered, the patients and their interests seemed to have entirely disappeared from the cases. Yet, the Justices did not reject specificity per se, but instead selectively expanded their view to include physicians and their medical concerns while declining to consider the social and political factors that contextualized the nature of the injuries alleged by the patients. In both sets of cases, then, the patients' charges were not so much heard on their merits as they were used to advance the interests of others—a quality seemingly at odds with justice.

Third, in abandoning the patients involved in these controversies, the Court also abandoned justice. In the Court's decisions in the cases following *Roe*, they ensconced legalized abortion in an abstract "right to privacy" and thereby isolated the patients, leaving some without the resources or the protection to access this procedure. In the PAS cases, the Court rejected the "right to die" and expressed the hope that further democratic debate as well as future changes in the delivery of medical care would one day respond to patients' needs. But these forsakings invite sad consequences. Summarized by an unlikely source (a promotional trailer for the movie *The Mask of Zorro*), the possibility is that "in a land where . . . justice is outlawed, the just must become outlaws." While this is a dramatic statement intended to explain the outlaw status of a fictionalized hero, it serves as an apt description for some who have felt abandoned by the Court concerning abortion or PAS. In the wake of the Court's failure to respond to the needs of pregnant women, some patients sought illegal abortions, lied to obtain them, or moved across state lines. When the Court ignored the plight of terminally ill competent adults seeking PAS, some turn to a Kevorkian, or shoot themselves, or stockpile medications, take an overdose, and ensure their demise by tying a plastic bag around their head. So it is that the hanger and the plastic bag stand as symbols of those who react to perceived judicial injustices by defying the law. These patients seem to understand that law must be both just and caring if it is to be either of these.

The Model

The goal, then, is to develop a jurisprudence that integrates the ethics of justice and care. My model begins with the understanding that at present the ethic of justice dominates law. In order, then, to integrate the ethic of care within the law, it is first necessary to identify the ways in which the ethic of justice has affected the process of judicial decision making. The most obvious and most widely recognized impact is in how the ethic of justice dictates how the Court regards, weighs, and utilizes the knowledge brought before it. Since the ethic of justice seems to demand that knowledge be universal, impartial, and reasoned, that which is particular, involved, and emotional knowledge is disregarded. Indeed, this contrast between the ethics of justice and care constitutes much of the focus of feminist scholarship critical of the law, and it must therefore be included in any model intended to counter justice with care. But the domination of the ethic of justice over the ethic of care shapes two other areas of legal practice at the Court that must be addressed as well. First, from the very beginning when the case enters the Court, the ethic of justice shapes how the Justices understand the case. That is, justice demands that the case be understood as presenting an *issue* to be resolved, and so, the focus turns to the process of how to resolve the conflict. In contrast an ethic of care would insist that the Justices understand the case as presenting first and foremost *people* in distress, and so, before the case begins, the Court must learn about those persons involved. The contrast, then, is quite clear in that while justice highlights the theoretical "federal issue" of the case, care reminds the Justices that at the heart of the case are particular people. So as justice abstracts the meaning of the case, care particularizes its meaning. Second, domination by the ethic of justice also influences how the Court translates the conflict into a specific legal question. Here, the ethic of justice confines the issue to one of rights—thereby stressing the constitutional meanings of the case. In contrast, care would insist on widening the Court's view to include the cultural context of the issue—thereby emphasizing the case's political meanings.

Therefore, in seeking to invigorate the ethic of care within the areas that the ethic of justice currently dominates, three points in the Court's decision making process must be addressed: the "micro level" analysis of the case by which the Court determines the circumstantial facts of the case; the "macro level" analysis of the case by which the Court places the case within a larger context in order to identify the legal issue(s) it presents;[7] and the consideration, assessment, and application of knowledge to form a decision about the case.

The Micro Level: Begin with the Patients. Right from the start of the case, the ethic of justice and the ethic of care pull the Court in different directions and ask the Court to adopt different perspectives from which to view the case. Justice insists that the Court focus on the facts of the case that include what happened to ignite the controversy, what the lower courts have done so far, and the textual bases for the litigation. In short, justice urges the Court to step back from the specifics of the case in order to survey the legal landscape to discover where this new case will fit in. In contrast, the ethic of care invites the Justices to come closer, to focus on the specifics of the case and to learn about the people involved—their experiences, needs, and lives. Seemingly, then, justice and care are at odds in guiding the Court as to how their introduction to the case should begin.

However, I contend that while these perspectives are certainly quite different, they are neither opposites nor mutually exclusive. In fact, they are interrelated in that concrete knowledge of the case can and should serve as the foundation for the legal abstractions. Since justice also demands that the Court distinguish among like and unlike cases, the Justices need to know as much about the facts as possible so that there is a sound basis for them to apply deductive reasoning. Therefore, in order for the Court to act justly, they must start by caring. A full accounting of what has transpired in these litigants' lives is necessary if the Court is to accurately assess which precedents, texts, and legal rules apply. And the source for this knowledge must be the litigants themselves.

In this sense, the ethic of care is not oppositional to justice. Caring also demands that litigants' needs, experiences, and information be at the heart of the decision

making process. As Joan Tronto puts it, "there is no simple way one can general-
ize from one's own experience to what another needs" (1995: 105). The only way
to know is through "knowledge that comes from others" (ibid.). This is especially
true since how we experience and view the world is dependent on socially significant characteristics that create differences among us (see Minow 1990). This
orientation toward appreciating others as knowers may originate within the ethic
of care, but it is not contrary to legal practices guided by justice—rather it is essential to its administration.

This integration of justice and care would have an effect on how the Court approaches cases like those presented by the abortion and PAS issues. To begin with
patients' knowledge mitigates against the privileging of medical knowledge over
that of patients. This is not to argue that medical (and other forms of) knowledge
should not be considered in these biomedical cases, but that patients' knowledge
should serve as the *starting point*. Disregarding medical knowledge would be a great
disservice to patients and practitioners alike, but the present state of affairs is that
patients' knowledge is dismissed in exactly that way. To recognize and use the
knowledge of patients is not to argue that it should replace other forms of knowledge but that it should be seriously considered by the Court during its weighing
of information. Indeed, these cases do not ask the Court to rely exclusively on either medical knowledge or patients' knowledge—but that the Court evaluate all
sorts of relevant knowledge (e.g., political, psychological, economic, ethical) in
coming to fully understand the facts of the case before it.

Therefore, the question of how to begin consideration of a case is crucial to the
outcome of the case. The beginning point must be patients. These cases are, after
all, about them. From this perspective, their knowledge is not contrary to legal
knowledge—it is its building blocks. When biomedical cases like abortion and PAS
enter the Court, the Justices should focus on the patients as the starting point for
the case and use them as a compass for staying on course as they move through
the case. The needle should consistently point in the direction of the patients, focusing on the question of what will happen to them. Both justice and care demand it.

The Macro Level: Add the Political Meanings. Depending on whether the ethic of
justice or the ethic of care is followed, the Court will translate the problem presented in a case into a legal issue emphasizing either constitutional or political
meanings. Under an ethic of justice, the Court hears litigants' concerns as claims
for constitutional rights. Thus it is that in *Roe*, women's requests for access to legal
abortion were framed in terms of a right to privacy. It also explains why the requests of terminally ill, competent adult patients for medical relief for their suffering were framed in *Glucksberg* as a claim to a right to suicide and in *Quill* as a claim
to a right to equal protection. Yet, in narrowing the issues to fit the language of
rights the constitutional meanings of the case are enhanced while its political

meanings are diminished, and sometimes even lost.[8] Following the feminist slogan that "the personal is political," I am using the phrase "political meanings" to refer to the cultural forces that intersect and interact to shape the issue. While the ethic of justice compels the Court to articulate case issues in terms of constitutional rights, the ethic of care would view this as an abridged version of the issue that can only be fleshed out by studying the problem as it is shaped by the culture.

The difference in orientation is quite dramatic. When a litigant claims that a right has been violated, that litigant is claiming a personal injury. Reliance on the ethic of justice alone averts the Court's gaze from the nature and extent of the injury claimed, to the question of the exact constitutional basis of the right asserted. This analysis is particularly intense when the right claimed lacks a firm textual basis, and such cases can be dismissed without ever seriously considering the nature of the harm. When the case is viewed instead from the perspective of an ethic of care, the alleged injury suffered by the litigant becomes the focus. Rather than focus on text and Founders' intent alone, the inquiry includes an examination as to how the litigant has been harmed and what can be done to alleviate it. Particular attention can be paid to the dynamics of oppression, especially when litigants claim a denial of rights that are not clearly contained within the language of the Constitution. In shifting from rights to injury, the focus is not on autonomous rights-bearing individuals but on the cultural forces that have contributed to the injury. The litigants are therefore no longer seen as separated from others, but as intimately connected to others by personal as well as social bonds. In this, the inclusion of the ethic of care offers the Court a richer sense of the injury alleged and perhaps a more relevant response to it as well.

This is evident in both the abortion and PAS cases. In focusing on the privacy right in the abortion cases, the Court sent the clear message that a woman's unwanted pregnancy is *her* personal problem and that the larger cultural context of the issue is irrelevant. Thus, the questions of how to afford the procedure, how to overcome the logistical problems (e.g., involving travel and housing) caused by the waiting period requirement, how to obtain parental consent or a judicial order, or how to deal with protesters outside the clinic are rendered personal problems left to her to resolve rather than social issues that need addressing. Therefore, the question of how a lack of access to abortion is connected to women's oppression is overlooked. When abortion is seen as a private matter, the response is private solutions. Left untouched are the roles that patriarchy, economics, religion, family, and cultural forces play in a woman's decision of whether to procure an abortion.

Likewise in *Glucksberg,* the Court's focus on the constitutional meaning of PAS—whether patients have a right to PAS—led the Court to ignore the cultural context that shaped patients' desire for PAS. Yet, the party briefs and many of the *amicus* briefs offered testimony as to how the decision to die is affected by medical practices, spiritual needs, social pressures, familial concerns, and economic policies. The advent of HMOs, the limitations imposed by health care insurance providers, and a lack of universal health care all figured in the dilemma of how to die. So too did patients' desires to define themselves by how they died; the social stigma of aging, illness, and dependency; and the desire not to financially burden loved ones. The Court's ruling, therefore, neither recognized the extent of the injury claimed by patients who sought and were denied PAS nor responded to it. Thus it was that by failing to offer a macro analysis of PAS, the Court appeared to be uncaring.

Therefore, drawing on care contributes to the analysis and the framing of the case. It is no longer enough to explore the meaning of rights, but now the nature of injuries must be examined as well. The constitutional meanings of the case are studied, but so too are its cultural contours. Analysis and understanding are enhanced. Individual circumstances can now be assessed within a comparative framework, and common cultural forces can be identified. In that this macro contextual analysis is more descriptive of the issues at hand, it should also lead to decisions more responsive to patients' needs. Otherwise, patients who ask for "care" may instead receive "justice" in the form of individual rights.

Draw on Knowledge from Justice and Care. Probably the best-known feature of an ethic of justice is how it directs the Court to value knowledge that is universal, impartial, and reasoned over that which is particular, involved, and emotional. Again, I am arguing that these tensions can be used to advantage by having them serve as checks on one another. Yet, the domination of justice over care in forming knowledge is so ingrained that it may be difficult for jurists to see the value of knowledge that is formed under an ethic of care. Therefore, it might be helpful for the Court to become more cognizant of how they already employ particular, involved, and emotional knowledge—and how such inclusion should be more deliberately and effectively extended to the knowledge offered by others.

Universals vs. Particulars. The question of whether the rule applied really fits the case is hardly contrary to legal norms since it is the very stuff of legal reasoning. Justices rely on the particulars of the case to suggest the use of principles or precedents, to challenge the applicability of others, and to test the universality of principles. The law's mandate that similar cases be treated alike and different cases be treated differently, also demands that particulars be scrutinized. Focus on the particulars, then, is not alien to judicial decision making, but an integral part of it.

Therefore, the Justices should bring this same appreciation of the particulars to bear on the knowledge brought before them. Knowledge that claims universality should be checked with knowledge stemming from the particular. Anecdotal evidence and personal stories can prevent the Justices from assuming universality where there is none. For example, in the abortion cases patients' stories told how class differences significantly affect what constitutes an "undue burden" on the abortion right, while in the PAS cases, the stories of patients' personal experiences contradicted much of the expert testimony of the medical organizations. Therefore, in trying to discover the "truth," the Court needs to test the universal claims with particularized knowledge.

Impartiality vs. Involvement. While impartiality is mandated by the ethic of justice, it does not require that Justices be detached from the litigants. While jurists must be fair and neutral in order to avoid either favoritism or discrimination, they should also recognize that they are in fact involved (see West 1997). The Justices have entered into a relationship with the litigants—they have been asked to care for them in a very public way. I am not suggesting that Justices personally meet with each and every litigant to get to know them and to develop relational bonds with them, but instead that they try to understand their perspective in evaluating their case and recognize that their obligations to the litigants places them in a relationship with them. Unbiased, therefore, need not mean detached, nor uncaring. In *Poetic Justice*, Martha Nussbaum (1995) adopts the figure of the "judicious spectator" (so named by the economist Adam Smith) to signify that while judges are not themselves parties to a case, they do view it, and to really understand it, they must employ the power of imagining what it is to be the litigant. Guided by both "empathetic participation" as well as "external assessment," the judge determines "the degree of compassion it is rational to have for the person" (ibid., 73). While this can be a helpful approach, imagining and empathy have limits, especially since differences in life experiences are linked to characteristics like race/ethnicity, class, and sexual orientation (see Harris 1991). Instead, Justices must first listen to the stories that litigants have to tell about themselves (see Delgado 1989).

If the Justices can recognize the value of their own involvement in a case as a source of knowledge, this may also help them appreciate the knowledge that others can bring based on their personal experiences. For example, in the PAS cases, one of the most personal *amicus* briefs filed was by Surviving Family Members. This document spoke of what it was like to have a family member suffer on and on before finally succumbing to a terminal disease. Similarly, the abortion case of *Thornburgh v. American College of Obstetricians and Gynecologists* (1986) included a brief filed by the National Abortion Rights Action League et al. that contained firsthand accounts of what it is like to choose between an illegal abortion and continuing an unwanted pregnancy. While the ethic of justice would demand that the Court disregard these stories, the "judicious spectator" would try to imagine what this situation must be like and draw on this information—not as the sole knowledge in making a determination, but as a part of the knowledge to be weighed. In this, impartiality is checked by involvement.

Reason vs. Emotion. Legal reasoning is a benchmark of law, but this does not mean that emotional knowledge should be excluded from judicial consideration. In fact, emotional knowledge is used by the Court precisely because it has something to tell (see Baer 1992). Emotional knowledge can tell the Court when the system has utterly failed: take for instance Justice Blackmun's lament of "Poor Joshua!" in *DeShaney v. Winnebago County Dept. of Social Services* (1989), a case in which the Court left no state actor responsible for the brain damage suffered by an abused child. Emotional knowledge can ensure that the Justices really face exactly what they are ordering, one example being Justice Brennan's ever-present reminder in the death penalty cases of the moral significance of allowing the state to take a human life (see *Furman vs. GA* 1972; *Gregg v. GA* 1976; *McCleskey v. Kemp* 1987). Emotional knowledge can speak the truth in a way objective terms cannot; recall Justice Marshall's sad rendering of the legacy of slavery in his separate opinion in the affirmative action case of *Regents of the University of California v. Bakke* (1978). While I do not argue in favor of having the Justices decide cases based on their gut feelings or emotional responses to issues without reference to other considerations, neither do I want the Justices ignoring their gut, their intuition, or their emotional reaction to a case—especially when it contradicts the "logical" outcome of a case.

Neither should they exclude the emotional knowledge of others. In fact, Alison Jaggar argues that the emotional knowledge of subordinated people should be weighed quite heavily:

> The perspective on reality that is available from the standpoint of the subordinated . . . is a perspective that offers a less partial and distorted and therefore more reliable view. Subordinated people have a kind of epistemological privilege in so far as they have easier access to this standpoint and therefore a better chance of ascertaining the possible beginnings of a society in which all could thrive. For this reason, I would claim that the emotional responses of subordinated people in general . . . are more likely to be appropriate than the emotional responses of the dominant class. (1997: 192)

Therefore, patients, as members of a subordinated group, are an important resource of emotional knowledge that the Court should value. The women patients in the abortion cases since *Roe* have emphasized again and again how the right to privacy does not adequately respond to their needs. Similarly in the PAS cases, the dying patients implored the Court to help them. That the Court's decisions left these pleas unanswered should stir something in not only the Justices but the rest of us. This feeling—whether of sadness, regret, or helplessness—can be instructive as we try to assess what has gone wrong and what should be done next. Law is, after all, a humanistic endeavor, not a social science (see Menkel-Meadow 1996: 75). Such emotional knowledge suggests that a test of legal decisions is not only how well the process stands up to standards of logic, but also how seriously the result addresses the needs of the litigants. In this, reason can be tempered by emotion.

CONCLUSION

As a whole, this model challenges the privileging of knowledge, returns to the oppressed their voice, and heightens not only care but justice. Far from resulting in unprincipled decision making, a caring jurisprudence would insist on the consideration of principles: What is the meaning and mandate of justice? What is the meaning and mandate of care? This is to the good. Without the constant tug of care, justice can lose its moral force. In its starkest form, legal justice has been reduced to the following of procedural guidelines and an obsession with maintaining objectivity. Yet, this seems to be a constricted view of justice. If justice is confined to the application of rules, how can unjust rules be challenged? If justice means neutrality, where is the commitment to right things that have gone wrong? At root, these questions ask us to consider the practical consequences of the ethic of justice. Martha Minow puts it well: "What does a perfect theory of justice matter if it operates miles above human experience?" (1997: 5). If the following of procedures and the stance of objectivity result in grave injustices, such as, the turning away of knowledge, the failure to recognize wrongs, and the willingness to allow injuries to continue, then legal justice as a principle seems to be a rather hollow one indeed. Therefore, the heightening of the ethic of care, rather than undermining justice, prods us to consider justice in its richest sense and in terms most connected with human experiences.

A good example of the model's transformative potential as well as its practicality is the concurring opinions of Justice Stevens in the *Glucksberg* and *Quill* cases. While I am not arguing that Stevens consciously utilized this model, his opinion tests the waters in that he found a way to incorporate patients' knowledge in the law by departing from the constraints of the ethic of justice. In evaluating the cases and weighing the evidence, Stevens seemed to employ elements similar to those of a caring jurisprudence: he began and ended the cases with the patients; he framed the issues so as to explore not only the constitutional meanings but the political meanings as well; and he drew on knowledge that was particular, involved, and emotional. That this orientation did not change the outcomes of the cases (indeed, he voted with the majority to uphold the state bans) was due to his judgment that the litigants failed to meet the requirements involved in posing facial challenges to the state laws. Yet, regardless of his votes, Stevens's opinion is distinctive in that it speaks to patients, their experiences, and their lives. It clearly tells them that while not voting in their favor, he heard them and considered their knowledge. In this, the opinion was striking in that it embraced both justice and care, thereby demonstrating that the integration of patients' knowledge within the law is not and should not be foreign to the Court.

My goal has been to argue that patients' knowledge should be seriously considered by the Court in cases like abortion and PAS because without it, the Court is in danger of acting unjustly as well as uncaringly. What I have hoped to show with this model for a caring jurisprudence is that by integrating the ethics of justice and care, patients' knowledge becomes an integral part of the Court's deliberations. The three components of the model—that the inquiry begin with the patients' knowledge, that the issue be framed with attention to both the constitutional and political meanings, and that knowledge be evaluated by drawing on both the ethics of justice and of care—all rely to some extent on the knowledge of patients. This approach may not be the only way for such knowledge to be heard, but it is a model that takes seriously the contributions of the ethic of justice to the law even as it strives to heighten the influence of the ethic of care. In this, the model does not replace justice with care, reason with emotion, universality with particularity, or impartiality with involvement. Instead, these contending forces are integrated to ensure that all elements of knowledge are heard, considered, and evaluated.

What is left to show in the following chapter, then, is three things: first, to illustrate how the model can be applied within legal practice by revisiting the abortion and PAS cases; second, to demonstrate how patients' accounts contribute to judicial decision making; and third, to make evident the models' moderate nature and to briefly respond to potential objections. Therefore, the final chapter is one of application. It calls on both Lady Justice and the Angel of Mercy to revisit the abortion and PAS cases. In this, it sets out to explore how law is transformed "when mercy seasons justice."

• 5 •

Listening to Patients:
The Abortion and Physician-Assisted
Suicide Cases Revisited

Forty minutes into the procedure the surgeon said, "If you can't handle this, tell us and we'll stop." I have to lie, I realized. They have to get that node. I knew this was a critical moment on my journey: whether I had the courage to endure it could determine whether I would live or die. A week's delay in treatment could tip the scales. "I'm okay," I called out weakly. "Just get this thing." As I strained to think of a way to get through it, the song "Amazing Grace" came into my head. I began to sing it in a soft, barely audible whisper, embarrassed lest the nurses hear. *Through many dangers, toils, and snares, I have already come. . . .* I heard the surgeon say quietly: "That's the tumor." *How precious did that grace appear the hour I first believed.*

Gale Warner, *Dancing at the Edge of Life*

*C*ataclysmic change and redemption are among the themes so poignantly captured in the lyrics of the hymn "Amazing Grace." They weave in and out of stanzas that speak of transformation, acceptance, the calming of fears, freedom, faith, and ultimately peace. The song enjoys an enormously wide appeal that seems to derive from the solace it offers to those in crisis—a spiritual message that is never forgotten. Written in the latter half of the 1700s by John Newton, a onetime slave trader turned Christian minister, the lyrics are a testament to the power of human beings to experience adversities in their lives and not only face them, but emerge with newfound knowledge—and perhaps, with grace as well.

Cataclysmic change and redemption are the same twin themes that I found in collecting, reading, and listening to the accounts of patients who have experienced an unwanted pregnancy or a terminal illness. While these are both dramatic events, patients' narratives indicate that they view these occurrences as something more— as seismic upheavals in the terrain of their lives after which nothing is ever again quite the same. The poet and journalist Gale Warner recorded such a moment in her memoir, a work that chronicles the last months of her life:

> I could see the difference on the chest X ray, the vague shadows leaning to the left. Bigger. But the gallium scan was the most dramatic. Four dark round spots in my chest, arranged in a little ring. Hot spots. Like Watts—like the West Bank. Rapidly dividing cells of destruction. And it was just at this moment when the full realization hit me somewhere in the belly. The universe shifted. We are not where we were fifteen minutes before. (1998: 62)

Indeed, patients' accounts stress that one does not have an *experience* of being a patient, but rather that one *becomes* a patient, and that such a becoming causes a shift not only in the world but within oneself.

Yet, patients speak not only of the sense of being caught in the jaws of this new universe, but of transforming it as well. In this, the crises presented by an unwanted pregnancy or by a terminal illness inspire more complex responses than may at first be assumed. While neither condition is a path willingly chosen, once the journey begins many patients claim the experiences as opportunities for discovery. While not all patients or their loved ones can find light in such moments of darkness, there are many accounts of people who find a kind of redemption even as they face a crisis. Amid the suffering they find peace; amid the sorrow they experience joy; amid the loss of life they discover meaning; and amid tragedy they embrace growth. This is not to say that the events "turned out for the best" or were not as tragic as they had at first seemed, but that many patients and their loved ones find a way to cope or to do the best that they can given their circumstances. Again, it is Gale Warner who tells of what it is like to experience such grace when fighting a deadly cancer:

> Under the dark sky last night, I danced with my reflection in the hospital window. So beautiful, the curve of the arm, the slow flowing power of the body. So beautiful, my shaved-short hair which gives me the face of a nun, stripped down to the single flame of pure devotion. The power of pure service, pure love, infusing my body with a new grace. This is my body, my vessel. This is my path. I am here! I have taken the leap and landed. . . . I have crossed a chasm, and I am going on.
>
> My soul was asked, on its deep travels through caves and labyrinths of the body, "Are you ready to be braver and stronger?" Deep in the body, deep in the dead seas of the tumor, my spirit said, "Yes." (1998: 64–65)

Patients, then, have stories to tell: disasters strike; the universe shifts; yet, some find grace. This language of change and redemption constitutes a perspective that sounds quite foreign to most medical and legal discussions of abortion and physician-assisted suicide (PAS). Physical conditions and appropriate treatments, legal precedents and the recognition of rights, these are the concepts that dominate the medical–legal discourse. The different perspective that patients offer, however, is not so much due to the language that they use but to the knowledge that they find within the experience of becoming a patient. Patients create knowledge by negotiating the waves of crises that rose up and seized them. While physicians, attorneys, and judges may brave these troubled waters to offer rescue, the success of the venture is primarily dependent on understanding that from which patients need saving—and this may differ from patient to patient. While experts may focus on wrenching these patients from the cataclysmic events that engulf them, patients may desire help in quite a different form—in a way that only they can tell.

This chapter, then, is about listening. What do patients have to tell us about abortion and PAS? How can their knowledge contribute to the legal deliberations and decisions of the U.S. Supreme Court? In order to highlight patients' voices, I apply the model of a "caring jurisprudence" that was developed in chapter 4 to the abortion and PAS cases that were discussed in chapters 2 and 3. The structure of this final chapter, then, follows the format of the model. First, I begin the examination of the abortion and PAS controversies by focusing the Court's attention on the micro level of analysis—i.e., the patients involved. What experiences have brought them to seek judicial resolution? Second, I frame the issues not only in terms of the constitutional meaning of the disputes, but also with an appreciation of the macro context of the issues, i.e., their "political" meanings. Third, employing both the ethic of justice and the ethic of care, I examine the knowledge of patients that is developed as they attempt to deal with their crises. In particular, I highlight where patients' knowledge contradicts or challenges the knowledge offered by medicine or assumed by the Court.

Since the model is intended to *integrate* and not blend the ethics of justice and care, the applications in this chapter explore these tensions by introducing the voices of patients. Therefore, it becomes absolutely necessary that patients be given an opportunity to "speak" of their experiences. While many of the Court documents claim to speak on their behalf or to construct a patients' perspective, I rely on firsthand accounts from the patients and their loved ones—the people who have experienced the crises created by unwanted pregnancies or terminal illnesses. I try as much as it is possible to have patients speak for themselves by quoting from legal and non-legal sources. From the legal sources, I rely most on the *amicus curiae* briefs that contain firsthand personal testimony. However, while these are rich sources of patients' knowledge, they are also limited in two ways. First, they are small in number, probably because such personal accounts have been discouraged as being at odds with the legal norms of objectivity, universalism, and reasoning. And second, they are limited in perspective, coming mostly from the pro-choice and pro-PAS sides of the cases which emphasized patients' knowledge in ways that the states on the other side did not. Therefore, I supplement these voices by drawing on some of the non-legal literature, coming from the pro and anti perspectives,[1] that is written by patients and their families. If a caring jurisprudence were to be employed by the Court, these are the types of outside resources that the Justices might draw on in assessing what patients know. Due to space considerations, I offer excerpts of patients' stories—a mere taste rather than a full course of patients' knowledge. In contrast, the Court could avail itself of these resources in their entirety.

It is through revisiting these cases that I hope to show that a caring jurisprudence contributes to judicial decision making. At the most obvious level, patients serve as new and important sources of knowledge, offering specific information and experiences concerning the issues. Yet, patients' knowledge would be an asset to the Court in at least two other ways. First, by refining the Court's sense of justice, and second by heightening its sensitivity to oppression. It is sometimes helpful to explore the meaning of the legal principle of justice by exploring the contours of injustice. Patients' personal stories of suffering are an important source of information on this nether side of justice. As Martha Minow explains,

> There is something about seeing and hearing violations of basic ideals enacted in life, with actual bodily and spiritual consequences, that alerts and refines the sense of injustice. Trials of injustice work best for me not merely as tests of general propositions but as tests for my own capacity to sense what is wrong and to push what must be changed. (1997: 5)

In addition, patients' knowledge reminds the Court of the human choices made—their suffering is not the result of misfortune alone, of fate or God's hand, but of human actions and decisions that regulate these issues (ibid.: 7). It is in speaking of what Minow calls the harms caused by "people's treatment of others" (ibid.) that patients' knowledge reminds the Court of its obligation to end oppression through judicial action.

While the purpose of this chapter is to illustrate a caring jurisprudence rather than to defend it, I hope that in the process of outlining its implementation that I will also answer some potential criticisms. While varied, most of these fall into two broad categories; namely that (1) the approach is not law but therapy, and that (2) it attacks rationally based knowledge while accepting the truth of personal stories. The first criticism (brought to my attention at a professional conference) argues that a caring jurisprudence is more like "Queen for a Day" jurisprudence in that patients seem to compete for a judicial ruling based on how pathetic they are or how sad their individual story is. However, what I believe the application will show instead is that not only do patients tell their stories with great dignity and with public rather than private concerns, but that the information can indeed be a valuable resource for the Court. The second criticism is that a caring jurisprudence radically reforms law by replacing reasoned knowledge with subjective, often atypical, storytelling (see Farber and Sherry 1997). Again, the applications below suggest otherwise since the model does not throw out the "objective," "universal," or "impartial" knowledge created by law or medicine, but challenges the claims implied by those labels by checking this knowledge with that of patients. In this, a caring jurisprudence offers a radical reshaping of judicial decision making in that it goes to the "root" of how knowledge is created and used, but it is moderate in its result in that it integrates knowledge derived from both the ethics of care and of justice.

With that said, then, it is time to listen. First to the patients involved in the abortion cases and then next to those experiencing life-threatening illnesses.

ABORTION REVISITED

The images of a turning point, a dividing line, or a chasm seem apt descriptions of the abortion issue on several levels—the personal, the societal, and the legal. For an individual woman, an unwanted pregnancy poses the challenge of what to do—and whether a woman continues the pregnancy through birth or ends it through abortion, a line has been crossed and there is no going back. Socially, abortion is an issue that has resulted in a breach that clearly separates those who support a woman's right to choose from those who support a fetal right to life; seemingly a divide that cannot be bridged.[2] Legally, *Roe v. Wade* (1973) also formed a chasm. As Anna Quindlen has noted, *Roe* constitutes a dividing line that marks the end of abortion as a crime and the beginning of abortion as a medical procedure—"the demarcation between one way of living and another" (Quindlen 1997: 5). Indeed, patients seem particularly attuned to this great shift in the law in that they cannot seem to speak of abortion without reference to what life was like before abortion was legalized and how it has changed since *Roe*. According to many patients, it is this history of lived experiences, and not the history of constitutional texts or the history of the American Medical Association's position on terminating pregnancies, that is central to the issue of whether abortion should be legal.

The Micro Level: Start with the Patients

While the proposition that the Court should begin its study of the abortion cases by focusing on the pregnant patients involved hardly seems a radical suggestion, it would in fact be a significant departure from how the Court has approached these cases. As described in chapter 2, the pattern that emerges from the Court's opinions is one in which the Justices consistently place physicians and their concerns at the center of the cases. In contrast, a caring jurisprudence would ask the Justices to begin these cases by remembering who the litigants in these cases are—women experiencing unwanted pregnancies.

While women have told their stories concerning their abortion experiences in Court documents as well as in books and articles intended for the general public, such speaking out is a relatively recent phenomenon. Both legal norms and cultural codes discouraged such public pronouncements of what it is to experience abortion—this being especially true in the days prior to *Roe* when abortion was still illegal. It is hardly surprising then that the early law cases were constructed without the inclusion of patients' stories. Nor is it surprising that although it is estimated that hundreds of thousands of women each year procured illegal abortions, many kept it a secret. Indeed, legal norms intersected with cultural norms to impose silence on those who would speak of something so shameful—perhaps even so evil—as the story of how they aborted their pregnancies.

Yet, the silence denied the Court as well as society the knowledge of those who had had abortions. Such storytelling by patients was not present in the legal documents presented in *Roe* or even in its progeny of the following decade (again, probably because such knowledge was not viewed as appropriate to file in Court documents given legal norms). But in 1986, the National Abortion Rights Action League (NARAL) adopted a strategy whereby the Court would come face to face with the women whose lives they affected. NARAL invited women who experienced abortions to send them letters that would then be compiled into an *amicus* brief to be filed with the Court (see "NARAL Amicus Brief" 1986). The "Abortion Rights: Silent No More" campaign resulted in what came to be known as the "voices brief" that was filed in *Thornburgh v. American College of Obstetricians and Gynecologists* (1986). As one scholar commented, the brief "paints a picture that gives the women not only bodies but jobs, families, schoolwork, health problems, youth, poverty, race/ethnic identity and dreams of a better life" (Petchesky 1986: 4). In summarizing the argument to be presented, the brief stated: "*Amici* submit this brief to place the realities of abortion in women's lives before this Court and to urge this Court to reaffirm *Roe v. Wade*" (1986: 12). NARAL submitted more of these letters as an *amicus* brief in *Webster v. Reproductive Health Services* (1989). The tone of these documents was different in kind than that assumed by the medical experts in their documents. Here was the personal speaking as knowledge:

> I am writing today to share my experience with abortion in the hope that it might, in some small way, help the Supreme Court understand why it is so important that abortion remain safe, legal and affordable. (Letter L-140, Brief for Women Who Have Had Abortions, *Webster*)

> This true story is written to those who have the power to deny women the right to a safe, legal abortion. (Letter L-296, *Webster*)

First I'd like to tell you a little bit about who I am because I am not just a statistic and because I might not fit your stereotype of a woman who would have an abortion. Most importantly, I'm alive thanks to safe, legal abortion. (Letter L-121, *Webster*)

The letters were intended to remind the Court of the fact that it would be *women* who would bear the brunt of the Court's decision:

It does not take a sperm + ova to create new life—it takes a *sperm, ova* and a *woman's uterus*. If that woman does not want to support that growth for whatever reason, she is the one who should decide what to do about it. (Letter L-209, *Webster*)

We must never go back to the days of back-alley, coat hanger abortions. Women should not have to pay the ultimate price of giving up their lives because of unwanted pregnancies. (Letter L-259, *Webster*)

An abortion should not be anyone's decision but the woman's—it's *her body, her health, her life*, at stake. (Letter R-26, *Webster*)

When lawyers and judges transformed the abortion controversy into a constitutional conflict over clashing rights, the personal experiences of those who had an unwanted pregnancy was largely lost. Again, this is an expected occurrence when the ethic of justice is employed without the tempering effect of the ethic of care. As an abstract conflict over rights, the issue of abortion becomes disembodied from the female bodies who experience it. As Rosalind Pollack Petchesky explains it, by focusing on the legal concept of "individual liberty" women were depicted "as asocial, bodyless abstractions whose 'choices' are immune from the pressures of poverty, moral and media crusades, or state power" (Petchesky 1986: 4). However, by adding patients' accounts of abortion to the legal discussions, the personal context is restored. These patients do not speak of their right to privacy, or to equality, or to due process—instead they speak in terms of cataclysmic personal change. And they do so in two ways. First, there are the changes caused by an unwanted pregnancy:

You cannot possibly know what it is like to be the helpless pawn of nature. (Letter 12, Brief for NARAL, *Thornburgh*)

It is difficult to adequately describe the difference between a wanted and an unwanted pregnancy. It is something like the difference between darkness and despair, and light and joy. (Letter 15, *Thornburgh*)

And second, there are the dramatic changes, both positive and negative, from procuring an abortion:

> On the ride home from the clinic, the relief was enormous. I felt happy for the first time in weeks. I had a future again. I had my body back. . . . I cannot stress strongly enough how that one personal decision allowed me to control my life. (Letter 36, *Thornburgh*)

> But I thought, "I'm never going to forget I've done this terrible thing. I'll never be who I was before—never be who I thought I was." (Bette in Mathewes-Green 1997: 93)

These stories of change are perhaps most acute regarding the differences in experiences between those women who obtained illegal abortions in the days before *Roe*, and those who were able to access safe and legal abortions since 1973. Many of the letters sent to the Court in *Thornburgh* and *Webster* recounted how family members and friends were killed, traumatized, injured, sickened, or rendered infertile by botched abortions. Such stories again place the emphasis not so much on constitutional rights but the meaning of abortion for women's individual lives. Without this safe and legal option, women and their families suffered:

> As children we were led to believe that my mother died of ptomaine poisoning. . . . That was a socially acceptable way to die, wasn't it?
>
> I learned that my mother died of an illegal abortion from my Aunt Alice when I was twenty-one and on active duty in the Marine Corps. I was shocked. That wasn't the kind of thing people did. That was the 1940s, and it was still a criminal act. If you found out that somebody had an abortion, it was because they weren't able to hide it, and the feeling was, shame on them. I felt ashamed that I didn't know of anybody else who'd had an abortion.
>
> . . .
>
> What makes me angriest about what happened to me is that everybody ignores the orphans. They don't even try to figure out how many children are orphaned by abortion, neither side, pro-life or pro-choice, not even a wild guess. Yet, you've got to think that, while we're sitting here right now, today, there's some four-year-old child like me out there, and the same damn thing is happening to him or her. (Jim Friedl in Bonavoglia 1991: 37-39)

Patients' stories highlight how a recognition of abstract rights makes a real difference in how lives are lived:

> I am 38 years old and have had 2 abortions—1 legal, 1 illegal. My first was when I was 19 years old. It was illegal. I had to drive from North Jersey to Philadelphia for what I understand now was an ineffective treatment by a doctor who sexually abused me while supposedly giving me injections to induce a miscarriage. After a week of treatments (64 injections a day) he used a scalpel to rupture the opening of my uterus.

I miscarried later that day. I was too frightened to go to the doctor and developed peritonitus. I almost died.

My second abortion was legal. When I discovered I was pregnant, I went to my doctor, who, with much concern and sympathy, told me of all the alternatives, including adoption. We both decided abortion would be best. The procedure was done in a hospital—it took three hours and I was back to work the next week. There was no trauma, other than the difficulty of making a decision that is always hard to make. (Letter 10, *Thornburgh*)

Adopting a jurisprudence, then, in which the Court begins with patients encourages the flow of such personal, firsthand knowledge into the Court. It is a step toward overcoming the legal norms that discourage the submission of such particular, involved, and emotional knowledge. Integration of justice and care occurs in that while the experiential knowledge of patients will be heard and assessed, the Justices will still turn to general rules and universal concepts in the course of their deliberations. The mandate of a caring jurisprudence requires the Court to treat patients' knowledge in a respectful way, but not in a deferential way. Knowledge is to be weighed—not necessarily accepted. Yet, serious consideration demands that the Court explicitly state why other knowledge is more or less persuasive. In short, to begin these cases with the patients promises that the Court will listen to them although not follow them. In practical terms this will complicate judicial deliberations by encouraging the Justices to see beyond the general issue of abortion to the individuals who experience it in their lives and to listen to the knowledge they offer. It asks them to view the controversy not only as a legal issue affecting litigants but as a cataclysmic event in the lives of people. To begin with patients, therefore, affects how the Court both sees and hears the cases.

The Macro Level: Add the Political Meanings

Once the Court has adopted its patient-centered focus and explored the micro context, the next step is to broaden the frame of reference to the macro level. While the constitutional meaning of the abortion issue received prominent attention in documents submitted to the Court as well as in the Court's opinions, less attention was paid to the "political" meanings of abortion for the lives of women. Again, I am using this term to indicate the cultural forces that shape the issue and the need for a macro level of analysis that goes beyond the question of legal rights to explore the nature of the injury alleged when abortion is restricted under law.

When the seemingly unconnected, individual stories of patients are pieced together, they begin to suggest the cultural contours of a gender oppression that is so pervasive as to make access to safe and legal abortions a necessity in women's lives. Four social factors in particular support the conclusion that an unwanted pregnancy is much more than just a personal problem. First, patients suggest that medicine is limited in its ability to offer women the means to prevent unwanted pregnancies:

> It hurt physically—what a joke, the idea that women have abortions for "convenience." We have abortions because we have unintended pregnancies, because our society has not created effective birth control. I was using a diaphragm when I got pregnant. (Letter 261, *Webster*)

> My husband and I take our responsibility to our children and any potential children seriously. I take no chance with my contraception except its own failure rate. And any of them can fail. I hunger for a time when this will stop, when we can know and not simply assume that our plans to prevent conception will work. But until that time we must have the right to choose, either to abort or to give birth. Without that choice we love in the shadow of fear. (Letter 14, *Thornburgh*)

Second, women indicate their awareness that it is they who will bear most if not all of the burden of an unwanted child. The man, as well as the society at large, will not "pay" for this pregnancy in the same terms as will the woman. Women who see the pregnancy to term often do so to the detriment of their educations, their economic stability, their personal ambitions, and their day-to-day lives.

> I have heard it said that abortion is just a convenience, especially for middle-class women. I assure you, pregnancy is no mere inconvenience. A pregnancy consumes a woman's body, energies and resources for nine months, many times with complications, sometimes at risk to the woman's life. After pregnancy, there is a child, life's most sacred responsibility, for eighteen years, for life. I am not well-to-do. I cannot offer my children the world on a silver platter, but I feel that I and every woman must have the right to offer her child the best chance for life that she can. Every woman must have the right to enter into this life-absorbing responsibility when she decides that she can. (Letter L-140, *Webster*)

> For those who wonder about possible Einsteins that could have been born, what about the female Einsteins that could have developed had their lives not been disrupted by an unplanned pregnancy? (Letter R-53, *Webster*)

> I was furiously angry, dismayed, by turns. I could not justify an abortion on economic grounds, on grounds of insufficient competence or on any other of a multitude of what might be perceived as "legitimate" reasons. But I kept being struck by the ultimate unfairness of it all. I could not conceive of any event which would so profoundly impact upon any man. Surely my husband would experience some additional financial burden, and additional "fatherly" chores, but his whole future plan was not hostage to this unchosen, undesired event. Basically his life would remain the same progression of ordered events as before. (Letter L-13, *Thornburgh*)

Third, women articulate their awareness that their pregnancy may not only "cost" them in economic terms but in social and personal status as well. While American culture celebrates and romanticizes sexual intercourse even among the young, it simultaneously punishes those who become pregnant outside the bounds of marriage. While the very wealthy may escape societal wrath, most women fall victim to the sexual double standard whereby men are expected to be sexually active but women must be sexually discrete. A pregnancy outside of wedlock is not only clear proof of sexual activity but implies a degree of irresponsibility in using birth control as well as carelessness in choosing an uncommitted sexual partner. The resulting shame or sense of helplessness is compounded when the pregnancy is the result of rape or incest. Yet, the cultural assumption still persists that women can control reproduction, and thus supports the view that an unwanted pregnancy is evidence of a woman's stupidity, irresponsibility, immorality, or promiscuity—in short, a cause for shame.

> More than anything else, what scared me about getting pregnant was the shame of being found out as being a bad girl, being a bad person. . . . The shame of it was so profound . . . it was a kind of terrorism that was practiced upon young women. That I was Puerto Rican made it even worse because Puerto Ricans were considered to be oversexed, dirty people. That hasn't changed a whole lot. (Rita Moreno in Bonavoglia 1991: 44, 46)

> Premarital sex is a secret. . . . The abortion is a secret. You mourn in secret. It's all a big dark secret, and that's not a healthy way to deal with it. (Bette in Mathews-Green 1997: 98).

> So by choosing abortion I could make sure I was the only one who knew that I wasn't noble and good and strong. (Bette in Mathewes-Green 1997: 94)

> You're thinking, "I don't have any *choice*, and now you have to tell me that I'm a *murderer* on top of the fact that I'm a *slut* and I have no *choice*." (Elizabeth in Mathewes-Greene 1997: 88)

Fourth, pregnant women speak of how all these social factors and pressures constrain the "choices" available to them. In particular, the testimony of women who have regrets about their abortion decision (including those who identify themselves as pro-life advocates) offer the Court a deeper understanding of the superficiality of "choice" and "rights" within a culture where most other options seem foreclosed (see Sweet 1985; Reardon 1987; Kelley 1996). These patients serve as reminders that abortion "choice" must run both ways—that abortion be an option and that continuance of the pregnancy be an option. Yet, this is not the experience of many women who "choose" abortion.

I was totally pro-life, I knew abortion was horrible. But when it happened to me, I just felt so trapped. (Cindy in Mathewes-Green 1997: 70)

Upset, depressed, tired, desperate, I took the path of least resistance. I adopted the attitudes of those around me. I accepted their decisions as my own. I simply floated along with "what had to be done." (Nancyjo Mann in Reardon 1987: xiv)

In sum, it is through patients' stories that the cultural context, what I call the "political" meaning of abortion, is added to the legal concerns of constitutional rights. This macro level analysis of abortion adds breadth to the framing of this issue. No longer can the language of rights, text, and precedent suffice, but required as well are the personal and social circumstances that shape women's inability or unwillingness to continue their pregnancies. No longer can medical knowledge be admitted as a pertinent legal source while patients' knowledge is deemed irrelevant. The personal nature of the stories is not a disqualification from consideration, rather, they are important because they tell of social problems regarding women's status and lives. Therefore, this knowledge argues against the usual understandings of legal injuries. Patients suggest that the injury of restrictive abortion laws is not so much a violation of privacy, but a disregard for what becomes of pregnant women within our society, especially those who are poor, of color, young, ill, stressed, or alone. Therefore, while the question raised by abortion litigation can be phrased in terms of constitutional rights of privacy or due process, to fully explore the meaning of these claims, the issue must be examined within its complex cultural context.

Knowledge from Justice and Care

Once the Court has developed an appreciation for both the micro and macro contexts of the issue—that is, the interconnected environments in which patients experience the abortion issue—the third step of a caring jurisprudence is to integrate into judicial decision making the knowledge that patients have formed from these experiences. In this, a caring jurisprudence instructs the Justices to adopt an inclusive approach to knowledge that hears as well as seriously considers the knowledge derived from an ethic of care as well as from an ethic of justice. Therefore, within this broadened circle of knowledge, patients' stories that are infused with particular, involved, and emotional components are as welcomed as medical or legal approaches that maintain universality, impartiality, and rationality. In the abortion cases, the addition of patients' knowledge to the Court's deliberations would result in several conflicts with medical and/or legal knowledge. This clashing of information would challenge some of the assumptions on which the Court based its decisions, and would therefore contest as well the soundness of these decisions themselves. Specifically, patients' knowledge contradicted medical and/or legal knowledge concerning two general aspects of abortion: the relationships at stake in the call for abortion rights, and the evaluation of whether state restrictions on abortion constituted "undue burdens" on women.

The Relationships at Stake. The *Roe* decision protected the right to abortion by safeguarding the sanctity of one particular association—the doctor–patient relationship. What seemed to ennoble this relationship in the eyes of the Justices was that it was based on rational expertise and professionalism. Yet, the Court's understanding of this particular "relationship" was derived from medical knowledge rather than patients' knowledge. True, physicians were threatened with criminal prosecution for performing abortions, and this clashed with their professional responsibilities. However, from the patients' point of view, what they sought through litigation was not so much a *relationship* with physicians (indeed, many had no preexisting relationship at all with clinic doctors), but guaranteed *access* to legal abortions by a trained medical professional in a clean, safe, and regulated environment. This concern is present in patients' accounts. Consider, for instance, the contrast between these two patients' statements:

> We all hear the stories about "what it was like" [before legalized abortion]. They are true. [The "doctor"] insisted I come by myself which I did. Is there any way I can describe my fear? He was unclean, he joked a lot, his hands were rough, his breath was bad. He forcefully approached me to have sex with him because "what harm would there be under the circumstance?" That, of course, explained his reason for insisting that I come alone. So on top of the fear for my physical safety in that situation, the agony of the decision about what I was doing, the need to keep this secret from everyone I knew and face it alone, there was the disgust, repulsion and deep fear that if I didn't do what he wanted he would send me away. (Letter L-130, *Webster*)

> The *legal* abortion was performed by my obstetrician at the . . . Hospital. I went into the hospital the night before; my doctor's attitude was practical and matter-of-fact. The procedure itself was done with sensitivity to my emotional as well as physical condition which allowed me to recover quickly and without added stress. (Letter L-125, *Webster*)

Understanding abortion litigation as women's demand for a doctor–patient *relationship* rather than as women's demand for *access* is more than a semantical distinction. With the former emphasis, the issue in *Roe* became whether states could prosecute physicians for performing abortions, and therefore the Court's answer (that the practice of abortion was legal) was responsive to this question. In contrast, if the case actually presented the latter question, that of access, then the answers in *Roe* and its progeny are less than satisfying since these decisions do not directly address whether a woman's right to access deserves protection.

This shifting of the issue could have been contested by hearing patients' knowledge regarding the relationships that they held to be most meaningful. The stories of pregnant women attest to how they frequently give great weight to interests of others (e.g., partners, existing children, future children, other family members, and even fetal life) in making the abortion decision and that they assess the consequences that the pregnancy will have on these personal relationships. These are relationships that evoke an array of emotions: love, nurturance, sacrifice, longing, guilt, and sadness. For these women, the call for legalized abortion, then, is not so much about preserving *relationships* with doctors, but about their ability to protect others with whom they share deeply felt emotional connections, by having *access* to safe, legal abortions:

> When I found out I was pregnant, quite a few years ago, I had my two boys to care for, and Norma, a baby girl. I already had all that I could handle, because my third child, our daughter, was a spina bifida baby, and I had made a promise to myself, when she was born with this condition, that I would take care of her until the end. I knew that such a baby will live two or three years at the most and I had a choice: I could place Norma in a hospital, or I could take care of her at home. I felt I owed it to my special baby to see she had the care she needed. . . . If I had not had that abortion, I would have been pregnant at the time I buried Norma, and I think I would have gone to pieces. . . . I did not believe that it was God's intention that I should have a fourth child, because I knew that it would break me and my family too. (Letter 26, *Thornburgh*)

> I have had two abortions and in each case I felt the decision was the most loving one I could make for myself, the unborn child, our family and the larger community. (Letter 11, *Thornburgh*)

Therefore, the inclusion of patients' knowledge offers another view of what is at stake in the litigation over abortion. While physicians asked for protection as they worked within the doctor-patient relationship, women asked the Court to give them clear access to abortion services so that they could protect relationships of emotional significance. The *Roe* decision respected the concerns of the physicians while ignoring those of the pregnant women.

The Identification of "Undue Burdens." Introduced in *Casey v. Planned Parenthood of Southeastern Pennsylvania* (1992), the undue burden test determined the constitutionality of state laws according to whether they have "the purpose or effect of placing a substantial obstacle in the path of a woman seeking an abortion of a nonviable fetus" (at 877). As applied, Pennsylvania's spousal notification rule was voided, but its mandatory counseling provision (that included a twenty-four-hour waiting period), and its parental consent requirement were upheld. Ironically, it was in evaluating the question as to whether these restrictions posed an undue burden on women that the Court ignored the knowledge of patients and instead relied on medical and legal testimony. Therefore, the introduction of patients' stories challenges judicial assumptions by offering a different assessment of what constitutes an "undue burden." They speak of the burdens of the waiting period and the mandatory counseling sessions:

> According to Louisiana law, I had to wait 24 hours from the point at which I signed some release forms. The neonatologist and ob-gyn each thought the other had given me the papers to sign.
> At that point I almost had a nervous breakdown. That this nightmare [aborting an anencephalic fetus] would last another 24 hours was almost more than I could take. I started screaming. I was so hysterical that my husband had to hold me down.
> We met with the ob-gyn. She gave us material to read and forms to sign. I was extremely angry, not at her, but at the law and the men who made it. I was supposed to calmly read all this information—anti-choice propaganda, really—and sign my name to each item. There were a couple of lines about options for adoption which, of course, was totally irrelevant in my case. It was a nightmare. (Shannon Lee Dawdy in Schneider 1997: 42-44)

They give accounts of the burden caused by the parental consent requirements:

> The coroner performed an autopsy and called us. "Your Rebecca Suzanne died from an illegal, botched abortion; dirty instruments had been used." And Bill said "No, no, not Beck." I said, "No, no, no, not my Becky. Oh my God, not Beck."
>
>   . . .
>
> Bill and I talked to Becky's friends and learned that she had sought an abortion at Planned Parenthood. They told Becky that they would help her but that because she was a minor, she had to get a parent's permission to comply with Indiana law. If she couldn't talk to a parent, she could seek permission from a judge. Becky told the counselor, "If I can't tell my mom and dad, how can I tell the judge?" They also told Becky that she could get a safe and legal abortion in Kentucky without telling her parents. But there was no way that Becky could get to Kentucky without us suspecting something. (Karen Bell in Schneider 1997: 24-25)

They depict the burdens due to funding restrictions:

> If you are a federal employee, you cannot choose a health insurance plan that covers abortion. The District of Columbia cannot use its own funds to pay for abortions for its low-income residents. And if you are stationed overseas in the military, you cannot have an abortion in a military hospital even if you paid for it with your own money.
> With these insidious votes—take a little bit of a right here, then a little bit of a right there—pretty soon you're left with a pretty empty right. (Elizabeth Furst in Schneider 1997: 39-40)

They describe how protests and a history of violent acts aimed at abortion providers, staffs, and facilities may in fact constitute a "substantial obstacle" to the abortion right.

> I was afraid to get out of the car. When I finally did, a group rushed at me and began shouting, "Don't do it—don't kill your baby!" and "You'll regret this for the rest of your life!" My boyfriend used his 6'4" stature to push my mother and me through the swarming crowd and toward the clinic entrance. As I neared the door, a slight man with thinning white hair grabbed my arm and in a raspy voice begged me not to go inside. Terrified, I looked at my boyfriend and noticed his clenched jaw. In one quick motion, he freed me from the man's hold and hurried us through the door.
>
> I was safe but an emotional wreck. I could see silhouettes of the protestors through the sheer curtains—arms flailing, signs bobbing—and I could hear their muffled chants. My eyes filled with tears—tears of fear and anger. How dare they harass me! How dare they grab me! The decision had been hard enough without this. (Krista Reuber in Schneider 1997: 33)

In short, patients' experiential knowledge challenges the Court's assessment of what constitutes an "undue burden" on the abortion right. Women's stories tell of how a denial of funding, consent and notification requirements, twenty-four-hour waits, biased counseling, and clinic protesters can be "substantial obstacles" to the abortion right. However, it was not so much a lack of this knowledge that influenced the Court's findings, but its preference for universal rules over particulars. The *Casey* Court knew the particulars:

> The findings of fact by the District Court indicate that because of the distances many women must travel to reach an abortion provider, the practical effect will often be a delay of much more than a day because the waiting period requires that a woman seeking an abortion make at least two visits to the doctor. The District Court also found that in many instances this will increase the exposure of women seeking abortions to "the harassment and hostility of anti-abortion protestors demonstrating outside a clinic." As a result, the District Court found that for those women who have the fewest financial resources, those who must travel long distances, and those who have difficulty explaining their whereabouts to husbands, employers, or others, the 24-hour waiting period will be "particularly burdensome." (at 885–886; citations omitted)

But with that said, the Court chose to ignore the particulars: "These findings are troublesome in some respects, but they do not demonstrate that the waiting period constitutes an undue burden" (at 886). Specifically, the Court disagreed with the District Court's conclusion that "the 'particularly burdensome' effects of the waiting period on some women require its invalidation" (at 886–887). Instead, the Justices maintained that "a particular burden is not of necessity a substantial obstacle. Whether a burden falls on a particular group is a distinct inquiry from whether it is a substantial obstacle even as to the women in that group" (at 887).

In this, the Court opted solely for the universality demanded by the ethic of justice while rejecting outright consideration of the particularity highlighted by the ethic of care. The particularized knowledge of patients challenged the Court's assumption that general principles could be justly applied to all without regard for specific circumstances. Indeed, these particularized stories questioned whether the generalizations that the Court employed in its application of the "undue burden" test undermined not only care, but justice as well. Given the differences in the degree of burden experienced by individual women, the Justices needed to explain how it is that by treating different people as if they were the same, they conformed with the judicial notions of either justice or care.

Summary

Applying a caring jurisprudence to the abortion cases not only invites patients' knowledge into the circle of consideration, but through this a more thorough assessment of the cases can result. By invoking the knowledge not only derived from the ethic of justice but also from that of the ethic of care, the Court has a richer context in which to survey and address the controversy. As identified above, if patients' knowledge was included in these cases, challenges would be made as to how the issue posed by the litigation is understood, whether restrictive state laws create "undue burdens" on women, and whether general rules can justly be applied without regard to particulars. But even beyond the addition of knowledge for its own sake, the inclusivity of the deliberations would also enhance the Court's ability to render justice. The persuasive power and even the moral force of the opinions would be heightened because patients' knowledge was given its due rather than excluded or ignored.

As a result of employing a caring jurisprudence, the Court would hear how an unwanted pregnancy is a crisis for women, and that each woman must seek her own way of coming to terms with this event. Recalling again the hymn "Amazing Grace," it is a solitary journey through "dangers, toils, and snares" to individual resolution. In this, the Court can enable women to find their way home or the Court can stand in their way. The former presents the possibility of grace; the latter precludes it.

PAS REVISITED

Contrary to Justice Scalia's flippant remark during oral arguments in *Glucksberg* and *Quill* that all of us are in fact dying, the diagnosis of a potentially life-threatening condition constitutes a shift in a person's reality. While we all know that we must eventually die, and while we know that each day brings us closer to our end, it is still quite a different thing when a person is informed that the actual dying process has begun. It is the difference between grasping the abstract concept of mortality versus experiencing the actual process of dying. The diagnosis of a terminal illness is so cataclysmic that it introduces the patient to an existence so different that it is commonly described as foreign territory:

> Everyone who is born holds dual citizenship, in the kingdom of the well and in the kingdom of the sick. Although we all prefer to use only the good passport, sooner or later each of us is obliged, at least for a spell, to identify ourselves as citizens of that other place. (Sontag 1990: 3)

> When we are sick or taking care of someone who is sick, we feel as though we are suddenly outside the borders of what we consider everyday life, and in another place. I call that place "Malady." (Lipsyte 1998: 3)

Patients have much to tell about the land of "Malady." Illness takes us on a journey, even as we are unwilling. It takes us to another place, even as we do not move. The journey is a solitary one, even as loved ones surround us. And again, in the midst of such seismic upheaval, we each must negotiate our own way.

The Micro Level: Start with the Patients

Because the legal wrangling over assisted suicide is usually framed in terms of *physician*-assisted suicide, the medical profession moves to the center of the controversy between state laws that ban PAS and ill patients who desire it. While medical practices and personnel are certainly implicated in PAS, questions concerning professional responsibilities and rights are quite different from those concerning patients' experiences and rights. It is precisely because the majority of the medical profession is opposed to PAS that it is critical that the Justices hear the counterbalancing voices of patients and remember that the litigation to legalize PAS, whether brought by physicians, patients, or family members, is being conducted in the name of those who are dying.

Yet, as in the early days of the abortion litigation, there are some difficulties in locating the voices of patients. One difficulty in obtaining the knowledge of these patients may be due to the very circumstances that render them expert—they are very ill, perhaps even near death. These are challenging circumstances in which to write. Still, some do. However, these voices seem to come from a narrow portion of the population because, not surprisingly, these authors tend to be writers or editors by profession (e.g., Broyard 1992; Brodkey 1996; Bauby 1997; Remoff 1997; Lipsyte 1998; Tilberis 1998; Warner 1998). What, then, of those who are not writers; those unconnected with the world of publishing; those not of means; and those who are inarticulate? Family members as well as attending physicians have tried to preserve the experiences and words of some of these patients (e.g., Rollin 1998; Quill 1996). Likewise, legal documents like those in the *Glucksberg* and *Quill* cases contained patients' testimony as well. However, while these sources yield rich information concerning PAS, they are as yet limited in number and in scope as they do not offer a complete range of experiences that explore the differences based on class, gender, race/ethnicity, illness or disability, religion, and even ideology. In the event that the Court indicates its willingness to consider such experiential knowledge in its future decision making, a more inclusive collection of stories would need to be invited and sought.

Yet, perhaps even more than the problem of recording the voices of patients, it may be the illegality of assisting a suicide that most restricts the stories that can be told. While the illegality of PAS may inspire the litigation, it also casts a shadow over the light that patients would shine on the issue. Unlike abortion that has moved from the realm of the illegal to the legal, assisted suicide whether performed by a physician or a family member is still a criminal activity throughout most of the United States (with the exception of the particular circumstances allowed in Oregon). Therefore, the accounts of dying told by patients, loved ones, and physicians are colored by this backdrop of illegality. Patients try not to implicate those who help them; loved ones do not want to incriminate themselves; and attending physicians risk prosecution if they reveal they participated in an assisted suicide. The illegality, then, may result in not only limited options but also in limited information about the reality of dying. Beneath this veil of illegality is fear, shame, and secrecy.

> On the 10th of November [my husband Jack] wrote his suicide note and we prepared the drugs. Jack died the next morning of a drug overdose in the room he loved with me but not our children by his side.
>
> The effect of the law against assisted suicide is to create a conspiracy of silence around the terminally ill at their time of ultimate loss and greatest need. It causes isolation, anguish, desperate acts, and prolonged suffering. I do not wish to go to jail but who is to speak for those who have died alone or those who fear prosecution if I do not.
>
> To classify me as a criminal because I refused to leave my husband's side at his time of greatest loss I find unconscionable. The law against assisted suicide is a travesty, a violation of my rights as an adult. The judicial system must find this law unconstitutional or be prepared to put people like me in jail. (Kay Beck, Appendix 4-1, Brief of Surviving Family Members, *Glucksberg* and *Quill* 1997)

The illegality of assisted suicide, then, is like a spectral presence in many of the testimonies of patients. Ironically, it is the illegality, rather than the dying, that shapes the plots of many of the stories told. Patients cope with the criminality of their desire in several ways. Some resort to self-inflicted violent or painful deaths.

My husband of twenty-five years, Emanuel J. ("Mac") McGeorge, had terminal cancer involving the spine, lungs and lymphatic system. . . . Because he was 72 years of age, he rejected massive chemotherapy and radiation and asked just for drugs to ease his then acute pain. . . .

During late spring of 1995, he broached the subject of suicide. It was not the first time suicide had been mentioned, but this time he was quite serious. He told me of his great concern for becoming incapacitated, or so ill that he would either be hospitalized or would not, for some other reason, be able to govern his own destiny. . . . Mac also brought up the possibility of assisted suicide with his doctor, but while his doctor was understanding, he was not supportive.

. . .

On the morning of February 9, 1996, he had made up his mind. . . . After a brief and very personal conversation, he gave me the note he had carried for months, attesting to the fact that his decision was his own; kissed me goodbye; went into the front yard; put a shotgun in his mouth and pulled the trigger. Since a peaceful death was not available, this was his way to ensure death with the dignity he valued so highly. Two months ago I was emotionally wrenched by finding a portion of his upper dental plate 50 feet from the site of his death—a testament to the violent alternative he was forced to choose.

. . .

I am thankful that he loved me enough to share his most personal emotions. I wish I could have been with him at the end, but he said no, "it will be messy." (Patsy McLaughlin McGeorge, Appendix 2-1, Brief of Surviving Family Members, *Glucksberg* and *Quill*, 1997)

Some patients protect doctors and loved ones by dying alone.

Sara and I were married for 49 years. She suffered from a very painful heart condition the last eleven years of her life. . . . Finally life became unbearable. . . . She wanted to die but we did not know how to do it.

. . .

We finally learned of the plastic bag method. On the day of her decision, I was with her up to the point of placing the bag over her head and she said, "Elvin, you must now go to the office because you cannot be implicated in this."

She had to die alone. I was denied my right to be with her when she died. This is not right.

. . .

A person has the right to control the conditions of their death as much as they have the right to control the conditions of their living. (Elvin O. Sinnard, Appendix 5-1, Brief of Surviving Family Members, *Glucksberg* and *Quill*, 1997)

Some family members at times take the risk, and they assist in the suicide or they stay with the patient as he or she commits the act.

I was arrested on December 4, 1995 in West Los Angeles after my lover of eight years committed suicide. Within hours of the arrest, I was charged with murder under California Penal Code section 187 and felony assisted suicide under California Penal Code section 401.

. . .

I am the one person who stayed by him while everyone else abandoned him as his condition worsened. I am the one person whose love was sufficient to withstand the horrible strain caused by his progressive illness. Despite all that, I am also the one person who was charged with a felony *and* faced a prison term of up to three years. In the end, the charges that were filed against me were the last thing that he would have ever wanted to happen. (Keith William Green, Appendix 12-3, Brief of Surviving Family Members, *Glucksberg* and *Quill*, 1997)

To begin with patients, then, is to be reminded of the consequences of the laws that prohibit assisted suicide and who suffer them. As Jane Roe, a patient-litigant in *Glucksberg*, said, "I do not want to have to die alone and unsupported" (Joint Appendix, p. 25). This concern echoes a point made by Dr. Quill: "No one should be forced to die alone, or to die with a plastic bag over his or her head, because we are afraid to fully address the practical implications of what we are allowing" (Quill 1996: 176). It is this reality of dying in the "real" world that patients' knowledge stresses at both the micro- and macro-levels.

The Macro Level: Add the Political Meanings

Again, once the micro level is addressed, the constitutional issues need to be set within their larger context. The Justices need to ask: what is the cultural context of the "injury" that is expressed in the case as a claim to rights? The answer to this question would lead to a critique of how our society views dying. While such critiques are available from social commentators as well as from medical professionals, patients and their families reinforce these messages with stories of their experiences. What they speak of suggests that when they are ill and/or dying, the culture causes them further injury and that these injuries constitute a form of oppression. Five interconnected cultural factors seem to exacerbate the suffering.

First, patients suggest that their suffering must be understood within the context of a society that is both death defying and death denying. That a terminal illness is experienced in American culture as a cataclysmic event rather than as a natural part of life is quite telling. It indicates a culture in which illness and death are seen as failures, as aberrations, and in which the aging, the sick, and the disabled are shunned as fearful reminders of mortality.

To tell the truth, for me, growing older is a lot scarier than dying. We treat our old people so badly. At the very time when you need the beauty of nature, with serenity and peace and birds singing and sunshine around you, we shut them up in these harshly lit, concrete bunkers with other old people half out of their minds, or terrible smells or bad cooking. It must be hell. To me that's much scarier than dying—to grow old, poor and abandoned. But it helps keep death out of sight. It helps us pretend it doesn't happen. (Lee Davis in Anderson 1996: 84)

The separation from society, the political marginalization and the financial thefts, the attacks to see what can be stolen from you, and the indignity—including social indignity—of AIDS suggest a partial, sometimes fluorescent and linoleumed version of the death camps. Those who postpone the final crescendoing of the humiliations—wasting, dementia, diarrhea, thrush, PML (which affects the brain), Kaposi's sarcoma, certain exotic glaucomas—for more than a year or two are sometimes called survivors, in what seems a recognition of cousinship. (Brodkey 1996: 44)

In a book that describes the role he played in his wife's suicide, George Delury sets the stage for their decision within the contradictions of American culture:

Yet for all [our] fascination with fictional and distant danger and death, the modern person seldom comes into immediate contact with real death. Real death is usually hidden away in hospitals and hospices and spoken of in hushed tones, if spoken of at all. Death has replaced religion and politics as the subject banned from polite conversation. It has replaced sex as the forbidden topic. Our TV talk-shows have no scruples about exhibiting the oddest kinds of sexual and political behavior, but seldom touch on death, unless it is violent, the kind of death we assume happens only to someone else. (Delury 1997: 1-2)

It was not always this way. Until the advances in medicine, death was ordinary, expected, commonplace. Children came of age with the experience of seeing loved ones sick, aging, and dying. The dying process took place at home; the body was prepared at home; the front parlor was the site of the wake; and the mourning period, with a host of rituals, was extensive. Now death has been removed from ordinary experience. Dying takes place in the hospital; funeral parlors strive to re-create a lifelike corpse, and "getting on with your life" is encouraged (Anderson 1996: 335). Since the 1950s, "it is likely that the average individual will reach forty years or older before experiencing the natural death of a spouse, parents, or close friend" (ibid.: 289). Given this expectation, the AIDS epidemic arrived as a cultural shock in that it "re-create[d] communities of people experiencing the frequent death of loved ones while in their youth (ibid.: 337).

Second, patients' stories tell us that the promises of modern medicine can only be obtained if one is willing to gamble. Unlike the finding that one is either pregnant or not, the demarcation between a condition that causes illness and one that will cause death is not always clear. Diagnoses of cancer or heart disease, once the equivalent of death sentences, may no longer be terminal conditions. Even infections like AIDS that will eventually claim the life of a patient may not do so with the swiftness that it did ten years ago. One of the hopeful yet problematic aspects of modern medicine is that there are options. Patients may employ new medical treatments in the hope of finding a miracle that delays or even revokes the death sentence. The problematic side of this triumph over death is that patients have the option of quite literally adopting the philosophy of "never say die." How does one know when to call off the fight against death and to concentrate on living the life that one has left?

> Nobody tells the full truth . . . which is that at its worst, chemo is punishing and spirit-sapping and still may not make a difference in your prognosis. At its best, it's the nuisance that saves your life. You'll never know where your treatment falls between those poles until you try it. (Lipsyte 1998: 55)

The possibilities offered by aggressive treatment necessitate that a decision be made as to whether to go this course. One reporter recounts why patient Valli Rice decided to forgo further treatment for a malignant brain tumor:

> Rather than spend her remaining time pursuing aggressive therapies that could run tens of thousands of dollars beyond what her insurance would cover Valli has decided to enter hospice, a program for terminally ill patients who reject curative treatment. She resents the impersonality of high-tech medicine, saying, "I never want to be the glioblastoma in room 102." And she is aware of its probable futility: "It won't prolong my life, only my death."
>
> But her parents, Ted and Muriel, and two of her three sisters feel differently. Though they are terrified at the prospect of the huge medical expanses that she may run up, they want Valli to fight for her life. (Luciano 1998: 85)

Indeed, families find it difficult to decide when to stop treatment for their loved one.

> We had already changed our order for [my father] from "put him on a respiration" to "D.N.R."—do not resuscitate. My father had said to put him on a respirator so long as there was a one-in-a-million chance he'd live. That day [the doctor told us], we lost that one-in-a-million chance.
>
> Once we made that decision, we were plagued with others. Did we want a feeding tube if it came to that? Did we want to withhold his insulin? His potassium? Would we agree to stop having his blood tested? Each decision brought my father closer to his inevitable death. (Hood 1997: 19)

Third, the close doctor–patient relationship that is presumed by the Court in the *Glucksberg* and *Quill* cases is spoken of with great longing by patients (as well as by some physicians; see Quill 1996; Nuland 1993; Groopman 1997). In wistful terms, these accounts imply that such a relationship, though desirable, is largely unattainable and rarely experienced today.

> I got the feeling that they would prescribe pain medicine for me but not that anyone would be willing to still have a relationship with me—a doctor–patient relationship

with me—and midwife me through the dying process if that's what it came to. (Cynthia in Quill 1996: 15)

While dying of prostate cancer, Anatole Broyard (1992) collected his thoughts on what an ideal doctor–patient relationship should be:

> I see no reason or need for my doctor to love me—nor would I expect him to suffer with me. I wouldn't demand a lot of my doctor's time: I just wish he would *brood* on my situation for perhaps five minutes, that he would give me his whole mind just once, be *bonded* with me for a brief space, survey my soul as well as my flesh, to get at my illness, for each man is ill in his own way. (44)
>
> . . .
>
> When a doctor refuses to acknowledge a patient, he is, in effect, abandoning him to his illness. (50)
>
> . . .
>
> In her essay "On Being Ill," Virginia Woolf wonders why we don't have a greater literature of illness. The answer may be that doctors discourage our stories. (52)
>
> . . .
>
> Every patient needs mouth-to-mouth resuscitation, for talk is the kiss of life. Besides talking himself, the doctor ought to bleed the patient of talk, of the consciousness of his illness, as earlier physicians used to bleed their patients to let out heat or dangerous humors. (53-54)

Fourth, patients' stories demonstrate the impact that economic resources have on the experience of illness and/or dying. At the most obvious level, money—or at least a comprehensive health insurance policy—buys access to medical care. The more the money or the better the insurance, the more options patients have in choosing facilities, specialists, and treatments. Such resources may not be able to buy a cure or to ward off death, but it can make the death sentence less certain. Patients recognize how the buying of health care is a privilege tied to economic resources.

> My experience with dying has been mostly about money. That sounds awful I know. Crass and cold. But the truth of it is, when my mother-in-law was dying, it all came down to money and trying to figure out how to pay for everything. When my parents die it will be the same. If I was going to die tomorrow, the biggest worry I'd have would be how to do it so it didn't cost too much for my family. (Shirley Stapleton in Anderson 1996: 179)

> I'm on a short medical leash because I have to get my [heart implant] battery checked regularly. Every two to three years they have to implant a new unit because the battery runs down. That costs about $20,000, for which I used to be insured but now I'm not. To an insurance company I'm your basic preexisting condition. (R.I.P. Hayman in Anderson 1996: 215)

As important as it is to have resources to buy health care, such resources can also make life during treatment more comfortable and more dignified. When the late Liz Tilberis, editor in chief at *Harper's Bazaar*, lost her hair to chemotherapy during her battle with ovarian cancer, she decided to get a long-haired wig. While such a decision is familiar to many chemo patients, her particular route to procuring a wig is unimaginable for most—she hired a Hollywood wigmaker who used her personal photos to re-create exactly her shoulder-length bob. Her response: "I was back!" (Tilberis 1998: 26). Patients remind us, therefore, that it is not only the treatments but their quality of life that is affected by economics.

Finally, those who provide care for their ill loved ones are soon initiated into the reality that they, like the patients, are largely alone. There is still little cultural support for care givers. Home health aides, visiting nurses, family and friends create fragile networks of patient care. Additional support may come from hospice care, a movement born in the United States in 1974, "develop[ed] primarily as a program designed to assist families to care for the dying in their own homes" (Anderson 1996: 337). Yet only about 20 percent of those who die this year will do so under the care of hospice (Wilkes 1997: 34). Without adequate support, a patient's desire to experience a "good death" at home may place unbearable strains on families and loved ones.

> Recently I saw something in the paper about people dying at home. The article made it sound so nice, like everybody used to live together in one big house and the babies were born there and the old people died there and they all had a great old time. I don't believe it. Not for one minute. I think the women had to take care of everybody and the only thing that made it work was if they had a lot of money. . . . And I think the only thing that makes it okay now is if you have a lot of money. Then you can get help and you can have a reasonable life and you can have this wonderful experience of being able to help the dying person or whatever. But if you don't have money, it's a real serious hardship. (Shirley Stapleton in Anderson 1996: 184)

George Delury, who later would be charged with assisting the suicide of his wife who suffered from multiple sclerosis (he agreed to a plea bargain and served six months in prison), wrote a letter to his wife's relatives describing his burden as a care giver and asking them for help:

> Much as it shames me to admit it, I am at the end of my resources—physical, emotional, and financial. . . .
>   I suppose I should not be surprised that a sixty-two-year-old man cannot work fifteen to sixteen hours a day for two years without a break, cannot continually bear the strain of putting on a brave front for his sick wife, cannot live in unending and growing grief, and continue to deal effectively with the constant rigamarole of Medicare, Medicaid, taxes and all the other bureaucratic requirements; shop, cook, keep track of

bills; work for money; and take care of the dozen of little details of household management, without finally failing on all fronts.

But I am surprised, and I am failing. Bills pile up, taxes are undone, contracts are
unfulfilled. I cannot focus or concentrate. I am often near tears and sometimes give
up to sobbing. I am short tempered. And angry at everything and everyone that makes
it unnecessarily harder. I am so very, very tired. Despairing. Drifting into the irrevo-
cable.

I haven't the vaguest idea of what I need or where to turn for help, except to you.
Help me! Please. (1997: 121)

Care givers and patients continue to require more support than is currently available to them. It is this aspect of medical care, that which is largely provided by
aides, volunteers, and family members, that patients' knowledge brings to the
Court. Although removed from medical settings, the hardship of this medical work
must be included in any examination of the forces that form the PAS issue.

Patients' knowledge, then, speaks not only of individual circumstances but also
of the cultural forces that shape illness and dying. Interestingly, the five social forces
studied above are emphasized not only by the patients who support PAS, but also
by those who oppose PAS. The anti-PAS patients point out how the death defying culture stigmatizes the ill, the aging, and the disabled; excessive medical intervention can threaten patients; the doctor–patient relationship is critical for patients' well-being; financial considerations can coerce patients into accepting an
early death; and concern for care givers causes patients guilt and stress. Where they
differ from the pro-PAS patients is in their conclusion as to what should be done
given this cultural context. The anti-PAS advocates argue in favor of changing the
conditions that lead patients to seek PAS. They point to statements from patients
who changed their mind about dying when their circumstances were improved
and who were grateful that physicians did not respect their requests to die:

The most valuable days of my life have been the last days I have spent. (A patient to
Dr. Pellegrino, Thomas 1997: 17)

You're looked upon as a second-rate citizen. People say, "you're using my taxes. You
don't deserve to be here. You should hurry up and leave." You reach a point where
you just can't take it anymore. (Larry McAfee in Brief of Not Dead Yet, *Glucksberg*
and *Quill*, 1997)

The *amicus* brief of Not Dead Yet suggests that some of Dr. Kevorkian's patients
might have wanted to live had they received appropriate services. This document
quotes one family member who says of a patient, "She did not want to be a burden to her husband and family," another patient who felt that she was "becoming
a burden on people," and another who told his doctor that "the quality of his life

had been compromised by an anxiety state" (at 13-14). Patients are also concerned that given the present environment where physicians discuss withholding treatment, their wishes for aggressive treatment may not be respected. One daughter reports that the first thing her ill father said when he regained consciousness in the hospital was "Make sure they keep giving me antibiotics. Even if they don't want to" (Hood 1997: 19). One spouse expresses her concern over the question of whose suffering is relieved by the death of a patient:

> At doses of 4 to 6 milligrams [of morphine], my husband tossed and turned and his breathing was ragged. I asked for 10 milligrams and he began to choke. I asked the nurse to push the morphine pump to 30 milligrams and my husband died, no longer struggling, within two hours.
> Did I kill him? I don't know. Did I push the morphine pump to warp speed to relieve his suffering or mine? I don't know. (Christina Campi 1998: A19)

Rather than capturing discord among patients, the statements quoted in this section demonstrate that patients on *both* sides of the PAS issue agree that these five social factors make the hardship of illness, disability, and/or dying all the more difficult. I want to stress, therefore, that should the Court decide to hear PAS cases in the future, a caring jurisprudence would insist that the Justices listen to the voices of patients from both sides of the issue. This inclusive embrace of patients' knowledge can underscore the existence of challenges within the medical profession (indeed, can reinforce the points made by some medical providers themselves) concerning the ethical limits of aggressive treatment, the impact of managed care, the distribution of resources, and the support available for patients and their families. Patients' knowledge can therefore enhance the Court's understanding of the PAS issue by supplementing the call for rights (whether it be a right to die or a right to life) with an appreciation of the social parameters in which those claims take place and the cultural forces that compel them.

Knowledge from Justice and Care

In the *Glucksberg* and *Quill* cases, there were two significant areas where medical knowledge clashed with patients' knowledge—whether medicine could ease patient's suffering and whether dying was understood as a medical event or as something more. In both of these instances, the Court assumed the validity of the medical knowledge. Again, this elevation of one source of knowledge over another may have been based on medicine's claim to universal, impartial, and rational knowledge over the patients' particular, involved, and emotional knowledge. The introduction of patients' knowledge by application of a caring jurisprudence would therefore force the Court to take this clash of information seriously by weighing it once again.

Suffering. One of the most obvious contradictions between medical and patients' knowledge in the PAS cases was the issue of whether suffering could be eased or controlled by medical intervention. The medical profession assured the Court that the answer was yes but patients told the Court that it wasn't so. The disagreement stemmed from two points: first, that there was a difference between what was possible and what was practiced; and second that while some medical experts focused on the narrow issue of pain, patients referred to the broader phenomenon of suffering.

That the issue of pain control is even an issue at all frustrates medical care providers. Hospice nurse Donna Howell maintains that modern medicine can ease much of the suffering associated with dying: "The irony of this to me is that this debate should come up now when we have such excellent means of supporting patients" (Lelyveld 1997: C4). The problem, then, is not so much of ability as it is of delivery. Even the AMA acknowledges the discrepancy between medical capability and providing adequate pain management stating that "the delivery of such care is 'grossly inadequate' today, and efforts to make such care universally available have not yet succeeded" (quoting the NYS Task Force Report, Brief of the AMA, *Glucksberg* and *Quill*, 1997, p. 7). Meanwhile, patients and their families ask the Court to consider not only what medicine can do in the abstract but what it actually delivers or fails to deliver in reality.

[My husband] was relatively comfortable until June of 1994 when a series of new problems developed. Following further diagnostic procedures it was ascertained that the cancer had spread to his ribs, spine and right femur. He was in considerable pain when walking, sitting or lying in bed. He had been given medication for the pain prior to this time but it now became a necessity if he was to have any measure of relief. His ribs gradually broke, and as he said to me many times, he could feel the broken edges of the bones rub together as he would sit or attempt to arise from the bed. He was in unbearable pain. He was an extremely intelligent, courageous and dignified man and he did not wish to suffer unbearable pain when there was no hope of recovery from this condition. . . . He felt that it was his right to say when he had suffered enough. (Dorothy B. Hoogstraat, Appendix 10-1, Brief of Surviving Family Members, *Glucksberg* and *Quill*, 1997)

A second point emphasized by patients is that suffering is more than experiencing pain. As one reporter put it:

A common misconception, even among doctors, is that palliative care focuses solely on keeping dying patients free of pain—"comfortable," as the euphemistic usage has it. In fact, the focus is much broader. According to a definition published by the World Health Organization in 1990, palliative care has to address not only pain, but also psychological, social and spiritual problems to achieve "the best possible quality of life for patients and their families." (Stolberg 1997: B7)

Patients reinforce exactly that point. For instance, suffering can be caused by the feeling of losing control. Heather Trexler Remoff, who was fighting ovarian cancer, wanted another CA-125 blood test to see if her levels had improved. While the results would not have changed her chemo treatment for that day she says "I wanted to know simply because I wanted to know" (1997: 53–54). The physician refused to order the test. She pleaded with the nurses and offered to pay for it on the spot. He kept sending the nurses back to refuse her.

> My anger and frustration mounted with each refusal. My tears were not of self-pity but of fury at the helplessness of my situation. "The blood is already drawn," I howled. "It's not as if you have to draw more blood. All he has to do is take that little order for lab work and check off one more box!" I kept glancing around the room, hoping to catch the eye of other patients equally tired of doctors making decisions that affected our lives, not theirs. I was sure I could get some kind of rebellion going, a storming of the palace gates, an overthrow, an uprising. Instead, patient after patient averted his or her eyes. It was clear I would get no support. (Remoff 1997: 54)

Suffering can come from the fact that a patient realizes he or she is dying. This fact may be quietly accepted by the patients, but it may cause sorrow or fear nonetheless.

> I am fading away. Slowly but surely. Like the sailor who watches the home shore gradually disappear, I watch my past recede. My old life still burns within me, but more and more of it is reduced to ashes of memory. (Bauby 1997: 77)

> And that fear; it's bottomless. It's a fear that knows no end because it's a fear that's dealing with the end of one's whole existence and all of one's experiences. So the fear potentially goes ad infinitum into a person's very being. It is so devastating that if one puts one's attention to it for any length of time, one could set oneself into an indefinite period of manic depression with very detrimental results to the immune system. That's why it is good to have anything that can pull a person out from that fear. (Eddie Mohr in Petrow 1990: 162)

Suffering can come not so much from any particular pain but from feeling terrible all over.

> I'm stuck—stuck in life. I don't want to be here anymore. I don't see why I can't get out. . . . I feel lousy. I feel lousy all the time. Sometimes it's more, sometimes it's less. These doctors don't understand what it *feels* like to be sick this way. All they know is your blood pressure and your temperature and the size of your tumor. They don't *hear* you when you tell them how you feel. And they definitely don't hear you when you tell them you want to take a powder. (Ida Rollin in Rollin 1998: 163)

In addition, some patients equate suffering with their inability to act on their choice or their inability to protect their loved ones from seeing them suffer.

> To withhold such choice, and the means to exercise it, from those who are suffering is to deny me my right to live and die humanely. . . . It is also inhumane to my loved ones, my family, to require them to watch helplessly as I am forced to endure such suffering. (Jane Roe, *Quill* Brief)

Dying as More Than Medical. Another point of disagreement between physicians and patients in the PAS cases arose over the meaning of death and dying. While most of the medical experts on the anti-PAS side instructed the Court as to the physical parameters of death and dying, patients spoke of death and dying within the context of the struggle for meaning. It is difficult here to cull illustrative excerpts from the books that have been written by dying patients because the books as a whole, rather than a specific sentence or paragraph, tell how in the face of death some patients succeed in finding meaning. Memoirs by authors like Gilda Radner (1990), Anatole Broyard (1992), Harold Brodkey (1996), Jean-Dominque Bauby (1997), and Gale Warner (1998), speak as much about life as they do about death, and deserve to be read in their entirety. Yet a few quotes may be instructive. For example, within most of these books is an attempt to answer what the illness or what their dying means.

> Susan Sontag insists that there is no meaning to cancer. "It's just a disease," she says. Others, like me, create elaborate symbols to support our healing and hope. Whatever your response, no one should ever tell you not to feel what you are feeling. (Warner 1998: 102)

> Death is a bore. But life isn't very interesting either. I must say I expected death to glimmer with meaning, but it doesn't. It's just there. I don't feel particularly alone or condemned or unfairly treated, but I do think about suicide a lot because it is so boring to be ill, rather like being trapped in an Updike novel. I must say I despise living if it can't be done on my terms. (Brodkey 1996: 152)

> Why did all this wisdom and beauty have to come so late? (Broyard 1992: 68)

Some patients fight against pain and incoherence so that they can bring their lives to a close in a meaningful way. It is not just that they want to avert pain, but that they want to maintain consciousness in order to "die well." Drawing on other literature, Anatole Broyard (1992) offers an explanation for these efforts:

> In *Death as a Fact of Life*, David Hendin maintains that a good death is an indispensable end to a good life, so much so that a German writer referred to the final moments as "the obstetrics of the soul." To die well is important not only to the patient but to

his survivors, for one of their strongest memories of him may be what Walter Benjamin called "love at last sight." (73)

Given the lack of options, and the fact that they are dying, patients may view suicide as a rational choice—as a way of taking care of themselves and of others. This understanding directly contradicts the Court's finding that a desire for suicide is itself proof of depression or mental incapacity.

My informed, rational choice is that my death from AIDS [when medicine can't help and the pain is intolerable] be as swift, painless and dignified as possible. I want to be able to hasten my own death in my own home, in a certain and humane way, surrounded with the people I love helping me make my passing comfortable and meaningful. I do not want my loved ones to watch me suffer needlessly. (George Kingsley, *Quill* Brief)

I don't think anyone knows where this tumor will go, which direction, or what will happen exactly. And I don't in any way maintain that I know what I would do in the end. But to have the option of having some pills there lowers my level of fear. It just gives me this feeling of relief. (Barbara Oskamp in Lelyveld 1997: C4)

This knowledge concerning pain and the meaning of dying, drawn from patients' experiences, tells the Court that the medical profession's position on pain relief and their understanding of dying as a medical event do not square with patients' realities. This is important information. Since the judicial system prides itself on its reliance on facts, this knowledge should be welcomed by the Court as it seeks to inform itself about PAS. In that patients' knowledge may contradict or supplement some of the medical knowledge entered into the cases, the Court is called on to integrate this knowledge to form an understanding of PAS. This is not only a caring approach to their role, but one required by justice as well.

Summary

My point is that patients' knowledge, though particular, involved, and emotional, is still knowledge and is still of value to the Court. A caring jurisprudence insists that the Justices hear and weigh this knowledge. Ironically, although I call upon patients' knowledge as a way to counter the anti-PAS testimony of the medical profession in the *Glucksberg* and *Quill* cases, it is some members of the medical profession who can serve as models for how to integrate seemingly contrary forms of knowledge. Some physicians employ their scientific knowledge and training yet listen closely to what patients have to teach them about healing and the practice of medicine (see Sacks 1985; Siegel 1990; Nuland 1993; Quill 1996; Campo 1997; Groopman 1997). Dr. Jerome Groopman tells how his father's death resulted in his forming a "powerful commitment to care for patients and their loved ones ... with genuine compassion and scientific excellence" (1997: 1). I'm asking that the Court approach the knowledge offered in the PAS cases in a similar way—with genuine compassion and judicial excellence. These physicians set an example for those in law who may object that the introduction of particular, involved, and emotional knowledge creates a hostile environment for universal, impartial, and reasoned knowledge. In this, these physicians are excellent role models for the Court in suggesting how to draw on the ethic of justice and the ethic of care to temper each other. Such an integration of knowledge would enhance the Court's ability to respond to the needs of the patients who initiated the PAS cases. As Anatole Broyard suggests, terminally ill patients ask not for love but for understanding:

> To a critically ill person love may begin to resemble an anesthetic. In a novel by Joy Williams called *State of Grace*, a character says, "There must be something beyond love. I want to get there." The sick man has got there: He's at a point where what he wants most from people is not love but an appreciative critical grasp of his situation, what is known now in the literature of illness an "empathetic witnessing." The patient is always on the brink of revelation, and he needs an amanuensis. (1992: 44)

Patients are asking the Court for an "empathetic witnessing"—an understanding of the fact that the dying have little else left to them than to shape how they die. It is hard work and meaningful work—far more than is captured in the claim of a "right to die." A caring jurisprudence asks the Court to respect this work and to consider how to help people find their way in this, their final act.

CONCLUSION

So, what would the application of a caring jurisprudence change regarding the abortion and PAS cases?

At the most obvious level, it would expand the Court's knowledge of the issues. Patients' knowledge demonstrates that the problem lurking beneath the abortion controversy is the lack of choices for pregnant women and the host of negative consequences they face in seeing a pregnancy to term. In this context, an unwanted pregnancy constitutes an injury. The Court, therefore, must do better than wave aside this claim with the assurance that restrictions on the abortion right do not constitute "undue burdens." Patients' knowledge also illustrates that the problem below the surface of the PAS controversy is inadequate social and medical care for the dying and their loved ones. In this context, the insistence that people suffer long, and sometimes painful, inevitable deaths constitutes an injury. The Court, therefore, must do better than refer to medicine's ability to ease suffering when faced with the reality that medicine frequently fails to deliver such care. Patients' knowledge insists that they face the realities of people's lives and address them.

Given the introduction of this knowledge, would the application of a caring jurisprudence change the outcome of the cases? Most assuredly, yes, it would. The outcome of the cases—the tone, the nature of the discussion, the points addressed, the reasoning used, the persuasiveness, and the moral force—would most certainly be affected though perhaps not the ultimate decision, that is, the vote. This is a crucial point, and one deserving of some explanation.

Throughout this book, I have tried to make my preferences clear. I favor a change in the Court's decisions so as to create an expanded right to abortion and to establish a right of terminally ill, competent adults to physician-assisted suicide. In my weighing of the medical, legal, and patients' knowledge, I am led to the conclusion that the Court should protect and respect patients' efforts to negotiate these troubled waters. However, when presented with the same knowledge, the Court need not be compelled to form the same conclusion. While a caring jurisprudence is concerned with the outcome of judicial decision making as well as the nature of the process itself, it is not strictly a result-oriented jurisprudence. In other words, I am not arguing that application of a caring jurisprudence will inevitably lead to my preferred outcomes. The Court may very well use this approach, integrate patients' knowledge, and still restrict access to abortion and still deny access to PAS. But this is not to say that a caring jurisprudence would therefore lack impact. I believe that regardless of the decision, the application of a caring jurisprudence would alter the work of the Court, and the outcome of the litigation, in other significant ways.

First, even if they find patients' knowledge less than persuasive when weighed against other knowledge, the Court can assure patients that it heard and considered their input. While this will not fully satisfy patients, it will be an improvement over the existing process since it will at least address patients' concerns directly, admit their testimony as knowledge, and evaluate their claims. This should result in a more truthful rendering of what exactly the Court considered, how it decided, and why. While the ultimate decision is indeed important, so too is the listening, the inclusion, and the rationale. This careful deliberation is a component not only of care but also of justice. The legitimacy of a system of law lies not in the guarantee that each individual will win (an impossibility), but that they will be heard and their knowledge taken seriously (an imperative).

Second, there is a potential for change when the Court hears the voices of patients that emanate from both sides of the issues. One cannot hear these voices without realizing that patients are not so neatly divided into two opposing camps as the litigation may suggest. In particular, the macro level analyses of abortion and PAS are fruitful areas in which to search for agreement. In the abortion cases, both pro-choice and pro-life women speak of the contradictions of a culture that sexualizes girls at young ages but that lacks support for pregnancy and motherhood. While I remain doubtful that such an agreement can open a path to resolving the abortion issue (since the answer to the fundamental issue of whether abortion should be legal cannot satisfy both sides), I do think that a shared cultural critique of the abortion issue would lead to outcomes more responsive to women's realities and women's concerns. I am more hopeful that a middle ground can be constructed in the PAS cases. There, patients' knowledge suggests that there may be a way of satisfying through strict safeguards both the wishes of terminally ill, competent adults who desire access to PAS and the concerns of the sick, disabled, and elderly who fear that legalized PAS will jeopardize them. This knowledge intimates that the demand that no one be forced to live and the demand that no one be sacrificed are not dichotomous claims. In any case, patients on both sides of these issues may be better served by a Court that listens carefully enough to discern not only the nature of the dispute but also the points of agreement.

Third, the Court can encourage or even insist that legislative bodies respond to the injuries of which patients speak. At minimum and consistent with a philosophy of judicial restraint, the Court can be emphatic that their refusal to establish rights is not a statement that there is no problem or no injury, but only a conclusion that the Court lacks the power to intervene. In this, the Justices can call upon elected officials to act. At the other end of the spectrum and more consistent with judicial activism, the Court can attempt to force legislative action by ruling that until legislatures do respond to these injuries suffered by patients, the Court (while not establishing specific constitutional rights) will use its power to protect people's liberties.[3] In both scenarios, the Justices would use their authority to provide the impetus, the moral leadership, for social change. They would do so by drawing from the authority of both the ethic of justice and the ethic of care.

A caring jurisprudence guides the Justices in how to hear patients' knowledge so that it can be included as a part of judicial considerations. Such an approach is not a call for a tearing apart of the law, a rending asunder, but an invitation to rethink our understanding of law's role and to reinvent it as a vehicle of justice and of care. This is to reconstruct law, not destroy it. Consider this: there is a verse of "Amazing Grace" that is of unknown origins; it was not authored by John Newton, but it is commonly known just the same:

> We lay our garments by,
> Upon our beds to rest,
> Though death may soon disrobe us all
> Of what we now possess.

This verse stands as an example of how people continue to create new verses for this meaningful, old song out of the experiences of their own lives ("Amazing Grace with Bill Moyers" 1995). Patients who are challenged with the crises of an unwanted pregnancy or of a terminal illness have asked the Court to do the same—to craft a legal response that speaks to their lives. Resolution of the issues of abortion and PAS requires both courage and creativity. Amid their personal crises, patients have ennobled themselves by embracing these attributes. The Justices of the U.S. Supreme Court should do no less.

Notes

1. By "personal" I mean that of patients. In equating personal with patient, my intent is to focus on the person who is actually experiencing the medical condition as a part of him- or herself. I do not mean to suggest that physicians and attorneys do not have a personal experience, role, or stake in the medical condition, but it is of a secondary nature in that the condition is that of another and not of them.

2. By "medical" I mean that of physicians. Since I am summarizing the dominant view of each perspective, I am deliberately focusing on the physician as the most recognized source of medical knowledge, while ignoring the knowledge of other medical care providers like nurses, physician's assistants, and technicians. I am aware of the gendered nature of this division of knowledge and confront this point in chapter 4.

3. Offensive labeling of patients either verbally or in written form on their charts appears to be commonplace. One index of terms includes: gomers—Get Out of My Emergency Room; crispy critters—children who are burn victims; dirtballs—a chronic alcoholic, drug abuser, bag lady or street person; and AMF—Adios Mother Fucker for a patient checking out against medical advice. (Konner 1987; see also Mizrahi 1986)

4. The threat of violence may be one of the reasons why the number of abortion providers has dropped. In a study for the Alan Guttmacher Institute, Stanley Hewshaw reported that as compared with the peak year of 1982 when there were 2,908 abortion providers in the United States, there were 2,380 in 1992 and 2,042 in 1996 (see "Fear Shuts Down Abortion Providers" 1998). In the wake of the October 1998 assassination of Dr. Barnett Slepian (the third physician to be slain), physicians along with all personnel who work at facilities that provide abortions are clearly being targeted in order to discourage them from continuing their work.

CHAPTER 2

1. Only the statutes in Alaska, Hawaii, New York, and Washington were unaffected by the ruling in *Roe* (O'Connor 1996: 47).
2. I focus here on the formal documents of the party briefs, *amicus* briefs, and oral arguments because these are the informational resources over which litigants and interested third parties exert the most control, and they are the formal records of information that are accessible to study in a way that the personal experiences and views of the Justices concerning abortion are not. I scrutinize these records for examples of what sort of medical and personal information were presented, how they were presented, and how their presentation was affected by legal norms. Because it is difficult, if not impossible, to conclude with certainty the different degree of influence that medical expertise and patients' expertise had on the Court, I refrain from arguing that a causal relationship exists between specific informational input and Court output (i.e., the decision). In other words, I am not arguing that certain types of information caused a certain decision. Instead, I accept at face value the Court's own explanation as to why they decided the cases as they did. Therefore, relying exclusively on the Court's own rationale in *Roe,* I attempt to determine how the Court actually used medical and patients' knowledge in the construction of the decision.
3. In actuality, this may have worked to the benefit of the pro-choice side since the particulars regarding Jane Roe, a.k.a. Norma McCorvey, may not have elicited sympathy: she had already lost custody of two children; she was a lesbian; she had a history of drug and alcohol abuse; and she was uneducated and poor. And while she had originally told Weddington and Coffee that she was pregnant as the result of a rape, she later recanted stating that she lied about the rape because she thought this would increase her chance of securing a legal abortion (McCorvey 1994: 179; see also Weddington 1992).
4. Congress appears to disagree with the Court's assessment, having passed into law with President Bill Clinton's signature the Freedom of Access to Clinics Entrances Act of 1994 (FACE), which makes it a federal crime to block access to clinics, or to harass or threaten with violence women who seek abortions or those who provide them.

CHAPTER 3

1. An April 1996 Gallup poll indicated that 75 percent of the respondents responded yes to the statement: "When a person has a disease that cannot be cured, do you think doctors should be allowed by law to end the patient's life by some painless means if the patients and his family request it, or not?"

The same question polled in July 1996 yielded an affirmative answer among 69 percent of the respondents. In this survey an additional, more specific question was then posed: "When a person has a disease that cannot be cured, do you think doctors should be allowed by law to assist the patient to commit suicide if the patient requests it, or not? Fifty-two percent answered yes, 42 percent answered no, and 6 percent offered no opinion. In addition, a study of oncology patients, oncologists, and the public published in Lancet found that about two-thirds of the patients and public viewed PAS as acceptable for patients with unremitting pain (Emanuel et al. 1996).

2. In choosing these descriptions, it is not my intent to erase the litigants from the cases but to avoid giving the perception that all patients or all physicians supported a single side of the PAS issue. I also hope that my selection of the terms "pro-PAS" and "anti-PAS" will not be interpreted as bearing the same judgmental assessments as those carried by the designations of "pro-abortion" or "anti-abortion" in that debate.

3. James Hoefler offers a clear description of this term: "The slippery slope refers to a continuum of ethical decisions; one end of the continuum, the high point of a slanted line, is defined by actions that are ethically acceptable. The further one moves down and away from this point, the more ethically suspect an action becomes. And the more steps one takes down the slope and away from the moral high ground, the easier it supposedly becomes to slide uncontrollably until entirely unethical actions at the lower end of the slope are practiced and accepted as the norm" (1997: 154). Hoefler also critiques this theory as overly simplistic and proposes in its stead a model that includes three inclines representing futility, autonomy, and dignity.

4. This was true despite the fact that Oregon voters had passed a referendum in 1994 to allow PAS since, rather than implement the Death with Dignity Act, the state legislature suspended its implementation and placed it on the ballot for another vote in October 1997. When the voters passed it again (and by a larger margin than the first time), the act became law. It was not until five months later, in March 1998, that a terminally ill patient became the first person to use legal PAS to end her life. In a study released by Oregon in August 1998, the state reported that during the first ten months of the act, ten patients used the act to receive fatal doses of prescription drugs, eight of these took their own lives, and two died without using these drugs.

5. To be successful a facial challenge must show that the law is not constitutional (i.e., permissible) under all or most constructions or applications. A facial challenge, is, therefore, a broad attack on the law and it is difficult to sustain. When the Court rejects a facial challenge, it is ruling that there are indeed circumstances under which the law is permissible. Therefore, such a ruling "does not foreclose the possibility that some applications of the statute might well be invalid" (Justice Stevens concurring in *Glucksberg*).

CHAPTER 4

1. Among those challenging the empirical validity of her study are: Kerber 1993: 103; Luria 1993: 200; Broughton 1993: 116; Greeno and Maccoby 1993: 196; Haan 1978; Brabeck 1993; Nunner-Winkler 1993; Walker 1993. Among those who defend Gilligan's methodology are Lyons 1982, 1983; Langdale 1983; and Baumrind 1993.

2. It would seem that empirical evidence showing a strong relationship between sex (i.e., male versus female) and guiding ethic (i.e., justice versus care) would be necessary before concluding that justice is masculine and caring is feminine. Even then, the question remains as to whether such differences are the product of biology or socialization. Yet, some scholars have argued that the correlative links between gender and the ethics are not necessary because the critical issue is the symbolic power of gender (see Friedman 1995: 62; Clemont 1996).

3. Scholars disagree as to whether the ethic of care is a stereotype that has both developed from and contributed to women's subordination (see Card 1995; MacKinnon in "Feminist Discourse" 1985; Kerber 1993: 107; Tronto 1993b: 112) or whether it has transformative power (see Ruddick 1989; Noddings 1984; Belenky et al. 1986; West 1997).

4. See Nicholson 1993; Stack 1993. For Gilligan's response see Gilligan 1993; "Feminist Discourse" 1985: 76.

5. While Gilligan goes on to link justice to men and care to women, it is not necessary for my purposes to follow suit. My purpose is not to establish how different genders engage in moral reasoning but to identify how these ethics influence legal norms and practices. That there is an imbalance in law whereby the ethic of justice dominates and the ethic of care is deliberately avoided is the point that interests me.

6. I am indebted to the students of my Spring '99 "U.S. Supreme Court" class for sharing their ideas on the ethics of justice and care and for testing mine. Their insights are reflected in the analysis that follows.

7. I am adopting here the language and description of two levels of analyses employed by Gayle Binion in her study of affirmative action policy. She describes "micro contextual analysis" as focusing "on the ways in which different circumstance or experience render imperative different conclusions or resolutions" (1998: 2). She proposes that a "macro contextual analysis" is complementary in that it places the particulars into an enlarged and comparative framework whereby the micro level distinctions can be assessed (1998: 3). I am following here Binion's suggestion that the two levels of analysis work together in conceptualizing the meanings of a case.

8. I am employing here terminology suggested by Judith Baer who distinguishes between constitutional meaning and political meaning (1992:

157–159). However, I am using the latter term in a broader sense than she does. While she refers to the "politics" of judicial decision making such as the ideology of the Justices, their understanding of the judicial role, efforts at persuasiveness, bargaining, etc., I mean the cultural context of the issue itself including its economic, moral, psychological, political, and historical dynamics.

CHAPTER 5

1. I want to be clear, however, that I am not striving to balance the patients' voices on the one side with those from the other side of these issues. In that I have focused on showing how the knowledge of the patients who were the actual litigants was left out of the case, and how their addition could change the case, I concentrate on discovering and adding these voices. However, if the Court were to take the model for a caring jurisprudence seriously, they would be obligated to seek the input of all patients who have something to say about the issue.

2. I say this with an awareness that there are groups composed of both pro-choice and pro-life advocates who seek to establish a "common ground" as well as scholars who have endeavored to close the gap between the two sides. While there has been some success in identifying shared values such as diminishing the number of unwanted pregnancies and supporting women who bring their pregnancies to term, the fundamental disagreement—whether abortion should be legal—resists resolution or compromise (see Behuniak-Long 1993).

3. This would, in fact, build on the concurrence of Justice O'Connor in the PAS cases who wrote that "there is no need to address the question whether suffering patients have a constitutionally cognizable interest in obtaining relief from the suffering that they may experience in the last days of their lives. There is no dispute that dying patients in Washington and New York can obtain palliative care, even when doing so would hasten their deaths" (138 L. Ed. 2d 772, at 798). Again, O'Connor is focusing on the fact that the law allows for such treatment and not whether such treatment is really available to patients.

Cases

Akron v. Akron Center for Reproductive Health, 462 U.S. 446 (1983).
Beal v. Doe, 432 U.S. 438 (1977).
Bellotti v. Baird, 443 U.S. 622 (1979).
Bigelow v. Virginia, 421 U.S. 809 (1975).
Bray v. Alexandria Women's Health Clinic, 506 U.S. 263 (1993).
Brown v. Board of Education, 347 U.S. 483 (1954).
Colautti v. Franklin, 439 U.S. 379 (1979).
Compassion in Dying v. Washington, 850 F. Supp. 1454 (W.D. Wash. 1994).
Compassion in Dying v. Washington, 49 F.3d 586 (9th Cir. 1995).
Compassion in Dying v. Washington, 79 F.3d 790 (9th Cir. 1996) (en banc).
Compassion in Dying v. Washington, 85 F.3d 1440 (9th Cir. 1996).
Cooper v. Aaron, 358 U.S. 1 (1958).
Cruzan v. Director, Missouri Department of Health, 497 U.S. 261 (1990).
DeShaney v. Winnebago County Department of Social Services, 489 U.S. 189 (1989).
Doe v. Bolton, 410 U.S. 179 (1973).
Furman v. Georgia, 408 U.S. 238 (1972).
Gregg v. Georgia, 428 U.S. 153 (1976).
H. L. v. Matheson, 450 U.S. 398 (1981).
Harris v. McRae, 448 U.S. 297 (1980).
Hodgson v. Minnesota, 497 U.S. 417 (1990).
Madsen v. Women's Health Center, 512 U.S. 753 (1994).
Maher v. Roe, 432 U.S. 464 (1977).
Mazurek v. Armstrong 520 U.S. 968, 117 S.Ct. 1865 (1997).
McCleskey v. Kemp, 481 U.S. 279 (1987).
National Organization for Women v. Scheidler, 510 U.S. 249 (1994).
New York v. Quill, 138 L.Ed 2d 834 (1997).
Ohio v. Akron Center for Reproductive Health, 497 U.S. 502 (1990).
Planned Parenthood of Central Missouri v. Danforth, 428 U.S. 52 (1976).
Planned Parenthood of Kansas City, Missouri v. Ashcroft, 462 U.S. 476 (1983).
Planned Parenthood of Southeastern Pennsylvania v. Casey, 505 U.S. 833 (1992).
Poelker v. Doe, 432 U.S. 519 (1977).
Quill v. Koppell, 870 F. Supp. 78 (S.D.N.Y. 1994).
Quill v. Vacco, 80 F3d 716 (2d Cir 1996).
Regents of the University of California v. Bakke, 438 U.S. 265 (1978).
Roe v. Wade, 410 U.S. 113 (1973).
Rust v. Sullivan, 500 U.S. 173 (1991).
Schenck v. Pro-Choice Network, 519 U.S. 357 (1997).

174   Cases

Simpoulous v. Virginia, 462 U.S. 506 (1983).
Thornburgh v. American College of Obstetricians and Gynecologists, 476 U.S. 747 (1986).
Vacco v. Quill, 135 L.Ed. 2d 1127 (1996) cert. granted.
Vacco v. Quill, 138 L.Ed 2d 834 (1997).
Washington v. Glucksberg, 135 L.Ed 2d 1128 (1996) cert. granted.
Washington v. Glucksberg, 138 L.Ed 2d 772 (1997).
Webster v. Reproductive Health Services, 492 U.S. 490 (1989).
Williams v. Zbaraz, 448 U.S. 358 (1980).

References

Albom, Mitch. 1997. *Tuesdays with Morrie: An Old Man, a Young Man, and Life's Greatest Lesson.* New York: Doubleday.

Alderman, Ellen, and Caroline Kennedy. 1997. *The Right to Privacy.* New York: Vintage Books.

Allende, Isabel, 1994. *Paula.* transl. Margaret Sayers Peden. New York: HarperCollins.

"Amazing Grace with Bill Moyers." 1995. Videorecording. Public Affairs Television.

Anderson, Margaret L. 1983. *Thinking about Women: Sociological and Feminist Perspectives.* New York: Macmillan Publishing Co.

Anderson, Patricia. 1996. *All of Us: Americans Talk About the Meaning of Death.* New York: Bantam Doubleday Dell.

Baer, Judith A. 1990. "What We Know as Women: A New Look at *Roe v. Wade.*" *NWSA Journal* 2: 558–582.

————. 1992. "How Is Law Male? A Feminist Perspective on Constitutional Interpretation," in *Feminist Jurisprudence: The Difference Debate,* ed. Leslie Friedman Goldstein, Lanham, MD: Rowman & Littlefield.

Baier, Annette. 1995. "The Need for More Than Justice." In *Justice and Care: Essential Readings in Feminist Ethics,* ed. Virginia Held. Boulder: Westview Press.

Bartlett, Katharine T. 1990. "Feminist Legal Methods." *Harvard Law Review* 103: 829–888.

Bartlett, Katharine T. and Rosanne Kennedy, eds. 1991. *Feminist Legal Theory: Readings in Law and Gender.* Boulder: Westview Press.

Bauby, Jean-Dominique. 1997. *The Diving Bell and the Butterfly,* transl. Jeremy Leggatt. New York: Alfred A. Knopf.

Baumrind, Diana. 1993. "Sex Differences in Moral Reasoning: Response to Walker's Conclusion that There Are None," in *An Ethic of Care,* ed. Mary Jeanne Larrabee. New York: Routledge.

Becker, Mary E. 1992. "The Politics of Women's Wrongs and the Bill of 'Rights': A Bicentennial Perspective." *University of Chicago Law Review* 59: 453–517.

Behuniak-Long, Susan. 1992. "Justice Sandra Day O'Connor and the Power of Maternal Legal Thinking." *Review of Politics* 54: 417–444.

————. 1993. "Review Essay: Abortion and Compromise." *Polity* 26: 141–151.

Belenky, Mary Field, Blythe McVicker Clinchy, Nancy Rule Goldberger, and Jill Mattuck Tarule. 1986. *Women's Ways of Knowing: The Development of Self, Voice, and Mind.* New York: Basic Books.

Bender, Leslie. 1988. "A Lawyer's Primer on Feminist Theory and Tort." *Journal of Legal Education* 38: 3.

————. 1992. "A Feminist Analysis of Physician-Assisted Dying and Voluntary Active Euthanasia." *Tennessee Law Review* 59: 520–546.

————. 1994. "Teaching Torts as if Gender Matters: Intentional Torts." *Virginia Journal of Social Policy and the Law* 2: 115–163.

Bickel, Alexander. 1962. *The Least Dangerous Branch*. Indianapolis, IN: Bobbs-Merrill.

Binion, Gayle. 1991. "Toward a Feminist Regrounding of Constitutional Law." *Social Science Quarterly* 72: 207–220.

————. 1998. "Affirmative Equality: Putting Policy in Context." Paper presented at the annual meeting of the Northeast Political Science Association, November 12–14, 1998, Boston, MA.

Biskupic, Joan. 1997. "Justices Skeptical of Assisted Suicide." Washington *Post* (January 9) A1, A17.

Black, Charles. 1960. "The Lawfulness of the Segregation Decision." *Yale Law Journal* 69: 421.

Blumenfeld, Laura. 1997. "At Dawn, Activists Greet Matters of Death in Shades of Gray." Washington *Post* (January 9) A1, A17.

Bolotin, Susan. 1997. "Slash, Burn and Poison." [review of *To Dance With the Devil*] New York *Times Book Review* (April 13), 8.

Bonavoglia, Angela. 1991. *The Choices We Made: Twenty-Five Women and Men Speak Out about Abortion*. New York: Random House.

Bonds, Curley. 1990. "The Hippocratic Oath: A Basis for Modern Ethical Standards." *JAMA* 264: 2311.

Bordo, Susan. 1987. *The Flight to Objectivity: Essays on Cartesianism and Culture*. Albany: State University of New York Press.

Brabeck, Mary. 1993. "Moral Judgment: Theory and Research on Differences between Males and Females," in *An Ethic of Care*, ed. Mary Jeanne Larrabee. New York: Routledge.

Brief *Amicus Curiae* of Not Dead Yet and American Disabled for Attendant Programs in Support of Petitioners, *Vacco v. Quill*.

Brief *Amicus Curiae* of Surviving Family Members in Support of Physician-Assisted Dying, *Washington v. Glucksberg* and *Vacco v. Quill*.

Brief for Petitioners, *Glucksberg*.

Brief for Petitioners, *Quill*.

Brief for Respondents, *Glucksberg*.

Brief for Respondents, *Quill*.

Brief for the *Amici Curiae* Women Who Have Had Abortions and Friends of Amici Curiae in Support of Appellees, *Webster v. Reproductive Health Services*.

Brief for the National Abortion Rights Action League et al. as *Amici Curiae* in Support of Appellees, *Thornburgh v. American College of Ostretricians and Gynecologists*.

Brief of the American College of Obstetricians and Gynecologists, et al., on behalf of Appellant, *Roe v. Wade*, 1971.

Brief of the American Medical Association et al. as *Amici Curiae* in Support of Petitioners, *Vacco v. Quill*.

Brief of 281 American Historians, on behalf of Respondent, *Webster v. Reproductive Health Services*, 1983.

Brodkey, Harold. 1996. *This Wild Darkness: The Story of My Death*. New York: Henry Holt and Company.

Brody, Howard. 1982. "Commentary on 'Error, Malpractice, and the Problem of Universals'." *Journal of Medicine and Philosophy* 7: 251–257.

————. 1987. *Stories of Sickness*. New Haven: Yale University Press.

Broughton, John. 1993. "Women's Rationality and Men's Virtues," in *An Ethic of Care*, ed. Mary Jeanne Larrabee. New York: Routledge.

Brown, Norman K. 1971. "How Do Nurses Feel About Euthanasia and Abortion." *American Journal of Nursing* 71 (July): 1415.

Broyard, Anatole. 1992. *Intoxicated By My Illness: And Other Writings on Life and Death*. New York: Clarkson Potter Publishers.

Byron, William, J., S.J. 1989. *Quadrangle Considerations*. Chicago: Loyola University Press.

Cain, Patricia A. 1988. "Teaching Feminist Legal Theory at Texas: Listening to Difference and Exploring Connections." *Journal of Legal Education* 38: 165–181.

Campi, Christina Walker. 1998. "When Dying Is as Hard as Birth." New York *Times* (January 5), A19.

Campo, Rafael. 1997. *The Poetry of Healing: A Doctor's Education in Empathy, Identity, and Desire*. New York: W.W. Norton & Co.

Card, Claudia. 1995. "Gender and Moral Luck," in *Justice and Care: Essential Readings in Feminist Ethics*, ed. Virginia Held. Boulder: Westview Press.

Cardozo, Benjamin. 1921. *The Nature of the Judicial Process*. New Haven: Yale University Press.

Cassell, Eric J. 1991. *The Nature of Suffering and the Goals of Medicine*. New York: Oxford University Press.

Clark, Brian. 1978. *Whose Life Is It Anyway?* New York: Avon Books.

Clemont, Grace. 1996. *Care, Autonomy, and Justice: Feminism and the Ethic of Care*. Boulder: Westview Press.

Coles, Robert. 1989. *The Call of Stories: Teaching and the Moral Imagination*. Boston: Houghton Mifflin Co.

Colker, Ruth. 1992. *Abortion and Dialogue: Pro-Choice, Pro-Life and American Law*. Bloomington: Indiana University Press.

Conant, James Bryant. 1964. *Two Modes of Thought: My Encounters with Science and Education*. New York: Trident Press.

Cook, Charles. 1975. "Introduction," in *The Sanctity of Social Life: Physician's Treatment of Critically Ill Patients*, ed. by Diana Crane. New York: Russell Sage Foundation.

Cook, Elizabeth Adell, Ted G. Jelen, and Clyde Wilcox. 1992. *Between Two Absolutes: Public Opinion and the Politics of Abortion*. Boulder: Westview Press.

Coombs, Robert H., and Joanne St. John. 1979. *Making It in Med School*. New York: SP Medical & Scientific Books.

Craig, Barbara Hinkson, and David M. O'Brien. 1993. *Abortion and American Politics*. Chatham, NJ: Chatham House.

Crenshaw, Kimberle. 1988. "Race, Reform, and Retrenchment: Transformation and Legitimation in Antidiscrimination Law." *Harvard Law Review* 101: 1331.

———. 1989. "Demarginalizing the Intersection of Race and Sex: A Black Feminist Critique of Antidiscrimination Doctrine, Feminist Theory and Antiracist Politics." *University of Chicago Legal Forum*: 139.

Dalton, Clare. 1991. "Deconstructing Contract Doctrine," in *Feminist Legal Theory: Readings in Law and Gender* ed. Katharine Bartlett and Rosanne Kennedy. Boulder: Westview Press.

Daly, Kathleen. 1989. "Criminal Justice Ideologies and Practices in Different Voices: Some Feminist Questions about Justice." *International Journal of the Sociology of Law* 17: 1–18.

Delgado, Richard. 1989. "Storytelling for Oppositionists and Others: A Plea for Narrative." *Michigan Law Review* 87: 2411–2441.

Delgado, Richard, and Jean Stefancic. 1993. "Critical Race Theory: An Annotated Bibli-ography." *Virginia Law Review* 79: 461.

Delury, George E. 1997. *But What If She Wants to Die? A Husband's Diary*. Secaucus, NJ: Birch Lane Press.

"Demonstrators Take Opposing Sides of Issue." 1997. Syracuse *Post-Standard* (January 9) A–10.

Duff, Raymond, and A.G.M. Campbell. 1976. "On Deciding the Care of Severely Handi-capped or Dying Persons: With Particular Reference to Infants." *Pediatrics* 57 (April): 487–493.

Edelstein, Ludwig. 1943. *The Hippocratic Oath: Text, Translation and Interpretation*. Baltimore: Johns Hopkins University Press.

Ehrenreich, Barbara, and Deirdre English. 1979. *For Her Own Good: 150 Years of the Experts' Advice to Women*. Garden City, NY: Anchor Books.

Ely, John Hart. 1980. *Democracy and Distrust: A Theory of Judicial Review*. Cambridge, MA: Harvard University Press.

Emanuel, Ezekiel J., Diane L. Fairclough, Elisabeth R. Daniels, and Brian R. Clarridge. 1996. "Euthanasia and Physician-Assisted Suicide: Attitudes and Experiences of Oncol-ogy Patients, Oncologists, and the Public." *Lancet* 347: 1805–1810.

Epstein, Cynthia Fuchs. 1988. *Deceptive Distinctions: Sex, Gender, and the Social Order*. New Haven: Yale University Press.

Estrich, Susan. 1987. *Real Rape*. Cambridge: Harvard University Press.

"Excerpts from the Supreme Court Decision on Physician-Assisted Suicide." 1997. Wash-ington *Post* (January 9) A16.

Farber, Daniel A. and Suzanna Sherry. 1997. *Beyond All Reason: The Radical Assault on Truth in American Law*. New York: Oxford University Press.

Farley, Lin. 1978. *Sexual Shakedown*. New York: Warner.

"Fear Shuts Down Abortion Providers." 1998. Syracuse *Post-Standard* (December 12) A–7.

"Feminist Discourse, Moral Values, and the Law—A Conversation." 1985. *Buffalo Law Re-view* 34: 11–87.

Finley, Lucinda. 1989. "Breaking Women's Silence in Law: The Dilemma of the Gendered Nature of Legal Reasoning." *Notre Dame Law Review* 64: 886.

Freidson, Eliot. 1970. *Profession of Medicine: A Study of the Sociology of Applied Knowledge*. New York: Dodd, Mead & Company.

Friedman, Marilyn. 1995. "Beyond Caring: The De-Moralization of Gender," in *Justice and Care: Essential Readings in Feminist Ethics*, ed. Virginia Held. Boulder: Westview Press.

Frug, Mary Joe. 1992. *Postmodern Legal Feminism*. New York: Routledge.

Gallup, George, Jr. 1996. *The Gallup Poll: Public Opinion*. Wilmington, DE: Scholarly Re-sources Inc.

Garrow, David J. 1994. *Liberty and Sexuality: The Right to Privacy and the Making of* Roe v. Wade. New York: Macmillan Publishing.

Gilligan, Carol. 1982. *In a Different Voice: Psychological Theory and Women's Development*. Cam-bridge: Harvard University Press.

———. 1993. "A Reply to Critics," in *An Ethic of Care*, ed. Mary Jeanne Larrabee, New York: Routledge.

Glendon, Mary Ann. 1991. *Rights Talk: The Impoverishment of Political Discourse*. New York: Free Press.

Gorovitz, Samuel, and Alasdair MacIntyre. 1976. "Toward a Theory of Medical Fallibility." *Journal of Medicine and Philosophy* 1: 51–71.

Gray, John. 1992. *Men Are from Mars, Women Are from Venus*. New York: Harper/Collins.

Greenhouse, Linda. 1997. "High Court Hears 2 Cases Involving Assisted Suicide." New York *Times* (January 9) A1, B9.

Greeno, Catherine G. and Eleanor E. Maccoby. 1993. "How Different Is the 'Different Voice?'" in *An Ethic of Care*, ed. Mary Jeanne Larrabee. New York: Routledge.

Groopman, Jerome. 1997. *The Measure of Our Days: New Beginnings at Life's End*. New York: Viking.

Guinier, Lani, Michelle Fine, and Jane Balin. 1997. *Becoming Gentlemen: Women, Law School, and Institutional Change*. Boston: Beacon Press.

Hann, Norma. 1978. "Two Moralities in Contexts." *Journal of Personality and Social Psychology* 36: 286–305.

Harmon, Louise. 1998. *Fragments on the Deathwatch*. Boston: Beacon Press.

Harris, Angela. 1991. "Race and Essentialism in Feminist Legal Theory," in *Feminist Legal Theory: Readings in Law and Gender*, ed. Katharine Bartlett and Rosanne Kennedy. Boulder: Westview Press.

Harvey, Nancy. 1991. *Tapestry Weaving: A Comprehensive Study Guide*. Loveland, CO: Interweave Press.

Hawkesworth, Mary E. 1989. "Knowers, Knowing, Known: Feminist Theory and Claims of Truth." *Signs* 14: 533–557.

Held, Virginia. 1993. *Feminist Morality: Transforming Culture, Society, and Politics*. Chicago: University of Chicago Press.

———, ed. 1995. *Justice and Care: Essential Readings in Feminist Ethics*. Boulder, CO: Westview Press.

Hilfiker, David. 1985. *Healing the Wounds: A Physician Looks at His Work*. New York: Pantheon Books.

Hoefler, James M. 1997. *Managing Death: The First Guide for Patients, Family Members, and Care Providers on Forgoing Treatment at the End of Life*. Boulder: Westview Press.

Hoffman, Robert. 1975. "Death and Dignity," in *Beneficent Euthanasia*, ed. Marvin Kohl. Buffalo: Prometheus Books.

Hood, Ann. 1997. "Rage Against the Dying of the Light." New York *Times* (August 2) 19.

Humphry, Derek. 1978. *Jean's Way*. New York: Quartet Books.

———. 1991. *Final Exit: Self-Deliverance and Assisted Suicide for the Dying*. Eugene, OR: Hemlock Society.

Hunter, Kathryn Montgomery. 1991. *Doctors' Stories: The Narrative Structure of Medical Knowledge*. Princeton: Princeton University Press.

Irons, Peter, and Stephanie Guitton, eds. 1993. *May It Please the Court: Transcripts of 23 Live Recordings of Landamrk Cases as Argued Before the Supreme Court*. New York: New Press.

Jaff, Jennifer. 1986. "Frame-Shifting: An Empowering Methodology for Teaching and Learning Legal Reasoning." *Journal of Legal Education* 36: 249–267.

Jaggar, Alison M. 1983. *Feminist Politics and Human Nature*. Totowa, NJ: Rowman and Allanheld.

———. 1995. "Caring as a Feminist Practice of Moral Reason," in *Justice and Care: Essential Readings in Feminist Ethics*, ed. Virginia Held. Boulder: Westview Press.

———. 1997. "Love and Knowledge: Emotion in Feminist Epistemology," in *Feminisms*, ed. Sandra Kemp and Judith Squires. New York: Oxford University Press.

Joint Appendix, *Glucksberg.*

Karst, Kenneth. 1984. "Woman's Constitution." *Duke Law Journal* 1984: 447.

Kelley, Maria Felicia. 1996. *The Choice I Made: A Week in the Life of a Young Woman Who Chose an Abortion.* New York: April Arts Press.

Kellough, Gail. 1996. *Aborting Law: An Exploration of the Politics of Motherhood and Medicine.* Toronto: University of Toronto Press.

Kennedy, Duncan, and Karl Klare. 1984. "Bibliography of Critical Legal Studies." *Yale Law Journal* 94: 461.

Kerber, Linda K. 1993. "Some Cautionary Words for Historians," in *An Ethic of Care*, ed. Mary Jeanne Larrabee. New York: Routledge.

Klass, Perri. 1987. *A Not Entirely Benign Procedure: Four Years as a Medical Student.* New York: G. P. Putnam's Sons.

Kluger, Jeffrey. 1997. "Mr. Natural." *Time* (May 12) 68–75.

Kohlberg, Laurence. 1981. *Essays on Moral Development.* Vol. 1: *The Philosophy of Moral Development.* San Francisco: Harper & Row.

Kohlberg, Laurence, and R. Kramer. 1969. "Continuities and Discontinuities in Childhood and Adult Moral Development." *Human Development* 12: 93–120.

Konner, Melvin. 1987. *Becoming a Doctor: A Journey of Initiation in Medical School.* New York: Viking Penguin.

Kubler-Ross, Elizabeth. 1969. *On Death and Dying.* New York: Macmillan Publishing Co.

———, ed. 1975. *Death: The Final Stage of Growth.* Englewood Cliffs, NJ: Prentice Hall.

Kushner, Eve. 1997. *Experiencing Abortion: A Weaving of Women's Words.* Binghamton, NY: Haworth Press.

Kutner, Luis. 1976. "The Living Will: Coping with the Historical Event of Death." *Baylor Law Review* 27: 39–53.

Langdale, Sharry. 1983. "Moral Orientations and Moral Development." Doctoral dissertation, Harvard Graduate School of Education.

Larrabee, Mary Jeanne, ed. 1993. *An Ethic of Care: Feminist and Interdisciplinary Perspectives.* New York: Routledge.

Lastrucci, Carlo L. 1967. *The Scientific Approach: Basic Principles of the Scientific Method.* Cambridge: Schenkman Publishing Co.

Law, Sylvia. 1984. "Rethinking the Constitution." *University of Pennsylvania Law Review* 132: 955–1040.

Lebacqz, Karen. 1986. *Six Theories of Justice.* Minneapolis: Augsburg Publishing House.

Lelyveld, Nita. 1997. "Debating the Right to Die." *Rutland-Herald* (November 2) C–1, 4.

Levi, Edward H. 1949. *An Introduction to Legal Reasoning.* Chicago: University of Chicago Press.

Lipsyte, Robert. 1998. *In the Country of Illness: Comfort and Advice for the Journey.* New York: Alfred A. Knopf.

Littleton, Christine. 1987. "Reconstructing Sexual Equality." *California Law Review* 75: 1279.

Luciano, Lani. 1998. "A Dying Woman and Her Family Ponder the Cost of Living." *Money* (April 1998) 85, 88, 90.

Luker, Kristin. 1984. *Abortion and the Politics of Motherhood.* Berkeley: University of California Press.

Luria, Zella. 1993. "A Methodological Critique," in *An Ethic of Care*, ed. Mary Jeanne Larrabee. New York: Routledge.

Lyons, David. 1993. *Moral Aspects of Legal Theory: Essays on Law, Justice, and Political Responsibility.* Cambridge: Cambridge University Press.

Lyons, Nona. 1982. "Conceptions of Self and Morality and Modes of Moral Choice." Doctoral dissertation, Harvard Graduate School of Education.

———. 1983. "Two Perspectives: On Self, Relationships, and Morality." *Harvard Educational Review* 53: 125–144.

MacKinnon, Catharine. 1979. *Sexual Harassment of Working Women.* Cambridge: Harvard University Press.

———. 1987. *Feminism Unmodified: Discourses on Life and Law.* Cambridge: Harvard University Press.

———. 1989. *Toward a Feminist Theory of the State.* Cambridge: Harvard University Press.

Mathewes-Green, Frederica. 1997. *Real Choices: Listening to Women, Looking for Alternatives to Abortion.* Ben Lomond, CA: Conciliar Press.

Matsuda, Mari. 1988. "Affirmative Action and Legal Knowledge: Planting Seeds in Plowed-Up Ground." *Harvard Women's Law Journal* 11: 1–17.

May, William F. 1991. *The Patient's Ordeal.* Bloomington: Indiana University Press.

McCorvey, Norma, with Andy Meisler. 1994. *I Am Roe: My Life, Roe v. Wade, and Freedom of Choice.* New York: HarperCollins.

McDonagh, Eileen L. 1996. *Breaking the Abortion Deadlock: From Choice to Consent.* New York: Oxford University Press.

Menkel-Meadow, Carrie. 1985. "Portia in a Different Voice: Reflections on a Women's Lawyering Process." *Berkeley Women's Law Journal* 1: 39–63.

———. 1988. "Feminist Legal Theory, Critical Legal Studies and Legal Education or the 'Fem-Crits' Go to Law School." *Journal of Legal Education* 38: 61–85.

———. 1996. "What's Gender Got to Do With It?: The Politics and Morality of an Ethic of Care." *Review of Law and Social Change* 22: 265–293.

———. 1997. "Women's Ways of 'Knowing' Law: Feminist Legal Epistemology, Pedagogy, and Jurisprudence," in *Knowledge, Difference, and Power.* ed. Nancy Goldberger et al. New York: Basic Books.

Mersky, Roy M. ed., 1996. *A Documentary History of the Legal Aspects of Abortion in the United States:* Planned Parenthood v. Casey, Vol. I–VI. Littleton, CO: Fred B. Rothman & Co.

Mersky, Roy M., and Gary R. Hartman, eds. 1990. *A Documentary History of the Legal Aspects of Abortion in the United States:* Webster v. Reproductive Health Services, Vol. I–VIII. Littleton, CO: Fred B. Rothman & Co.

———. 1993. *A Documentary History of the Legal Aspects of Abortion in the United States:* Roe v. Wade, Vol. I–III. Littleton, CO: Fred B. Rothman & Co.

Miller, Arthur S., and Ronald F. Howel. 1960. "The Myth of Neutrality in Constitutional Adjudication." *University of Chicago Law Review* 27: 661.

Minda, Gary. 1995. *Postmodern Legal Movements: Law and Jurisprudence at Century's End.* New York: New York University Press.

Minow, Martha. 1986. "Law Turning Outward." *Telos* 73: 79.

———. 1987. "The Supreme Court 1986 Term—Foreword: Justice Engendered." *Harvard Law Review* 101: 10.

———. 1990. *Making All the Difference: Inclusion, Exclusion, and American Law.* Ithaca: Cornell University Press.

————. 1997. "Introduction: Seeking Justice," in *Outside the Law: Narratives on Justice in America.* ed. Susan Richards Shreve and Porter Shreve. Boston: Beacon Press.

Mizrahi, Terry. 1986. *Getting Rid of Patients: Contradictions in the Socialization of Physicians.* New Brunswick, NJ: Rutgers University Press.

"National Abortion Rights Action League *Amicus* Brief for *Richard Thornburgh v. American College of Obstetricians and Gynecologists.*" 1986. *Women's Rights Law Reporter* 9: 3–24.

Nedelsky, Jennifer. 1993. "Reconceiving Rights as Relationships." *Revue d'etudes constitutionnelles* 1: 1–26.

New York State Task Force on Life and the Law. 1994. *When Death Is Sought: Assisted Suicide and Euthanasia in the Medical Context.*

Nicholson, Linda J. 1993. "Women, Morality, and History," in *An Ethic of Care,* ed. Mary Jeanne Larrabee. New York: Routledge.

Noddings, Nel. 1984. *Caring: A Feminine Approach to Ethics and Moral Education.* Berkeley: University of California Press.

Nuland, Sherwin B. 1993. *How We Die: Reflections on Life's Final Chapter.* New York: Vintage Books.

Nunner-Winkler, Gertrude. 1993. "Two Moralities? A Critical Discussion of an Ethic of Care and Responsibility versus an Ethic of Rights and Justice," in *An Ethic of Care,* ed. Mary Jeanne Larrabee. New York: Routledge.

Nussbaum Martha C. 1990. *Love's Knowledge: Essays on Philosophy and Literature.* New York: Oxford University Press.

————. 1995. *Poetic Justice: The Literary Imagination and Public Life.* Boston: Beacon Press.

O'Connor, Karen. 1996. *No Neutral Gound? Abortion Politics in an Age of Absolutes.* Boulder: Westview Press.

Okin, Susan Moller. 1989. *Justice, Gender, and the Family.* New York: Basic Books.

Olsen, Frances. 1984. "Statutory Rape: A Feminist Critique of Rights Analysis." *Texas Law Review* 63: 387.

Osler, William. 1903. "On the Need of a Radical Reform in Our Methods of Teaching Senior Students." *Medical News* 82: 48–53.

Patterson, Edwin W. 1951. "The Case Method in American Legal Education: Its Origins and Objectives." *Journal of Legal Education* 4: 1–21.

Petchesky, Rosalind Pollack. 1984. *Abortion and Women's Choice.* New York: Longman.

————. 1986. "Introduction: NARAL *Amicus* Brief: *Richard Thornburgh v. American College of Obstetricians and Gynecologists.*" *Women's Rights Law Reporter* 9: 3–6.

Petrow, Steven. 1990. *Dancing Against the Darkness: A Journey through America in the Age of AIDS.* Lexington, MA: Lexington Books.

Pickard, Toni. 1983. "Experience as Teacher: Discovering the Politics of Law Teaching." *University of Toronto Law Journal* 33: 279–314.

————. 1987–88. "Is Real Life Finally Happening?" *Canadian Journal of Women and Law* 2: 432.

Quill, Timothy E. 1996. *A Midwife Through the Dying Process: Stories of Healing and Hard Choices at the End of Life.* Baltimore: Johns Hopkins University Press.

Quindlen, Anna. 1997. "Preface," in *Choices: Women Speak Out About Abortion* ed. Karen A. Schneider. Washington, DC: NARAL Foundation.

Radner, Gilda. 1990. *It's Always Something.* New York: Simon and Schuster.

Rawls, John. 1971. *A Theory of Justice.* Cambridge: Harvard University Press.

Reardon, David C. 1987. *Aborted Women: Silent No More.* Chicago: Loyola University Press.

Remoff, Heather Trexler. 1997. *February Light: A Love Letter to the Seasons During a Year of Cancer and Recovery.* New York: St. Martin's Press.

Resnik, Judith. 1988. "On the Bias: Feminist Reconsiderations of the Aspirations for Our Judges." *Southern California Law Review* 61: 1877–1955.

Rhode, Deborah L. 1990. "Feminist Legal Theories." *Stanford Law Review* 42: 617.

Rifkin, Janet. 1980. "Toward a Theory of Law and Patriarchy." *Harvard Women's Law Journal* (3) 83: 95.

Rollin, Betty. 1976. *First You Cry*. Philadelphia: Lippincott.

———. 1998. *Last Wish*. New York: PublicAffairs.

Rosenblatt, Roger. 1992. *Life Itself: Abortion in the American Mind*. New York: Random House.

Ruddick, Sara. 1989. *Maternal Thinking: Toward a Politics of Peace*. New York: Ballantine Books.

———. 1995. "Injustice in Families: Assault and Domination, in *Justice and Care: Essential Readings in Feminist Ethics*, ed. Virginia Held. Boulder: Westview Press.

Sacks, Oliver. 1985. *The Man Who Mistook His Wife for a Hat and Other Clinical Tales*. New York: Summit Books.

Sarachild, Kathie. 1995. "Consciousness Raising: A Radical Weapon," in *Women: Images and Realities, A Multicultural Reader*, ed. Amy Kesselman, Lily N. McNair, and Nancy Schniedewind. Mountain View, CA: Mayfield Publishing Company.

Scales, Ann C. 1981. "Towards a Feminist Jurisprudence." *Indiana Law Journal* 56: 375.

———. 1986. "The Emergence of Feminist Jurisprudence: An Essay." *Yale Law Journal* 95: 1373–1403.

Schneider, Karen A., ed. 1997. *Choices: Women Speak Out About Abortion*. Washington, DC: NARAL Foundation.

Schwartz, Bernard. 1996. *Decision: How the Supreme Court Decides Cases*. New York: Oxford Press.

Selzer, Richard. 1993. *Raising the Dead*. New York: Penguin Books.

Sherry, Suzanna. 1986. "Civic Virtue and the Feminine Voice in Constitutional Adjudication." *University of Virginia Law Review* 72: 543.

Siegel, Bernie S. 1990. *Love, Medicine and Miracles*. New York: Harper Perennial.

Sontag, Susan. 1990. *Illness as Metaphor and AIDS and Its Metaphors*. New York: Doubleday.

Stabiner, Karen. 1997. *To Dance With the Devil: The New War on Breast Cancer*. New York: Delacorte Press.

Stack, Carol B. 1993. "The Culture of Gender: Women and Men of Color," in *An Ethic of Care*, ed. Mary Jeanne Larrabee. New York: Routledge.

Stolberg, Sheryl Gay. 1997. "Cries of the Dying Awaken Doctors to a New Approach." New York *Times* (June 30) A1, B7.

———. 1997. "The Good Death: Embracing a Right to Die Well." New York *Times* (June 29) Section 4, 1, 4.

"Supreme Court Proceedings. Arguments Before the Court. Health Care." 1997. *United States Law Week* 65: 3481.

Sweet, Gail Grenier. 1985. *Pro-Life Feminism: Different Voices*. Toronto: Life Cycle Books.

Talerico, Susette. 1988. "Women as Offenders and Victims in Criminal Justice," in *Women in the Judicial Process*, ed. Beverly B. Cook, Leslie Friedman Goldstein, Karen O'Connor, and Susette Talerico. Washington, DC: American Political Science Association.

Tannen, Deborah. 1990. *You Just Don't Understand: Women and Men in Conversation*. New York: William Morrow and Company.

Thomas, Gary. 1997. "Deadly Compassion." *Christianity Today* (June 16) 14–21.

Tilberis, Liz with Aimee Lee Ball. 1998. *No Time to Die*. Boston: Little, Brown and Company.

Tong, Rosemarie. 1993. *Feminine and Feminist Ethics*. Belmont, CA: Wadsworth Publishing Company.

Toulmin, Stephen. 1961. *Foresight and Understanding: An Enquiry into the Aims of Science*. Bloomington: Indiana University Press.

Tronto, Joan. 1993a. *Moral Boundaries: A Political Argument for an Ethic of Care*. New York: Routledge.

———. 1993b. "Beyond Gender Difference to a Theory of Care," in *An Ethic of Care*, ed. Mary Jeanne Larrabee. New York: Routledge.

———. 1995. "Women and Caring: What Can Feminists Learn About Morality from Caring?" in *Justice and Care: Essential Readings in Feminist Ethics*, ed. Virginia Held. Boulder: Westview Press.

Tushnet, Mark. 1991. "Critical Legal Studies: A Political History." *Yale Law Journal* 100: 1515.

Unger, Roberto. 1975. *Knowledge and Politics*. New York: Free Press.

"Vacco Argues for Reinstatement of New York's Assisted-Suicide Ban." 1997. Syracuse *Post-Standard* (January 9) A–10.

Van Praagh, Shauna. 1992. "Stories in Law School: An Essay on Language, Participation, and the Power of Legal Education." *Columbia Journal of Gender and Law* 2: 111–144.

Walker, Lawrence J. 1993. "Sex Differences in the Development of Moral Reasoning: A Critical Review," in *An Ethic of Care*, ed. Mary Jeanne Larrabee. New York: Routledge.

Walker, Lenore. 1984. *The Battered Woman Syndrome*. New York: Springer.

Walker, Margaret Urban. 1995. "Moral Understandings: Alternative 'Epistemology' for a Feminist Ethics," in *Justice and Care: Essential Readings in Feminist Ethics*, ed. Virginia Held. Boulder: Westview Press.

Warner, Gale. 1998. *Dancing at the Edge of Life: A Memoir*. New York: Hyperion.

Wasby, Stephen L. 1993. *The Supreme Court in the Federal Judicial System*, 4th ed. Chicago: Nelson-Hall Publishers.

Wechsler, Herbert. 1959. "Toward Neutral Principles of Constitutional Law." *Harvard Law Review* 73: 1.

Weddington, Sarah. 1992. *A Question of Choice*. New York: G. P. Putnam's Sons.

West, Robin. 1988. "Jurisprudence and Gender." *University of Chicago Law Review* 55: 1.

———. 1997. *Caring for Justice*. New York: New York University Press.

Wilkes, Paul. 1997. "Dying Well Is the Best Revenge." New York *Times Magazine* (July 6) 32–38.

Williams, Joan C. 1992. "Deconstructing Gender," in *Feminist Jurisprudence: The Difference Debate*, ed. Leslie Friedman Goldstein. Lanham, MD: Rowman & Littlefield.

Williams, Patricia J. 1991. *The Alchemy of Race and Rights: Diary of a Law Professor*. Cambridge: Harvard University Press.

Williams, Wendy. 1985. "Equality's Riddle: Pregnancy and the Equal Treatment/Special Treatment Debate." *New York University Review of Law and Social Change* 13: 525.

Wishik, Heather Ruth. 1986. "To Question Everything: The Inquiries of Feminist Jurisprudence," *Berkeley Women's Law Journal* 1: 64–77.

Woodward, Bob, and Scott Armstrong. 1979. *The Brethren: Inside the Supreme Court*. New York: Simon and Schuster.

Index

AAPPP. *See* American Association of Planned
Parenthood Physicians
abortion, xii, xix, 1, 137–49; access to, 57,
140, 145, 146; choosing, 49, 143; court
opinions on, 46–50; cultural context of,
61, 138, 144; as equality issue, 41–42;
illegal, 40, 47, 124, 129, 138, 139, 140;
legal, 36, 124, 139, 140, 141, 145, 146;
legal knowledge/reasoning and, 18;
macrolevel analysis of, 141–44, 165;
medical/legal authorities and, 32, 46, 134;
as medical issue, 39, 41, 51, 52–53, 54, 59,
137; microlevel analysis of, 137–41; as
moral issue, 41–42; mortality rate of, 47;
PAS and, 66–67; personal knowledge and,
25, 138–39; politics of, 62, 63, 141; as
private issue, 108, 127; resolution of, 166,
167; restrictions on, 32, 55, 141, 165; right
to, 25, 35–36, 58, 145, 148, 165; safety of,
10, 39, 42–43, 53; as social issue, 137; state
funding for, 52; substantial obstacle to, 61,
62, 148. *See also* unwanted pregnancy
abortion laws, 62, 116, 144, 150; changing,
33–34, 35, 47; freedom of speech and, 60;
physicians and, 29
"Abortion Rights: Silent No More"
campaign, brief by, 138
ACOG. *See* American College of
Obstetricians and Gynecologists
Acree, Glynn, 103
affirmative action, 130, 170n7
AIDS: assisted suicide and, 154; death from,
75, 163
AMA. *See* American Medical Association
"Amazing Grace" (Newton), 133, 149, 166
American Association of Critical Care
Nurses, PAS and, 83

American Association of Homes & Services
for the Aging, brief by, 83, 85
American Association of Planned Parenthood
Physicians (AAPPP), brief by, 43
American Bar Association, *Roe* and, 47
American College of Legal Medicine, PAS
and, 83
American College of Obstetricians
and Gynecologists (ACOG), 67; abortion
and, 37; brief by, 42, 43, 44;
doctor-patient relationship and, 42
American College of Physicians, PAS and, 78
American Disabled for Attendant Programs
Today, brief by, 85
American Ethical Union, 43
American Geriatrics Society: brief by, 85; PAS
and, 78
American Law Institute Model Penal Code,
50, 70
American Medical Association (AMA): abortion
and, 37, 46, 137; brief by, 94; PAS and, 67,
68, 78, 83; terminal sedation and, 98
American Medical Student Association, PAS
and, 83
American Medical Women's Association, brief
by, 43
American Nurses Association, PAS and, 83
American Osteopathic Association, PAS and, 83
American Psychiatric Association (APA), 45;
brief by, 43; PAS and, 83
American Society of Clinical Pathologists,
PAS and, 83
American Suicide Foundation, brief by, 85
Americans United for Life, 43; brief by, 38
amici briefs, 135; abortion, 33, 36–42, 45, 70; PAS,
68, 75, 79–80, 81 (table), 82 (table), 83, 84
(table), 85, 86 (table), 87–88, 90, 99, 127, 129

Angel of Mercy, 103, 104, 132
APA. *See* American Psychiatric Association
argumentation, 14, 36; abortion, 33, 37; PAS, 74
assisted suicide: arrest for, 152–53; cultural
    context of, 153–54; prohibiting, 153. *See
    also* physician-assisted suicide
Association of Texas Diocesan Attorneys, 43;
    brief by, 38
autonomy, 24–25; PAS and, 76

Baer, Judith, 119, 170n8
Barth, William A., 69
Bartlett, Katharine, 116; on ethics of justice/
    care, 121
Bauby, Jean-Dominique, 162
Beeson, Lucille Stewart, 103, 104
beginning of life, 43–46, 48
Benjamin, Walter, 163
Bickel, Alexander: on countermajoritarian
    difficulty, 12
Binion, Gayle: on contextual analysis, 170n7
bioethicists, PAS and, 83
Bioethics Professors, brief by, 85
Blackmun, Harry, 63; abortion and, 52, 53;
    DeShaney and, 130; *Doe* and, 50; medical
    knowledge and, 49; *Roe* and, 31, 41, 45,
    46, 47, 48–49, 51, 53
Bolotin, Susan: on personal experience, 21
Bork, Robert: judicial restraint and, 13
Brennan, William: on death penalty cases,
    130; judicial activism and, 13; *Roe* and, 45
Breyer, Stephen: on medical technology, 95;
    on palliative care, 95; PAS and, 88, 91, 92,
    94, 95, 96
briefs. *See amici* briefs; party briefs
Brodkey, Harold, 162
Broughton, John: on justice/care, 116, 122
Brown v. Board of Education (1954), 12, 122
Broyard, Anatole: on doctor–patient
    relationship, 156; on dying well, 162–63;
    on understanding terminally ill, 164
buffer zones, 58, 61
Burger, Warren: dissent by, 49; *Roe* and, 45
Byron, William, S.J.: on justice, 121–22

California Penal Code, violating, 153
Campo, Rafael, 21
"Cancer: A Personal Voyage" (Morgan), 21
care: feminist critique of, 108, 112–19;
    guiding principles of, 25; images of, 122;
    justice and, 107, 116, 122, 128; knowledge

from, 128, 144–49, 159–63; law and, 119,
    166. *See also* ethic of care
care givers: burdens for, 157–58; cultural
    support for, 157
Caring for Justice (West), 121
caring jurisprudence, xi, xiii; abortion and,
    149, 164–65; development of, 106, 112,
    118, 120, 136–37, 141, 165; judicial
    decision making and, 136, 165; model for,
    xii, 107, 119–30, 132, 171n1; PAS and, xii,
    xiii, 159, 163, 164–65; patients' knowledge
    and, 135, 165, 166; transformative
    potential of, 131
case study method, 15
*Casey v. Planned Parenthood of Southeastern
    Pennsylvania* (1992), 71, 73, 74, 92, 93; clinic
    protests and, 60–61; substantial obstacles
    and, 148; undue burden test and, 146
cataclysmic change, redemption and, 133–34
certain physicians, professors and fellows of
    ACOG, 43; brief by, 38, 42
chemotherapy, 157, 161
choice, 24–25, 92; freedom of, 142, 143
Clark, Brian, 22
Clemont, Grace: care/justice and, 115, 120
Clinton, Bill: FACE and, 168n4
CLS. *See* Critical Legal Studies
Coalition of Hospice Professionals, PAS and, 83
Coffee, Linda, 168n3; party brief by, 38; results
    oriented stance and, 37; *Roe* and, 34
Coles, Robert, 1
Compassion in Dying, 69
Compassion in Dying v. Washington (1994), 69
conception, 115; life and, 48
consciousness raising, 23, 109
consent restrictions, 55, 57–58, 119, 146, 147
constitutionalism, legal knowledge and, 11
controversies, 33, 34
Cooper v. Aaron (1958), 62
coping, strategies for, 5–6
Council on Ethical and Judicial Affairs
    (AMA), 94
countermajoritarian concerns, 12, 13
criminal law: abortion issue and, 42–43;
    women and, 116
Critical Legal Studies (CLS), 16
Critical Race Studies (CRS), 16
Cruzan, Nancy Beth, 72, 97
*Cruzan v. Director, Missouri Department of
    Health* (1990), 67, 71, 73, 74, 92, 96, 99
culture: as gendered, 26; life/death and, 26–27

Dancing at the Edge of Life (Warner), quote from, 133
death: fear of, 26, 27; fighting, 155; good/bad, 27, 96; meaning of, 27, 91; medicalized, 96; physicality of, 96. *See also* dying
Death as a Fact of Life (Hendin), 162
death penalty cases, xiii; moral significance and, 130
Death with Dignity Act (1994) (Oregon), 169n4
decision making: end-of-life, 92; patients' knowledge and, 25. *See also* judicial decision making
deductive reasoning, using, 17
Delgado, Richard: on outgroups, 22
Dellinger, Walter: on PAS, 88, 89
Delury, George: charges against, 157–58; on cultural contradictions, 154
DeShaney v. Winnebago County Dept. of Social Services (1989), 130
different voice, 107, 112–14, 116, 117, 118
dignity, 87, 92, 95; PAS and, 76
discrimination: legal knowledge about, 16; sexual, 109, 117, 143
distance, principle of, 17
divisions, intersections and, 26–27, 29–30
doctor–patient relationships, xi, 111; abortion and, 41, 51, 52, 60, 145, 145, 146; government regulations on, 59–60; PAS and, 90, 105, 155–56; *Roe* and, 53, 54; sanctity of, 42
Doe v. Bolton (1973): physicians/medical discretion and, 50; progeny of, 54 (table); restrictions imposed following, 55–57 (table)
domestic violence law, 116
Douglas, William, 45, 49
due process: abortion and, 139, 144; PAS and, 71, 74, 88, 90, 93; women and, 116
dying: aid in, 90; controlling process of, 92, 99, 154; dignity in, 76, 87, 92, 95; as medical issue, 162; money and, 156; PAS and, 162; suffering and, 161; suicide and, 163; understanding, 96, 163. *See also* death

Edelstein, Ludwig, 46
Eighth Amendment, 38
emotional distance, 5–6
emotional knowledge: abortion and, 141; drawing on, 25–26; excluding, 130; PAS and, 159, 164; privacy rights and, 130; reason and, 117, 129–30

empathetic participation, 129
empathetic witnessing, 164
Epstein, Cynthia Fuchs, 118
equality, 119; abortion and, 139
equal protection, 18, 71, 122; PAS and, 74, 75, 88; women and, 117
ethic of care, x, xiii, 113; abortion and, 144, 149; ethic of justice and, xi, 114–16, 119, 120–21, 124–25, 126, 149, 164, 170nn5, 6; feminine, xii, 118; feminists and, 106, 108, 119; following, 115, 126, 131, 135; justice and, 106, 125–26; law and, 114; limitations of, 115; political meanings and, 127; stereotype of, 170n3
ethic of justice, ix–x, xii, 11, 14, 24, 113, 117; abortion and, 33, 144; ethic of care and, xi, 114–16, 119, 120–26, 149, 164, 170nn5, 6; feminists and, 106, 108, 119; following, 115, 126, 135; impartiality and, 129; judicial approach with, 106; judicial decision making and, 124, 125; Lady Justice and, 114; limitations of, 115; political meanings and, 127; reliance on, 127
ethics, 9; gendered, 113; medical, 83
euthanasia, 66, 67, 76, 78, 87; prohibiting, 79
experiential knowledge. *See* personal knowledge

FACE. *See* Freedom of Access to Clinics Entrances Act
facial challenges, 94, 96
facts, relying on, 16
fairness, ix, 11
feelings, knowledge and, 25
Fem Crits, CLS and, 16
feminism: challenge by, 112, 116; inclusive knowledge and, 109, 110, 117; marginalization and, 23; patients' knowledge and, 107–11; relational/cultural, 117; Second Wave, 109
feminist jurisprudence, 113, 116–19; challenge by, 16
fetal personhood, 43–46, 48
fetus, protecting, 48, 58, 59
Fifth Amendment, 18, 47
Finley, Lucinda: on legal voice, 17
First Amendment, xiii, 18, 47; abortion issue and, 62; protestors and, 58, 60, 61; restrictions, 55, 58
Flowers, Robert G., 44, 45
Floyd, Jay, 44; on abortion safety, 39

Fourteenth Amendment, 18, 47; PAS and, 71, 74; terminally ill and, 69; testing, 35–36

Fourth Amendment, 18, 47

Freedom of Access to Clinics Entrances Act (FACE) (1994), 168n4

Frug, Mary Joe, 118

fundamental rights, 35

funding restrictions, 55, 57; undue burden from, 147

Gay Men's Health Crisis, brief by, 85

gender: hidden, 111; moral reasoning and, 112; oppression, 141; public/private dichotomy and, 110–11; symbolic power of, 170n2

Get Rid of Patients orientation (GROP), 5

Gilligan, Carol: different voice of, 107, 112–14, 116, 117; feminine voice and, 117; moral reasoning and, 112, 114, 115

Ginsburg, Ruth Bader, 89; on dying process, 90; PAS and, 91, 94, 95, 96

Glucksberg, Harold, 69, 70, 75, 88. See also *Washington v. Glucksberg*

grace, 133, 134

Gray, John, 112

Gray's Anatomy, 24

GROP. See Get Rid of Patients orientation

Gropman, Jerome: on PAS, 164

Grossman, Howard A., 69

Hallford, James Hubert, 40

Halperin, Abigail, 69, 75

healing, professionalization of, 6

health care, buying, 156

health insurance, 9, 128

Hemlock Society, 90

Hendin, David, 162

Hewshaw, Stanley: on abortion providers, 167n4

Hippocratic oath, 8, 45, 46

HMOs, advent of, 128

Hoefler, James: on slippery slope, 169n3

hospice movement, 157

Howell, Donna, 160

How We Die (Nuland), 22, 65

impartiality: involvement and, 129; law/medicine and, 137

In a Different Voice (Gilligan), 107, 112, 114–15

inclusive knowledge, feminism and, 109, 117

integrationist approach, using, 120–24

intuitive, drawing on, 25–26

Jaggar, Alison: on ethics of care, 120; on justice thinking, 115

judicial activism, 13, 166

judicial decision making, ix, 14, 61, 107; abortion and, 33, 62; bias in, 11; caring jurisprudence and, 136, 165; commitment to, x, 12; ethic of care and, 123; ethic of justice and, 124, 125; fair/objective, 12; knowledge and, 144; model for, xii; objectivity/impartiality of, 17; PAS and, 99; patients' knowledge and, xi, 36; politics of, 171n8; result-oriented, 122

judicial restraint, 13

justice: achieving, 123; administration of, 11, 104; care and, 107, 116, 122, 128; caring jurisprudence and, xiii; ethic of care and, 125–26; feminist revisionings of, 108, 112–19; impartial/reasoned/universal, ix; knowledge from, 128, 144–49, 159–63; law and, 119, 166; love and, 116; mercy and, 104; understanding, 104. *See also* ethic of justice

Karst, Kenneth, 117

Kellough, Gail: *Roe* and, 51

Kennedy, Anthony: *Casey* and, 61; PAS and, 65, 72, 91

Kingsley, George, 69

KKK Act, 58

Klagsbrun, Samuel G., 69

knowledge: approaches to, 2, 17; constraints on, 8; construction of, 13, 15, 109, 117; cultural context of, 26–27; feelings and, 25; feminine form of, 109, 110, 114; gender division of, 6–7; interplay of, 32–46; judicial decision making and, 144; law and, 116; medicine and, 7; PAS and, 68–80, 83, 85, 87–91; privileging, 107, 108–9, 131; reason and, 22; scientific method and, 109; subjective/objective, 18; trust in, 7; weighing, 141

Kohlberg, Lawrence, 112; on love/justice, 116; moral reasoning and, 114

Kubler-Ross, Elizabeth, 26–27

Lady Justice, 11, 132; ethic of justice and, 114; sculpture of, 103, 104

Langdell, Christopher Columbus: case study method and, 15

law: art of, 121; feminist approaches to, 118; impartial knowledge from, 137;

justice/care and, 119; knowledge and, 116; medicine and, 27, 29; paternalism and, 109–10; patients' knowledge and, 20, 120; personal and, 24; science of, 11–16
law professors, PAS and, 83
law schools: feminism within, 117; teaching at, 14–15
Lee, Gary: brief by, 85
legal education, 16, 116; feminist approaches to, 118; objective of, 14; personal knowledge and, 17
legal epistemology, 16–17, 105, 116; and personal/medical epistemologies compared, 27, 28 (table), 29–30
legal knowledge, xiii, 1, 2: abortion and, 62–63; acquiring, 10–19; limits of, 17–19; medical knowledge and, 29, 105; PAS and, 74, 87; patients' knowledge and, xi, xii, 16, 63, 106; shaping, 12
legal norms: abortion, 33–36, 105, 123, 138; bias in, xi; challenging, 107, 114; PAS, 71, 73, 94, 105, 123
legal system: epistemology of, 11; politics and, 14
Levi, Edward: on knowledge construction, 13
life: meaning of, 91; sanctity of, 93
life support, 72; PAS and, 78; removing, 70, 74, 76, 89, 98, 100
Ludwig, Alfred O.: quote of, 1

MacKinnon, Catherine, 118, 119
malpractice law suits, 10
managed care, 9, 159
mandatory counseling: challenging, 146; undue burden of, 147
marginalization, 22; challenging, 23
Marshall, John, 11, 130
McCorvey, Norma. See Roe, Jane
McGeorge, Emanuel J.: death of, 152
medical, defined, 167n1
medical education, 5; healing knowledge and, 6; science and, 4
medical epistemology, 7–8, 105; and legal/personal epistemologies compared, 27, 28 (table), 29–30
medical knowledge, xiii; abortion and, 10, 32–35, 40–42, 44–46, 51, 62–63; acquiring, 2–10; influence of, 7, 168n2; law and, 104–5; limits of, 8–10, 22; PAS and, 74, 83, 87, 93, 99, 163; patients' knowledge and, xi, xii, 1–2, 9, 20, 23, 30,

36, 63, 106, 126, 159; preference for, x–xi; science and, 3–7, 8; transfer of, 7
medical profession: ethics of, 44; PAS and, 163; reliance on, 7; restrictions on, 55, 58; science and, 4
medicine: alternative, 7; economics and, 10; knowledge and, 7, 137; law and, 27, 29; paternalism and, 109–10; professionalization of, 6; science/technology and, 3, 4
Men Are from Mars, Women Are from Venus (Gray), 112
Menkel-Meadow, Carrie, 117
Merchant of Venice (Shakespeare), quote from, 103
mercy, justice and, 104
minorities, protecting rights of, 13
minors, protecting rights of, 60
Minow, Martha: on patients' knowledge, 136; on theory of justice, 131
Model Penal Code, 50, 70
morality, 112, 113; abortion issue and, 42
moral reasoning, 114, 115, 122; different voice of, 113; gender and, 112
Morgan, Peter, 21

National Abortion Rights Action League (NARAL), brief by, 40, 129, 138
National Hospice Association, brief by, 85
National Legal Center for the Medically Dependent & Disabled, brief by, 85
National Legal Program on Health Problems of the Poor, 43; brief by, 38
National Right to Life Committee, brief by, 38
National Spinal Cord Injury Association, brief by, 85
Newton, John, 133, 166
New Women Lawyers, brief by, 37, 38, 39
New York Academy of Medicine, brief by, 43
New York State Task Force on Life and Law, report by, 78–79, 93, 94
New York *Times*, on PAS, 88
New York Times Book Review, on Stabiner, 21
Nightingale, Florence, 6
Ninth Amendment, 18, 47
Not Dead Yet, 90; brief by, 85, 158
Nuland, Sherwin B., 65; on medical knowledge, 22
Nussbaum, Martha: judicious spectators and, 129

objectivity, 10, 63, 65, 116, 123, 131, 135; emphasis on, 14; politics of, xii; principle of, 17; reason and, 22
obligations, guiding principles of, 8
O'Connor, Sandra Day: *Casey* and, 61; different voice of, 118; on dying process, 90; PAS and, 65, 72, 91, 92, 94, 95, 96, 171n3; *Quill* and, 26; *Roe* and, 53
"On Being Ill" (Woolf), 156
oppression, dynamics of, 107, 110–11
oral arguments: abortion, 33, 36, 37, 39, 41, 45, 66; PAS, 68, 88–91, 90
Oresteian Trilogy, The (Aeschylus), 11
Osler, Sir William: on experiential, 23
Our Bodies, Ourselves, 24

pain, 123, 160; controlling, 95, 105, 160; knowledge about, 163; treatment for, 96
palliative care, 94, 95, 98, 160
parental consent requirement: challenging, 146; undue burden of, 147
partial, drawing on, 25–26
particulars, universals and, 128–29
party briefs: abortion, 33, 36, 37, 38, 41; conflicting knowledge of, 73–79; PAS, 68, 90, 99
PAS. *See* physician–assisted suicide
paternalism, medicine/law and, 109–10
patients: disempowering, 111; epistemology of, 24–26; ethic of care and, 125–26; experiential knowledge and, 20–24; information on, 5; wishes of, 10, 21
patients' knowledge: abortion and, 19, 20, 23, 29, 32, 33, 37–40, 62–63, 106, 123, 131–32, 135, 146, 164; access to, 6; acquiring, 19–26, 126, 132, 135; caring jurisprudence and, 135, 165, 166; excluding, 30, 106; guiding principles of, 29; information from, xi, 9, 21, 136, 168n2; law and, 104–5, 120; legal knowledge and, xi, xii, 63, 106; limits to, 19–20; medical knowledge and, xi, xii, 1–2, 9, 23, 30, 36, 63, 106, 126, 159; medicine/law and, 23; PAS and, 68, 77–78, 86 (table), 87–88, 101, 105, 106, 123, 131–32, 135, 159, 164, 166; personal experience and, x; persuasiveness of, 165; *Roe* and, 55; validating, 22. *See also* personal knowledge
patients' voices, 36, 165, 171n1
patriarchy, 109–10
Patterson, Edwin: on legal pedagogy, 15

per curium opinions, abortion and, 54
personal: defined, 167n1; science/law and, 24
personal epistemology, and medical/legal epistemologies compared, 27, 28 (table), 29–30
personal knowledge, 1, 2; abortion and, 138–39, 148; legal knowledge and, 16, 17, 105–6; patients and, 20–24, 29; reason and, 22. *See also* patients' knowledge
Petchesky, Rosalind Pollack: on individual liberty, 139
physical, start with, 7–8
physician-assisted suicide (PAS), x, 1, 122, 169n2; abortion issue and, 66; banning, 68, 72, 79, 128, 150, 151–52, 165; caring jurisprudence and, xii, xiii; constitutional meaning of, 73, 127; debate over, 75, 99, 169n1; framework for, 70–71; gender and, 26; impact of, 87; judicial tests for, 71; legalization of, 27, 78, 88, 91, 100; legal knowledge and, 18, 72–73, 134; macrolevel analysis of, 128, 165; medical knowledge and, 10, 134; microlevel analysis of, 150–53; opposition to, 158, 159, 163; patients' knowledge and, 19, 20, 23, 25, 29; political meanings of, 153–59; precedents for, 71–73; as private issue, 108; revisiting, 124, 132, 149–64, 167; support for, 77–78, 80, 158, 159, 165
physician–patient relationship. *See* doctor–patient relationship
Physicians' Desk Reference, The, 24
physicians' discretion: protecting, 54–55, 57–62, 60; regulations impeding, 59
Poe, John, 69, 75
Poetic Justice (Nussbaum), 129
Poetry of Healing, The (Campo), 21
Powell, Lewis, 43
PPFA: brief by, 38, 42, 43; statistics from, 43
Preston, Thomas A., 69, 75
privacy: abortion, 139, 144; emotional knowledge and, 130; right to, 18, 31, 35–36, 40, 48, 53, 58, 124, 127; violation of, 144
professionalization, 24, 145; gender split and, 6
protection bubbles, 58, 61
protestors, 62; First Amendment and, 58, 60, 61; as substantial obstacles, 148
public/private dichotomy: feminist critiques of, 108, 110–11; gender differences and, 110–11; separation of, 107–8

Quadrangle Considerations (Byron), 121
quickening, 47
Quill, Timothy E., 69, 70, 74, 75, 89, 98, 153;
brief by, 78; PAS and, 9, 76. See also *Vacco v. Quill*
Quindlen, Anna: on *Roe*, 137

Radner, Gilda, 162
reason, 17, 123, 135; emotion and, 117,
129–30; emphasis on, 14; experience and,
22; knowledge and, 22; legal, 15;
methodology of, 8; moral, 11, 113, 114,
115, 122; objectivity and, 22
redemption, cataclysmic change and, 133–34
Regents of the University of California v. Bakke
(1978), 80; affirmative action and, 130
Rehnquist, William, 43; *Glucksberg* and, 92;
PAS and, 65, 91, 92, 93, 94, 100; *Quill*
and, 92, 93–94; *Shenck* and, 61
relationships, guiding principles of, 25
Remoff, Heather Trexler, 161
Rice, Ted and Muriel, 155
Rice, Valli: treatment refusal by, 155
RICO Act, 58
Rifkin, Janet: on power/ideology of law, 118
rights: abstract, 140–41; defining, 119;
framework of, 16–17; negative/positive,
35
right to die, 67, 71, 92, 123, 124, 164
Roe, Jane, 18, 69, 75, 153, 168n3; standing
for, 34
Roe v. Wade (1973), x, xii, 30, 37, 46, 68, 79,
80, 105, 124, 126, 168n2; Blackmun on,
31; challenges to, 54; investigation of, 33;
legacy of, 137, 138; maternal health and,
59; medical knowledge and, 51, 55; oral
arguments for, 66; physician–child
relationship and, 53; physician–patient
relationship and, 54; progeny of, 32,
54–55, 54 (table), 57–62, 63 restrictions
imposed following, 55–57 (table)
rule of law, 13, 15

St. Denis, Richard, 90
Sassone, Robert L., 43; brief by, 38
Scalia, Antonin: on dying process, 89;
Glucksberg and, 149; judicial restraint and,
13; PAS and, 90, 91; *Quill* and, 149
science: medical knowledge and, 3–7, 8;
medicine and, 4; objective knowledge of,
22; personal and, 24

scientific knowledge: application of, 5, 9;
government regulations on, 59;
scientific method, 3, 9; described, 4;
knowledge and, 109; law and, 15
Second Wave feminism, contributions of, 109
self-determination, 20, 24–25; right to, 71
sexual discrimination, 109, 143; challenging,
117
Shalit, Peter, 69, 75
Slepian, Barnett: assassination of, 167n4
slippery slope, 169n3; PAS and, 100
Smith, Adam, 129
Socratic Method, 15
Sontag, Susan: on cancer, 162
Souter, David: *Casey* and, 61; facial challenge
and, 94; PAS and, 72, 91, 92, 95, 96
speech, freedom of, 57, 60
spousal notification, 57–58, 59, 60;
challenging, 146
Stabiner, Karen, 21
State Communities Aid Association, brief by,
38
State of Grace (Williams), 164
Stevens, John Paul: caring jurisprudence and,
131; on *Cruzan*, 97; on doctor–patient
relationships, 98; facial challenges and, 96;
Glucksberg and, 131, 169n5; PAS and, 91,
92, 95, 97, 98, 99, 106; patient-centered
approach of, 106; *Quill* and, 131
Stewart, Potter, 39; Weddington and, 44
strict scrutiny test, 35, 61, 72
substantial obstacles, 61, 62; undue burden
and, 148
suffering, 123, 162; dying and, 161; easing, 94,
96, 164–65; PAS and, 76, 77, 160; patients'
knowledge and, 25; stories of, 134, 136.
See also pain
suicide, 78; assisted, 152–54; defining, 74;
dying and, 163. *See also* physician-assisted
suicide
Surviving Family Members, brief by, 87, 129
symptoms, knowledge and, 7–8

Tannen, Deborah, 112
technology, 10; faith in, 7; PAS and, 73, 83, 95
terminal illness, 94, 165; cataclysmic impact
of, 150; crisis of, 134, 135; legal
knowledge and, 10, 167; medical
knowledge and, 2; PAS and, 66, 74, 75, 78,
87, 91, 98, 100; patients' knowledge and,
19, 166; understanding, 164

terminal sedation, 76, 98
tests, using, 35–36
Texas Penal Code, challenging, 32
theoretical-deductive, imaginative use of, 4
Thirteenth Amendment, violation of, 38
Thomas, Clarence: PAS and, 91
Thornburgh v. American College of Obstetricians and Gynecologists (1986), 40, 129, 140; brief for, 138
Tilberis, Liz, 157
To Dance with the Devil (Stabiner), review of, 21
Torcaso, Roy R., 90
treatment, stopping, 78, 155
Tribe, Laurence, 89, 97; judicial activism and, 13
Tronto, Joan, 126; on caring, 115
Tucker, Kathryn L., 91; on dying, 89; on PAS, 88

undue burden, 61, 72, 74; abortion and, 128, 142, 145, 148, 149, 164; identification of, 146–49; PAS and, 128–29; substantial obstacles and, 148; types of, 147
U.S. Constitution, as reference, 34–35
U.S. Supreme Court, x; legal norms of, xi; PAS and, 65, 66, 67, 70, 91–99, 100
universals, 14, 135; particulars and, 128–29
unwanted pregnancy, 66, 123; changes caused by, 31, 139–40, 142–43; crisis of, 134, 135; legal response to, 167; medical knowledge and, 2; patients' knowledge and, 19; preventing, 142; privacy and, 116, 127. *See also* abortion

Vacco, Dennis: on PAS, 88–89
Vacco v. Quill (1997), x, 26, 65, 67, 72, 73, 75, 99, 105, 126, 131, 150, 151; brief for, 80, 81 (table), 82 (table), 84 (table), 86 (table), 87; doctor-patient relationship and, 155; legal knowledge from, 82 (table); medical knowledge from, 84 (table), 159; medical profession and, 163; New York State Penal Law S. 125.15 (3) and, 69; PAS and, 63, 66, 68, 79, 91; patients' knowledge from, 86 (table), 159; reformulation in, 18
viability, 48–49, 53, 58, 59
Voices brief, 138

Wade, Henry, 32; brief for, 37–48, 42. See also *Roe v. Wade*
waiting period, 58; undue burden of, 147, 148
Warner, Gale, 133, 134, 162
Wasby, Stephen: on neutral principles, 12
Washington *Post*, on PAS, 88
Washington State Psychological Association, PAS and, 83
Washington v. Glucksberg (1997), x, 67, 69, 70, 72, 73, 92, 94, 99, 105, 126, 131, 150, 151, 169n5; brief for, 80, 81 (table), 82 (table), 84 (table), 86 (table), 87; doctor–patient relationship and, 155; Joint Appendix in, 77; legal knowledge from, 82 (table); medical knowledge from, 84 (table), 159; medical profession and, 163; PAS and, 63, 65, 66, 68, 79, 91, 127; patients' knowledge from, 86 (table), 159; reformulation in, 18
Webster v. Reproductive Health Services (1989), 70, 80, 140; brief for, 138
Wechsler, Herbert: on neutral principles, 12
Weddington, Sarah, 34, 168n3; ethical guidelines and, 43–44; oral arguments by, 39; party brief by, 38; policy making and, 39; results oriented stance of, 37
Weil, Andrew, 7
West, Robin, 117; on ethics of justice/care, 121, 123; on images of care, 122
When Death Is Sought: Assisted Suicide and Euthanasia in the Medical Context, 78–79
White, Byron: dissent by, 49, 52–53; *Roe* and, 41, 45
"Whose Life Is It Anyway?" (Clark), 22
Williams, Joan, 118
Williams, Joy, 164
Williams, Wendy, 118
Williams, William, 88, 89
Wishik, Heather Ruth, 119
Wittig, Monique, 119
Women for the Unborn, 43; brief by, 38, 41
Women's Organizations and Named Women, brief by, 38
women's rights, 62; abortion issue and, 39; expansion of, 31
Woolf, Virginia, 156
World Health Organization, palliative care and, 160

You Just Don't Understand (Tannen), 112

About the Author

Susan M. Behuniak is professor of political science and member of the women's studies program at Le Moyne College, Syracuse, New York. She is the past recipient of two teaching honors, the Monsignor A. Robert Casey Teacher of the Year Award from Le Moyne College (1994) and the Carpenter Award for the Outstanding Teacher of the Year from Wilkes College (1987). Her articles have appeared in journals including *Judicature, Policy Studies Review, Review of Politics,* and *Women and Politics,* as well as in several books.

Behuniak, Susan M., 1956-
A caring jurisprudence :
listening to patients at the
Supreme Court